D1596254

New Directions in Slavery Studies

NEW DIRECTIONS
IN
SLAVERY STUDIES

*Commodification,
Community, and
Comparison*

EDITED BY
JEFF FORRET
AND
CHRISTINE E. SEARS

LOUISIANA STATE UNIVERSITY PRESS   BATON ROUGE

Published by Louisiana State University Press

First printing

DESIGNER: Michelle A. Neustrom
TYPEFACE: Adobe Caslon Pro
PRINTER AND BINDER: Maple Press

LIBRARY OF CONGRESS CATALOGING-IN-PUBLICATION DATA

New directions in slavery studies : commodification, community, and comparison /
edited by Jeff Forret and Christine E. Sears.

    pages cm

  ISBN 978-0-8071-6115-9 (cloth : alk. paper) — ISBN 978-0-8071-6116-6 (pdf) —
ISBN 978-0-8071-6117-3 (epub) — ISBN 978-0-8071-6118-0 (mobi) 1. Slavery—
United States—History. 2. Slaves—United States—Social conditions. I. Forret, Jeff,
1972– editor, author. II. Sears, Christine E., 1969– editor, author.
  E441.N48 2015
  306.3'620973—dc23

                                                                    2015019696

CONTENTS

ABBREVIATIONS

ACBG/MOS   Arquivo Casa Borba Gato / Museu do Ouro de Sabará, Sabará, Minas Gerais, Brazil

AHU   Arquivo Histórico Ultramarino

APM   Arquivo Público Mineiro, Belo Horizonte, Minas Gerais, Brazil

BCC   Baltimore County Court

BLIC   Baltimore Life Insurance Company

CMS   Câmara Municipal de Sabará

CSO   Cartório do Segundo Ofício

FCRL   Virginia Room Rare Book Collection, Fairfax City Regional Library, Fairfax, VA

GArch   Georgia Archives, Morrow, GA

LC   Library of Congress, Washington, DC

LSU   Hill Memorial Library, Louisiana State University, Baton Rouge, LA

LVA   Library of Virginia, Richmond, VA

MDAH   Mississippi Department of Archives and History, Jackson, MS

MHS   Maryland Historical Society, Baltimore, MD

MSA   Maryland State Archives, Annapolis, MD

NARA   National Archives and Records Administration

PASC-HSP   Pennsylvania Abolition Society Collection, Historical Society of Pennsylvania, Philadelphia, PA

PCA   Philadelphia City Archives, Philadelphia, PA

SCDAH   South Carolina Department of Archives and History, Columbia, SC

SCHS   South Carolina Historical Society, Charleston, SC

SCL South Caroliniana Library, University of South Carolina, Columbia, SC

SHC Southern Historical Collection, Louis Round Special Collections Library, University of North Carolina, Chapel Hill, NC

VHS Virginia Historical Society, Richmond, VA

New Directions in Slavery Studies

INTRODUCTION

JEFF FORRET AND CHRISTINE E. SEARS

Since the early 1970s, scholarship on slavery has proliferated to the extent that it is difficult for most people to remain fully versed on developments in the field. Readers from both inside and outside the academy embark upon well-intentioned efforts to try, only to realize the enormity of the task confronting them. Only a few exceptionally devoted and uniquely talented scholars have undertaken the Herculean mission of synthesizing the enormous body of work on slavery for the literate masses. Peter J. Parish's *Slavery: History and Historians* (1989), Peter Kolchin's *American Slavery, 1619–1877* (1993), and Mark M. Smith's *Debating Slavery: Economy and Society in the Antebellum American South* (1998) are three of the most noteworthy examples. In the twenty-first century, slave studies have pursued such imaginative and disparate paths that no one has yet dared attempt a similarly ambitious accounting of where the field stands. The tenth-anniversary edition of Kolchin's book, published in 2003, brought with it a welcome new preface and afterword, but the rapid pace at which historians continue to churn out important work on slavery renders labors to remain current with slave historiography almost Sisyphean.[1]

Like other edited collections, this anthology zeroes in on important themes currently explored in slave studies, both to reflect scholarly roads being traveled and to encourage further journeys down those same avenues.[2] In different ways, the three themes identified in the title—commodification, community, and comparison—all gained traction in the wake of Stanley M. Elkins's seminal work *Slavery: A Problem in American Institutional and Intellectual Life* (1959). Elkins portrayed slaves in the U.S. South as infantilized Sambos—docile, childlike, dependent, and utterly dominated by the will of their masters.[3]

In reaction, a generation of revisionist scholarship beginning in the 1970s examined slaves as agents who shaped the contours of their own lives. Both culturally and physically, slaves proved resilient in the face of oppression and contested the terms and conditions of bondage as imposed by their owners.[4] So effective were the revisionists in transforming slaves from passive objects into active subjects that the literature bordered on forgetting that bondpeople were slaves at all. By 1993 one pair of distinguished scholars felt compelled to publish an edited volume to remind readers that slavery was, at root, a system of labor.[5]

Now a growing number of scholars are not only rediscovering that slaves were indeed the property of their masters but also elaborating upon the many ways in which slaves were commodified. The slave trade is the most readily apparent form of slaves' objectification as property. A spate of recent studies has elucidated many facets of the domestic slave trade from the Upper South to the Lower and from the eastern seaboard slave states to those in the Old Southwest.[6] Calvin Schermerhorn's opening essay takes a different tack by examining the coastwise slave trade in the United States and its broader place in transatlantic commercial networks, even after the termination of the lawful international traffic in human cargoes.

Yet the slave trade was merely one means through which masters commodified their labor force. For as growing numbers of scholars are making clear, slaves represented not only a form of labor but also a form of capital. In chapter 2, Bonnie Martin demonstrates slaves' centrality to the borrowing and lending practices of Virginia slaveholders from the colonial era to the Civil War. The mortgaging of slaves and the use of human collateral grew increasingly significant in her sample communities from the seventeenth through the nineteenth century. Dovetailing nicely with Martin's work is Karen Ryder's account in chapter 3 that shows some masters purchased life insurance on their slaves—policies that lubricated the machinery of slave-based credit arrangements in the antebellum decades. Compared to the first three chapters, chapter 4, dealing with the slave as a subject in modern-day cinema, approaches commodification from a fundamentally different perspective. Kenneth S. Greenberg offers a firsthand account of his experiences as a historian and expert consultant for a documentary on the Nat Turner slave revolt. In light of two recent feature films, director Quentin Tarantino's unapologetically absurd revenge fantasy *Django Unchained* (2012) and the vastly more sobering and more realistic portrait of bondage in the Oscar-winning *12 Years a Slave*

(2013), Greenberg supplies valuable insights into the process and challenges of translating the history of slavery onto the screen.

As historians refuted Elkins through an emphasis on agency, they also stressed the significance of the "slave community." Revisionist scholars upheld slaves' close familial networks, religious beliefs and gatherings, and rich culture as means of coping with the brutal excesses of bondage. Historians uncovered ample evidence of slaves' camaraderie and a cooperative ethos, information that profoundly reoriented the historiography but seemed to neglect the undeniable fact of bondpeople's continued enslavement. By the early 1980s, historian Peter Kolchin could justly criticize the "celebratory tone" of many revisionist works and their "exaggerated picture of the strength and cohesion of the slave community."[7] He cautioned students of slavery against glorifying the harmony imputed to the quarters through the slave community paradigm; indeed, mounting evidence now shows that community was neither monolithic nor forged automatically in the crucible of bondage. In chapter 5, John Davies examines the process of community formation in Philadelphia among ex-slave refugees from Saint Domingue. Jeff Forret's research provides, in chapter 6, explicit evidence of division within the slave community by documenting thefts internal to the slave quarters and the violent encounters among bondpeople that ensued. The stealing Forret documents was very much the product of slaves' internal economy, which supplied one method through which hardworking, enterprising slaves could distinguish themselves from others in bondage. As Kathleen M. Hilliard demonstrates in chapter 7, the ingenuity and techniques of the slave economy served bondpeople well amid the turmoil of Civil War–era Richmond, so much so that blacks' rising fortunes sparked anxiety among whites, whose economic futures dramatically soured in wartime. Much of the scholarship on the slave economy has described it as a foundation for slaves' autonomy—their ability to forge lives outside masters' control. Yet in the analysis presented in chapter 8, Anthony E. Kaye takes aim at the theme of autonomy itself—pervasive in the revisionist literature on slavery—and charts a path toward a postliberal historiography unfettered by autonomy's ideological burdens.

Part III of this collection turns to the comparative history of slavery, a methodological approach launched by Frank Tannenbaum's *Slave and Citizen* (1946). Tannenbaum identified two contrasting varieties of slavery in the Western Hemisphere. In Latin America, he argued, the institutions of church and state interfered in the master-slave relationship, buffering bondpeople from the worst brutalities of enslavement. By contrast, in the United States, no such institutional constraints protected slaves from severe treatment and abuse by the master. Building upon Tannenbaum's foundation, Stanley Elkins ascribed the infantilized Sambo personality type among slaves in the American South to the region's "closed" system of slavery. Whereas church and state mitigated the severity of slavery under the relatively more "open," mild form of slavery practiced in Latin America, he explained, in the American South no similar institutions were available to restrain the excesses of capitalist production for market. Hence, southern slavery was so harsh and oppressive that the unspeakably brutal conditions slaves endured transformed them into Sambos. Elkins famously drew an analogy between southern slaves and the inmates of Nazi concentration camps. The psychic strains both groups suffered, he claimed, reduced them to Sambos as they struggled to adjust to the realities of absolute power wielded by their oppressors.[8]

Although subsequent scholarship largely refuted Tannenbaum's and Elkins's characterizations of the differences between slavery in the United States and in Latin America, the comparative methodology as a tool of historical analysis remains valuable because it lends itself to two seemingly antithetical but related goals. First, comparative work uncovers details distinct to the regions and time periods being compared. Juxtaposing Caribbean and U.S. slavery, for example, reveals demographic differences, such as a natural increase in the U.S. slave population and a natural decrease in that of the Caribbean. Second, the comparative method enables a big-picture understanding of the past. In the case of slave systems, comparative work has shown just how flexible the institution proved to be and has pointed to the fact that the plantation system model in the New World was in fact a historical aberration rather than the norm.

The four chapters in the last third of the book answer Peter Kolchin's call for more "broad-based comparative studies."[9] Three show pointedly how, in the words of Ira Berlin, slavery "varied from time to time and from place to place."[10] In chapter 9, Mariana Dantas indicates how female slaves' urban work shaped Atlantic economies. Enslaved women in Sabará, Minas Gerais, Brazil, used their labor as a pathway to freedom, whereas their female counterparts in Baltimore, Maryland, contended with forces that seldom permitted their manumission. Like Dantas, Christine E. Sears notes in chapter 10 that urban slavery had no inherent, definitive nature. As with its rural equivalent, city slavery was not monolithic. Sears investigates the eighteenth-century Ottoman Algerian enslavement of Christians to show that slavery was not incompatible with the urban setting. Nothing about slavery in the city inevitably led to the institution's demise. To the contrary, urban slavery in the Ottoman Algerian context thrived for centuries. In chapter 11, Enrico Dal Lago embarks upon a three-way comparison of nineteenth-century separatist movements launched by slaveholders in the American South, the Rio Grande do Sul province of Brazil, and Cuba. Less focused on slave life than other chapters, his work highlights three alternative visions of modern state-building in which slavery and slave property figured prominently.

But as Peter Kolchin observed, work on comparative slavery encompasses "not just transnational comparisons with other slave societies but also internal comparisons within the South."[11] Damian Alan Pargas takes the latter approach in chapter 12. His study of the "forced break-ups" of slave families, whether through estate divisions or through local or long-distance sales, in northern Virginia's Fairfax County and in Georgetown District of low-country South Carolina reveals shared processes as well as distinct regional differences. No less than comparisons that cross national boundaries, internally comparative research such as Pargas's is valuable for the insights that result. The use of the comparative methodology, in whichever form, "increases the accuracy of our knowledge of the past," Kolchin explained, which, he added, "is what history is all about."[12]

Kolchin, a professor at the University of Delaware, a Bancroft Prize–winning historian, and a recent president of the Southern Historical Association, inspired this collection of essays. Many of the contributors are former doctoral students of his or were aided by him, either directly or indirectly, in their research. Few practicing historians of slavery today have escaped the influence of Kolchin's work. The themes explored here reflect those mined in his scholarship and explored in his graduate courses. In recognition of Peter's tireless devotion to his students, to his subject, and to the historical profession, we dedicate this anthology to him.

NOTES

1. Peter J. Parish, *Slavery: History and Historians* (New York: Harper & Row, 1989); Peter Kolchin, *American Slavery, 1619–1877* (1993; New York: Hill and Wang, 2003); Mark M. Smith,

Debating Slavery: Economy and Society in the Antebellum American South (Cambridge: Cambridge University Press, 1998). See also Robert W. Fogel, *The Slavery Debates, 1952–1990: A Retrospective* (Baton Rouge: Louisiana State University Press, 2003).

2. See, for example, Edward E. Baptist and Stephanie M. H. Camp, eds. *New Studies in the History of American Slavery* (Athens: University of Georgia Press, 2006). For those struggling to keep abreast of the many directions slave studies have taken and to harness our ever-accumulating knowledge of the peculiar institution, recently published handbooks and encyclopedias provide another source of information. See, for instance, Robert L. Paquette and Mark M. Smith, eds. *The Oxford Handbook of Slavery in the Americas* (New York: Oxford University Press, 2010); Junius P. Rodriguez, *Slavery in the United States: A Social, Political, and Historical Encyclopedia*, 2 vols. (Santa Barbara, CA: ABC-CLIO, 2007); Orville Vernon Burton, ed., *Gale Library of Daily Life: Slavery in America* (Detroit: The Gale Group, 2008).

3. Stanley M. Elkins, *Slavery: A Problem in American Institutional and Intellectual Life*, 3rd ed. (Chicago: University of Chicago Press, 1976).

4. John W. Blassingame, *The Slave Community: Plantation Life in the Antebellum South*, rev. ed. (New York: Oxford University Press, 1979); Eugene D. Genovese, *Roll, Jordan, Roll: The World the Slaves Made* (1974; New York: Vintage, 1976); Herbert G. Gutman, *The Black Family in Slavery and Freedom, 1750–1925* (New York: Pantheon, 1976); Leslie Howard Owens, *This Species of Property: Slave Life and Culture in the Old South* (New York: Oxford University Press, 1976); Lawrence W. Levine, *Black Culture and Black Consciousness: Afro-American Folk Thought from Slavery to Freedom* (New York: Oxford University Press, 1977); Albert J. Raboteau, *Slave Religion: The "Invisible Institution" in the Antebellum South* (New York: Oxford University Press, 1978); Sterling Stuckey, *Slave Culture: Nationalist Theory and the Foundations of Black America* (New York: Oxford University Press, 1987).

5. Ira Berlin and Philip D. Morgan, eds. *Cultivation and Culture: Labor and the Shaping of Slave Life in the Americas* (Charlottesville: University Press of Virginia, 1993).

6. Michael Tadman, *Speculators and Slaves: Masters, Traders, and Slaves in the Old South* (Madison: University of Wisconsin Press, 1989); Walter Johnson, *Soul by Soul: Life inside the Antebellum Slave Market* (Cambridge, MA: Harvard University Press, 1999); Robert H. Gudmestad, *A Troublesome Commerce: The Transformation of the Interstate Slave Trade* (Baton Rouge: Louisiana State University Press, 2003); Steven Deyle, *Carry Me Back: The Domestic Slave Trade in American Life* (New York: Oxford University Press, 2005).

7. Peter Kolchin, "Reevaluating the Antebellum Slave Community: A Comparative Perspective," *Journal of American History* 70 (December 1983): 581. See also Kolchin, *American Slavery*, 148–55; and Clarence E. Walker, *Deromanticizing Black History: Critical Essays and Reappraisals* (Knoxville: University of Tennessee Press, 1991), xi–xviii. It should be noted that Blassingame, *Slave Community*, recognized disputes and divisions within the quarters that many others inspired by his work often overlooked.

8. Frank Tannenbaum, *Slave and Citizen: The Negro in the Americas* (New York: Knopf, 1946); Elkins, *Slavery*.

9. Kolchin, *American Slavery* (2003), 248.

10. Ira Berlin, "Time, Space, and the Evolution of Afro-American Society on British Mainland North America," *American Historical Review* 85 (February 1980): 78.

11. Kolchin, *American Slavery,* 248.

12. Peter Kolchin, "Comparing American History," *Reviews in American History* 10 (August 1982): 78.

I

COMMODIFICATION

COMMODITY CHAINS AND CHAINED COMMODITIES

The U.S. Coastwise Slave Trade and an Atlantic Business Network

CALVIN SCHERMERHORN

In the decade after the War of 1812, commerce in cotton linked the American South to northwest England. The American republic's fortunes rose on a tide of cotton lint, while agents of the British Industrial Revolution sped cloth and debt instruments through global arteries of commerce. The resulting cotton chain included cotton fibers, textiles, and conveyances such as ships, along with manufacturers, mariners, merchants, planters, and workers. Credit, knowledge, and trust formed the links. They were capitalist constructions, magnificently creative yet monumentally destructive. Enslaved people were a hidden but central component, and their commercial transport from the eastern seaboard of North America to the Lower South was vital to the process.

Scholars investigating slavery and capitalism have disagreed sharply over capitalism's historical characteristics and how directly slavery was involved in modern commercial development. This chapter takes a microhistorical approach to a world system, investigating concrete connections within the broad processes of Atlantic world commerce and the expansion of slavery in the early United States. An analysis of merchant voyages connects the bondpersons who shouldered the burdens of unpaid labor to the businessmen who orchestrated and financed the larger system. Systems of money and credit that made possible the rise of the transatlantic cotton economy of the 1820s were also part of the infrastructure of the interstate slave trade.[1]

The cotton economy took shape rapidly after the War of 1812. In 1815 food was the primary U.S. export, mainly flour shipped to the British West Indies. Ten years later, cotton was the largest by a factor of two or more. Most American cotton went to England. England imported cotton from all over the globe, and American cotton competed with West Indian and Brazilian lint. By the last half of the 1820s, three-quarters of Britain's imported cotton came from the United States.[2]

Financial mechanisms, maritime technologies, and manufacturing processes all underwent significant changes that shaped the process. The Second Bank of the United States and later state banks expanded credit, though that expansion was cyclical. Shipping firms rationalized markets over time, and vessels became more capacious. English manufacturers improved technology using power looms, which turned out abundant varieties and prodigious quantities of cloth. American agriculturalists experimented with higher-yielding strains of cotton. At either end of the transatlantic cotton chain were workers whose productivity rose substantially. Spinners and weavers in England increasingly worked in factories for wages that fluctuated with markets, while enslaved field hands in the United States were forced to produce ever more cotton per person.[3]

Like the Internet of a later age, the resulting cotton chain was an abstraction, the sum of a multitude of market actors, relationships, and materials. Anyone in the second or third decade of the 1800s seeking concrete evidence of it could find it in a wooden sailing ship docked at Baltimore, Maryland's premier city. Merchant ships carried the commercial world in miniature. The *Hyperion* of Baltimore was one such vessel. Built in 1820, it was described as an "elegant and swift sailing brig" with two tall masts and a capacious 413-ton cargo space. Perhaps the ship's name was inspired by John Keats's epic poems featuring the Titan god of the sun. Owner Thomas Tenant was one of Baltimore's leading merchants, a participant in the Baltimore Exchange and the city board of trade. He was a councilman and captain of the Seaman's Union Bethel Church in Fell's Point. Tenant initially sent his new ship to Rotterdam, Holland, but the *Hyperion* returned without cargo.[4] That was a losing venture emblematic of the tough economic times following the panic of 1819, which capped half a decade of natural and unnatural disasters.

Following the War of 1812, the Chesapeake region was hit hard by a terrible harvest, restricted trade, and constricted credit, all of which gave Maryland slaveholders incentives to sell slaves at the same time as their flour exports flowed to the other end of the national slave market, the lower Mississippi Valley. Thanks to the cataclysmic volcanic eruption of Mount Tambora and a confluence of other natural phenomena, 1816 became known as the year without a summer. Poor wheat harvests in the Northern Hemisphere sent prices rising and farmers into bankruptcy. Farmers sold slaves to make debt payments, but their finances were further damaged after Britain threw up tariff barriers to the American flour trade to the West Indies, which had filled Baltimore's commercial sails. The Bank of England constricted credit, causing textile exporters to sell consignments in cities such as New York for less than their value to remit debt payments, undercutting American merchants and glutting the market. Then times worsened. In 1819 a loss of confidence in banks on both sides of the Atlantic brought on a financial panic. Many Baltimore merchant houses failed, and others scrambled for new opportunities. It soon became clear that slave-grown cotton rather than foodstuffs would be the nation's chief export. In search of revenue, Tenant put the *Hyperion* on a new route that took advantage of the reorientation in Chesapeake trade. His ship would haul flour to New Orleans and cotton to Liverpool, returning with manufactured goods. Part of that voyage involved shipping enslaved Marylanders thousands of miles from home on a voyage of no return.[5]

The economic hard times for the Chesapeake region were flush times for the interstate slave trade. After the Revolution, the population of enslaved African Americans grew as the demand for slave labor slackened. By the early nineteenth century, Chesapeake slaveholders moaned that surplus bondpeople burdened them with upkeep costs like food, clothing, and shelter. Hard times at home and a flourishing cotton economy to the south and west presented golden opportunities to those masters. Upper South slaveholders relieving themselves of excess bondpersons formed a complementary interest to Lower South countrymen taking on mountains of debt to buy slaves and land. The domestic slave trade surged in the 1820s. About 155,000 enslaved Americans crossed state lines by force in that decade, and the maritime slave trade from cities like Baltimore and Norfolk, Virginia, was expanding rapidly. Professional traders moved in, offering "CASH FOR NEGROES." They scoured the countryside, assembling enslaved Marylanders in coffles and marching them overland to the Lower South or else consigning them to merchant voyages. Shippers suffering in the hard times took advantage of revenues from human cargoes.[6]

Many Marylanders became alarmed at the new commerce. The proliferation of newspaper advertisements worried some citizens that Marylanders of African descent were being spirited out of Baltimore illegally. Maryland's laws of slavery permitted slaves for life to be transported but forbade those under bond of manumission to be sold out of state. Slave owners were nevertheless breaking promises and selling bondpersons to slave traders. Kidnappers prowled the northern borderlands in search of victims to enslave. Commerce in people caused a demographic catastrophe as it split apart thousands of families. Cash for slaves amounted to "CASH FOR BLOOD," screamed Baltimore editor Hezekiah Niles, a Quaker, in 1821. Niles was an economic nationalist whose paper celebrated the growth of agriculture and industry, but he detested its side effects. Slave traders "have a number of dens in the suburbs of the city," he growled, "wherein misery personified is groaning in chains."[7] Baltimore's Quakers worried that too many African-descended Marylanders were disappearing into the holds of ships like the *Hyperion* never to be seen again.

Some decided to investigate. In 1820 Quaker George Ellicott policed the Baltimore shipping district of Fell's Point. In early November, Ellicott and a customs inspector arrived at Tenant's Wharf to inspect the *Hyperion,* which had been cleared to sail to New Orleans with slaves. As they approached the wharf on a crisp November morning, the inspectors beheld a forest of ships' masts rising above the warehouses on the waterfront. Peering into the *Hyperion*'s hold, Ellicott and the inspector saw critical parts of the cotton chain in the form of several enslaved people consigned by a local merchant. The inspector asked whether they were being smuggled out of Baltimore. All "acknowledge[d] themselves to be slaves for life," he reported, "except James Spencer who says that he had the promise of a former master that he would be free at some future period but what time he cannot say." Six-foot-one-inch-tall Spencer had seen plenty of promises broken in his forty years in slavery. But this one was shattering. After holding out a promise of freedom as an incentive to work diligently, his owner, a local grain dealer, sold Spencer to a city merchant. Not wanting to risk his running off, the merchant decided to sell him in New Orleans. Misery filled the *Hyperion*'s hold. Among Spencer's companions was twenty-five-year-old Bill Short and four-year-old Eliza with her twenty-four-year-old mother Hagar. Their stories were not recorded, but all were being taken from loved ones and their homeland.[8]

The *Hyperion* was freighted with commodities and consumer goods. Tenant owned much of that cargo, including wine, raisins, and six hundred barrels of flour. Wine and raisins would sell well at the holidays. So would hams and the fifty barrels of apples put aboard. Chesapeake flour was reputed to be some of the finest in the world, and instead of shipping it to the British West Indies to be consumed by enslaved people, Tenant shipped it to fellow Americans in the Mississippi River Valley. Hundreds of thousands had moved west from 1810 to 1820, taking a taste for wheat bread with them. Flour and other bulk commodities were difficult to haul over the Appalachian Mountains and along the dirt roads leading west. The Erie Canal would not be finished for five more years, and in the meantime the city of New Orleans was the dominant transshipment point for goods entering the Mississippi Valley. Much of the *Hyperion*'s cargo would be steamed upriver for sale. Natchez citizens, for instance, could enjoy a Virginia ham, French wine, and loaves of wheat bread at Christmastime. Perhaps to ameliorate the consequences of holiday excess, the *Hyperion* also carried medicines. The merchant who owned most of the slaves also shipped boxes and barrels of other goods as well.[9]

The *Hyperion* landed in New Orleans three weeks before Christmas, completing one leg of the so-called cotton triangle linking eastern seaboard cities with southern cotton ports and British or European ones. After Christmas, shipmaster Francis Blackwell oversaw the loading of 890 bales of cotton. Before steam presses were employed to compress bales of cotton into about half the size they generally occupied, a North American bale of cotton took up about thirty cubic feet. The *Hyperion* was nearly filled to capacity. It took an experienced mariner to load a vessel correctly. Heavy in the bow or stern, the ship could not navigate effectively. Few things sunk merchant ships quicker than improperly packed cargoes. Blackwell sailed for Liverpool in early January 1821.[10]

For merchant seafarers, the Atlantic was a series of strategic sea lanes. Blackwell could be thankful that this passage was in winter. Fogs were less dense during winter crossings. Icebergs were scarcer. The eastbound route across the North Atlantic was faster than the return. Ships sailed to the northeast with the winds and ocean currents off of Cape Hatteras, North Carolina. The Gulf Stream and the North Atlantic Drift could speed a ship sailing from Louisiana to Liverpool along thousands of miles of ocean in less time than it took to sail from Baltimore to New Orleans.[11] After clearing the southwestern tip of Ireland and sailing through St. George's Channel, the *Hyperion* entered the River Mersey. The passage had taken just thirty-one days.[12]

Liverpool was about three times the size of Baltimore and extended for three miles along the banks of the Mersey estuary. Wide and well-kept streets were home to commodious houses constructed of dark yellow bricks. The skyline was punctuated by church spires. In mid-February, Blackwell's ship landed at the recently opened Prince's Dock, built especially for the U.S. cotton trade. There a throng of workers unloaded the cargo. Blackwell delivered 571 bales of cotton to William and James Brown and Company. Smaller consignments went to other merchants, and 200 would be auctioned.[13] Whether William Brown or his brother James oversaw the *Hyperion*'s unloading is unclear, but their firm had much to do with the voyage's success.

C redit was largely responsible for the strength of the cotton chain. A merchant such as Thomas Tenant could not stay in business long if he invested money in one voyage and then waited four or six months to reap a return and reinvest. Small merchants were self-financed, but that was an obstacle to growth. William and James Brown and Company was the Liverpool branch of Alexander Brown and Sons, one of the largest merchant banking houses in the United States. Alexander Brown was Thomas Tenant's Baltimore neighbor at 128 Baltimore Street, several minutes' walk from the Basin (now Inner Harbor), in the commercial center of the city. Brown was an Irish immigrant who began in business by buying and selling consignments of finished goods in Baltimore. His firm sold goods on commission, speculated in commodities, and extended short-term credit to merchants in the transatlantic trade between the United States and Ireland or Britain.[14]

Brown's ambitious strategy led him into merchant banking, which supplemented his import-export business. Brown got into the shipping business as well. With his sons, the firm branched out into financing others' consignments and eventually into the letter-of-credit business. Letters of credit were endorsements guaranteeing payment by Brown's firm if the creditor did not pay. Such arrangements built merchants' creditworthiness under Brown's patronage. Alexander Brown and Sons's financial services included dealing in bills of exchange, drawn in pounds sterling, against exports of commodities such as tobacco and flour, and accepting payment in dollars. Bills of exchange were orders for a third party to pay a designated sum at a certain time after the bill was accepted. Such private money became public currency. Merchants and bankers who created such debt instruments multiplied liquidity and thus credit. And in good economic times such arrangements were a mix of efficiency and sophistication as bills went from hand to hand, paying for a variety of goods and services before reaching the payee.

The Browns quickly understood that credit, the most expansive resource in human history, enabled the creativity at the heart of merchant capitalism. Over time the Browns discovered that the business of credit held more profit and growth potential than the business of trading cotton and other tangible commodities. Each of Alexander's four sons rose in the family business. In 1815 William partnered with his three brothers in Baltimore, and the Liverpool firm became known as William and James Brown and Company. The William and James Brown and Company was in the vanguard of Liverpool's surging postwar commodities market. By 1825 the firm had branches in Baltimore, Liverpool, London, New York, and Philadelphia. It also employed agents in New Orleans. The company's directors and agents shared knowledge, allocated decision-making responsibilities, and cooperated strategically.[15] As they grew, they discovered that some of the most valuable commodities traversing the North Atlantic were intangible.[16]

C redit gave the cotton chain its strength, but knowledge gave it its integrity. In an age before credit-reporting agencies, firms like Alexander Brown and Sons and their London competitor Baring Brothers and Company kept what amounted to an index of merchants' reputations, which they shared internally. William and James Brown and Company cooperated with other branches of the Brown partnership in sending and receiving tidbits on merchants' creditworthiness and other market intelligence. It was critical to know when and what to ship, whose bills were sound, and whose credit was shaky.[17]

The cotton chain was knowledge intensive. Merchants sought competitive advantages through strategic intelligence. As the cotton economy matured, so did a network of business information such as public circular letters, private correspondence, and commercial reports. British merchants had published prices in newspapers such as the weekly *Course of the Exchange* beginning in 1803. Americans published prices as well. After the financial crisis of 1825—a crisis resolved by a banking system based on cotton derivatives—British financier Henry Burgess began to publish in 1828 the weekly newspaper *Circular to Bankers*, a digest of laws and industry news. Another paper begun the same year, *Perry's Bankrupt and Insolvent Weekly Gazette*, reported on failures. But such information traveled along lines of communication coextensive with the routes of merchant sailing ships.[18]

In the age of sail, whoever commanded the fastest ships held a competitive advantage. Merchant vessels fell into three categories: transients or tramps, regular traders, and packets. Tramp ships sailed wherever the owner or operators detected a hint of revenue. They were on the bottom rung. Regular traders plied a regular route but not on a schedule. Precisely when sailing ships departed depended upon the weather, and merchants seeking to maximize their capacity often delayed departure in hopes of a last-minute cargo. Passengers often languished for weeks before their ship sailed. But the increasingly competitive transatlantic cotton market required that news and cargoes sail on schedule. Packets made that happen. The Black Ball Line from New York to Liverpool was the first packet line, begun in 1817. Alexander Brown competed with New York City–based textile merchants who owned the Black Ball Line by forming his own packet line, into which he incorporated Thomas Tenant's *Hyperion.*[19] While the *Hyperion* was docked at Baltimore in 1822, Alexander Brown wrote his sons in Liverpool, "Tenant's *Hyperion,* is going back to [New] Orleans and may possibly go from there to Liverpool," and indicated that he wanted William and James Brown and Company to operate the vessel. By the end of the year the House of Brown organized such ships into a line sailing on schedule between Philadelphia and Liverpool, supplemented by regular traders carrying commodities in which they had an interest. Packet service demanded punctuality. "You must have a fast ship and a pushing captain," Alexander Brown counseled.[20] In Liverpool, William and James Brown and Company advertised that their ships would sail from Philadelphia on the twentieth of each month, January excepted, and from Liverpool on the eighth of each month.[21]

Over time the Browns and Baring Brothers and Company, a large, London-based merchant bank, competed to operate packet lines that delivered commodities and information on a prearranged schedule. The convenience they offered transatlantic passengers was tertiary. Their organizational experience was a model of knowledge-creation and its diffusion in public and proprietary forms. Partly as a result of organizing information concerning merchants and commodities markets, Alexander Brown and Sons became the leading Baltimore exporter of cotton to Liverpool by 1827. It soon became the second-largest exchange merchant in the country, behind the Second Bank of the United States. In Liverpool, William and James Brown and Company (later Brown,

Shipley, and Company) was the second-leading cotton merchant in 1820, 1830, and 1839 and the main competitor to Baring Brothers. As for market strategy, the Browns built their status by undercutting competitors and funneling the export trade to the United States on ships operated by Brown partnerships.[22]

The growth of the transatlantic cotton chain led to specialization that rationalized the market. If a Baltimore or Liverpool merchant printed a business card in 1800, it might be filled with various occupations. Ship owners were also insurance underwriters. Merchants who bought and sold flour, salt, or lumber also bought and sold dozens of other commodities depending on the season and market. Over time, merchants who dealt in only one commodity gained advantages over their generalized competitors. Occupational specialties narrowed. Between 1820 and 1839, the number of Liverpool merchants who dealt in cotton declined by more than 40 percent. In the same time frame, there were one-quarter fewer regular dealers, those who bought cotton on six occasions during any one year. As time went on, a smaller pool of importers consolidated a dominant share of the cotton trade for themselves. As merchant bankers specialized in financing a transatlantic trade in cotton and other North American commodities, Liverpool replaced London as England's main entrepôt.[23]

The strength and integrity of the cotton chain also depended on the actual cotton lint that landed in Liverpool. Prince's Dock was located adjacent to Liverpool's Exchange, where the produce of the *Hyperion* and thousands of other voyages was sold. Often, the cotton dealers' were the first white hands to touch samples of cotton or tobacco that had been cultivated, processed, packed, and ported by enslaved laborers. The process of grading and selling cotton linked the quality of lint traded in Liverpool to the fortunes of shippers, merchants, factors, planters, overseers, and, ultimately, enslaved people. British cotton buyers sought dry, cream-colored lint that was not discolored by parasite or environmental damage and had been ginned to keep the fibers intact and with only a minimum of dirt and debris. The top grade was fair. Producers desperate to get cotton to market after a rain sometimes packed the lint before drying. Such fiber often arrived rotten and putrid, turning otherwise middling cotton into ordinary or bottom-grade lint. Cotton buyers tested samples of particular consignments, negotiated prices, and exchanged information about the market.[24] From the houses of financiers, the United States' domestic slave trade was nearly invisible, its violence concealed in bales of cotton and hogsheads of tobacco. But the commercial processes that applied to cotton also applied to enslaved laborers.

Thousands of miles from the Liverpool Exchange, Americans appraised fellow enslaved human beings, inspected their bodies, and haggled over their prices. Most enslaved Americans were bought and sold in private transactions, but the slave market was most conspicuous at auctions. Americans auctioned just about everything, and in cities and towns a crimson banner hanging outside a doorway was an auction sign. When Scottish journalist William Chambers visited Richmond, Virginia, one autumn, he looked for a slave auction. He found several. Off a busy city street, he ducked into one auction room where a mother and her three children were being sold along with several other slaves. "Already a crowd had met," Chambers recalled, "composed, I should think, of persons mostly from the cotton-plantations of the south." Men thronged a fireplace on that cold morning. The building was "dilapidated" and the private brick jail across the alley was "shabby."[25]

But what slave auctions lacked in elegance they made up for in theatrics. Each auction was a commercial theater that obscured its subjects' histories and identities. As Chambers watched, a "mulatto" assistant "ushered in" the several bondpeople offered for sale, he recalled. "I saw no whips, chains, or other engine of force." The lack of overt coercion was part of the show. "Nor did such appear to be required," Chambers remarked. The captives sat down on benches adjacent to a wood stove. The visitor was struck by the fact that "none shewed any sign of resistance; nor did any one utter a word." Silence was often part of the script. "Their manner was that of perfect humility and resignation." Would-be bidders crowded in, groping body parts, peering at teeth and gums, "and investigating the quality of their hands and fingers—this last being evidently an important particular." Nimble fingers were of the utmost importance. Cotton bolls were sharp, and while cotton picking did not require much strength, it demanded considerable manual dexterity.[26]

The slaves for sale wore costumes, which were like packaging. A young woman auctioned with three children "was neatly attired," Chambers recalled, "with a coloured handkerchief bound round her head, and wore a white apron over her gown." "Her children were all girls, one of them a baby at the breast, three months old, and the others two and three years respectively, rigged out with clean white pinafores" or aprons. Chambers stepped forward to interview the woman offered for sale. She was from a rural county about eighty miles northwest of the city. Her life's story was one of displacement and family destruction. She had given birth to seven children and had been separated from her husband just two days before. The owner wanted money, she supposed. Chambers asked if she was sorry to part from her husband. "'Yes, sir,' she replied with a deep sigh; 'my heart was a'most broke.'"[27]

After an initial review, the performance began. The auctioneer gathered a throng of potential bidders as the assistant ushered the woman and three children to an elevated block. "There she stood with her infant at the breast, and one of her girls at each side," Chambers recalled. On a raised platform the auctioneer struck a commanding pose. "'Well, gentlemen,' began the salesman, 'here is a capital woman and her three children, all in good health—what do you say for them? Give me an offer.'" He asked $850 to start the bidding for the four. No one bid. He had his assistant grab the baby from the mother's nursing breast and hold the infant up to the audience to show its apparent health. The bidding started. It advanced in ten-dollar increments up to $890. "That won't do, gentlemen," the auctioneer warned. "I cannot take such a low price," after which he ordered the assistant to dismiss the woman and her children.[28] They would come up again or else be bought in a backroom deal that satisfied the auctioneer and his client. The first act was over.

As the commercial spectacle proceeded, buyers imagined their future in the flesh-and-bone goods offered for sale and bet their money on their ability to read bodies. The next scene in that morning's auction featured a man whom bidders asked that he strip naked so they could perform a thorough examination. Before the man ascended the block, the assistant ushered him behind a canvas screen near a window. "About a dozen gentlemen crowded to the spot while the poor fellow was stripping himself," Chambers recorded, "and as soon as he stood on the floor, bare from top to toe, a most rigorous scrutiny of his person was instituted. . . . There was no part of his body left unexamined." Buyers wanted skin unblemished by disease or abrasions, eyes free of sickness or rage, and hands nimble and dexterous enough to make them money. As Chambers observed, "The man was told to open and shut his hands, asked if he could pick cotton, and every tooth in his head was scrupulously looked at." Once purchased by a slave trader, the enslaved were confined in jail until a sufficient quantity existed to make up a coffle or consignment aboard a merchant vessel.[29]

The theatrics of the auction room contrasted with the banalities of maritime commerce. In May 1822, the *Hyperion* was again docked at Tenant's Wharf, Baltimore, after another voyage to New Orleans. From its hold emerged an abundance of slave-grown commodities, including sugar, cotton, and tobacco. Much of the cotton would be transshipped to Liverpool aboard ships operated by Alexander Brown and Sons. Distance measured in dollars was shorter between New Orleans and Liverpool by way of Baltimore or New York City than the geographic distance between Louisiana and England. That was because merchants like the House of Brown extended credit on favorable terms.[30] While the Browns were incorporating the *Hyperion* into their transatlantic packet line, the ship was loading slaves. Its voyage in the fall of 1820 had included 10 captives. In the fall of 1821, the ship sailed from Baltimore with 37. Six months later, professional slave traders embarked 55.[31] Production of cotton lint and textiles was soaring, but something odd was happening.

Slave prices were falling as the cotton chain globalized. So were the prices of cotton and cloth. In the 1820s, inexpensive agricultural lands recently taken from American Indians yielded abundant cotton produced by forced labor. Planters worked bondpeople harder and demanded more of them. High-yielding cotton varieties generated more lint per acre, while British production technologies turned out the most abundant and cheapest fabrics in human history. Suppliers auctioned them off, some taking losses if it meant undercutting competitors. Credit became abundant, and British merchants sought new markets in Africa, South America, and South Asia. Local textile manufacturers all over the globe succumbed to the cotton chain. They could not compete with cheap goods that were becoming necessities. That deflationary process was roughly analogous to the way in which large retail chains of the twenty-first century depress prices while flooding the market with inexpensive foreign manufactures. As in the Wal-Mart age, few consumers could resist. Prices for cotton and slaves fluctuated in the mid-1820s and then rose substantially between 1830 and 1836, along with American economic and financial expansion. The domestic slave trade also peaked in the 1830s.[32]

For those packed aboard the *Hyperion* in May 1822, the larger process of commercial development was scarcely perceptible. Immediate concerns presented themselves as slave traders embarked new mothers with infants. George was just four days old when he and his mother were ushered aboard. Eliza and Eleanor were both in their twenties, and one of them had given birth sometime between her sale and embarkation. George thus spent the first month of his life confined aboard a slave ship. Before they left Tenant's Wharf, more captives joined them.[33] An agent acting for professional slave trader Austin Woolfolk loaded seven captives, including six young men and women, ages eighteen to twenty-four. The seventh was a two-month-old infant. They were consigned to his uncle, John Woolfolk, and his younger brother Samuel in New Orleans.[34]

The Woolfolks were at the time the slave-trading counterparts to the House of Brown. Austin Woolfolk, along with his uncle John and four younger brothers, led a loosely knit firm that bought enslaved people in the Chesapeake region and transported them to cotton ports such as Savannah, Charleston, and New Orleans. Woolfolk's competitor David Anderson embarked a coffle of twenty-eight captives aboard the *Hyperion* as well. Lacking the Woolfolks' corporate form, Anderson consigned his captives to a New Orleans merchant firm. The *Hyperion* sailed from Baltimore but touched at Norfolk, where Richard T. Woolfolk embarked six more captives. A Louisiana planter put aboard a final five. Conditions must have been wretched. There was no neonatal care for a new mother and infant, and strangers, even if sharing the same horrific fate, were hardly a substitute for family or friends. By the time newborn George reached New Orleans, he had spent most of his life aboard ship and would likely never see his father. But enslavers' eyes were firmly fixed not on emotional bonds or familial ties but on dollars.[35]

As with the cotton chain, credit was essential to the strength of the slave market. While the *Hyperion* was sailing, Samuel M. Woolfolk sold five enslaved people to a New Orleans city gentleman for thirty-three hundred dollars. Instead of cash, the buyer gave him a note payable the following March and endorsed by another city gentleman. That was a nine-month loan to the buyer, which Woolfolk factored into the price of the slaves. Such promissory notes carried significant advantages over cash sales. Enslaved people were perishable goods. Humans sickened and died; bondpeople ran off. Bills or promises to pay were durable. They were recognized in law. Instead of waiting for buyers to come up with cash, slave traders such as the Woolfolks willingly exchanged human beings for paper promises.[36]

The violence of slavery corresponded in large measure to debt service. Slaveholders in Maryland liquidating human assets to meet debt obligations tore families apart. Merchants under pressure to meet their margins sold transport. Planters in Louisiana intensified violence to increase productivity. There was a perverse irony to the relationship between violence and debt. The humiliation, misery, trauma, and terror experienced by the enslaved as they passed through a supply chain mirrored the optimism of agents of the cotton economy. Debt ballooned in a rising market. When confidence eroded, as during the panic of 1819, liquidity dried up and commerce slowed. As the supply chain in slaves lengthened, however, problems emerged for interstate traders.

The magic of returns was often overwhelmed by the realities of distance. Paper money posed difficulties for commerce over geographic space. Most money was local, and no one took it for granted. Paper money tended to travel local or regional circuits, and banknotes tended to decline in value the farther they traveled from the issuing institution. A planter's promissory note or a merchant's bill of exchange also tended to depreciate the farther it traveled from the issuer. The Woolfolks solved the problem of distance by expanding their corporate form. The New Orleans branch of the firm functioned as its bank, accepting and holding or discounting paper while remitting the proceeds to Chesapeake branches. Other interstate slave traders formed strategic alliances with commission merchants in New Orleans and other cities in order to diminish what amounted to a tax on distance.[37]

Remitting revenues from Louisiana to Maryland was no simple matter. When David Anderson consigned captives to the *Hyperion* or any other vessel, to be sold in New Orleans, he employed city merchants to act as his sales agents and financial agents. From about 1815 through the early 1820s, Anderson consigned captives to fellow Kentuckian Hector McLean. Hector McLean and Company was a commission merchant of New Orleans that sold bondpeople, collected bills, and acted as a banker and accountant. McLean's services permitted Anderson to keep more of the proceeds from Louisiana slave sales and to offer local bank notes to Maryland slaveholders. In January 1820, for instance, Anderson drew a bill on McLean and Company for fifteen hundred dollars, payable sixty days after sight. That was an efficient way for Anderson to claim what he thought McLean owed him. After drawing the bill and having it endorsed by a Baltimore merchant, Anderson discounted the bill at the Baltimore branch of the Second Bank of the United States. There the cashier gave Anderson a percentage of the face value. In return, Anderson received some of the best bank money in the country, which he could use to buy more captives. While his consignments of bondpersons were sailing to New Orleans for sale,

Anderson could continue to purchase more. He drew more bills on McLean and Company later that spring. McLean protested, and by 1822 Anderson was consigning captives to another firm.[38]

T he cotton chain that brought miseries to so many enslaved Americans delivered freedom and convenience to consumers. After disembarking captives in New Orleans, the *Hyperion* sailed to Liverpool and then home to Baltimore. The return trip took sixty days. At Fell's Point in early January 1823, porters unloaded containers of salt and textiles. Merchants who bought the cotton cloth arriving from England would not immediately catch a whiff of slavery in a cornucopia of calicoes, quilts, shirtings, and shawls.[39]

The cases of textiles shipped from Liverpool and unloaded at Tenant's Wharf were packed with ironies as well. They were tangible components of the towering achievements of nineteenth-century capitalism: the rational organization of time and space and of markets spanning thousands of miles of land and sea. That commerce was founded on transparency and trust, mediated by knowledge and transportation technologies, linked by a network of merchants, manufacturers, producers, and bankers, delivering cheap manufactured textiles to customers hungry for them. To American consumers, ready-made fabric embodied democracy. It was a sign of the wearer's emerging status. Cheap fabric relieved home spinners and weavers—mostly women—of domestic drudgery.[40] The cotton chain was emblematic of a great nineteenth-century leap in technology and commercial growth, one that showered beneficiaries with cheap consumer goods and shouldered bondpeople with the human costs.

NOTES

1. Joseph C. Miller, *The Problem of Slavery as History: A Global Approach* (New Haven, CT: Yale University Press, 2012), ch. 4; Anthony E. Kaye, "The Second Slavery: Modernity in the Nineteenth-Century South and the Atlantic World," *Journal of Southern History* 75 (August 2009): 627–50; Immanuel Wallerstein, *The Modern World-System IV: Centrist Liberalism Triumphant, 1789–1914* (Berkeley: University of California Press, 2011), ch. 2; Brian Schoen, *The Fragile Fabric of Union: Cotton, Federal Politics, and the Global Origins of the Civil War* (Baltimore: Johns Hopkins University Press, 2009); Dale W. Tomich, *Through the Prism of Slavery: Labor, Capital, and World Economy* (Lanham, MD: Rowman and Littlefield, 2004), chs. 1–2; Joseph I. Inikori,

"Slavery and the Development of Industrial Capitalism in England," in *British Capitalism and Caribbean Slavery: The Legacy of Eric Williams,* ed. Barbara L. Solow and Stanley L. Engerman (Cambridge: Cambridge University Press, 2004), 79–102; Eric Williams, *Capitalism and Slavery* (1944; Chapel Hill: University of North Carolina Press, 1994), chs. 7–10.

2. Scott Reynolds Nelson, *A Nation of Deadbeats: An Uncommon History of America's Financial Disasters* (New York: Knopf, 2012), ch. 5; Walter Johnson, *River of Dark Dreams: Slavery and Empire in the Cotton Kingdom* (Cambridge, MA: Harvard University Press, 2013).

3. Edward E. Baptist, "The Whipping Machine," paper delivered at Slavery's Capitalism Conference, Harvard University, April 9, 2011; John K. Walton, *A Social History of Lancashire, 1558–1939* (Manchester: Manchester University Press, 1987), ch. 6; Robert Greenhalgh Albion, *Square-Riggers on Schedule: The New York Sailing Packets to England, France, and the Cotton Ports* (Princeton, NJ: Princeton University Press, 1938), chs. 1–2.

4. *Baltimore Patriot,* August 1, 1822, 2 (quotation); Londa Schiebinger, *Plants and Empire: Colonial Bioprospecting in the Atlantic World* (Cambridge, MA: Harvard University Press, 2004), 8; Toni Ahrens, *Design Makes a Difference: Shipbuilding in Baltimore, 1765–1835* (Bowie, MD: Heritage Books, 1998), 137; William S. McFeely, *Frederick Douglass* (New York: Norton, 1991), 59–63; Jeff Markell, *Unusual Vessels* (Annapolis, MD: Light House Press, 2003), 77–90; Thomas N. Layton, *The Voyage of the Frolic: New England Merchants and the Opium Trade* (Stanford, CA: Stanford University Press, 1997), 44–45; J. Thomas Scharf, *History of Baltimore City and County, from the Earliest Period to the Present Day* (Philadelphia: Louis J. Everts, 1881), 187, 214, 246, 407, 437–38, 577.

5. *Baltimore American and Commercial Daily Advertiser,* July 1, 1820, 1; *Baltimore Patriot,* October 14, 1820, 3; Max Grivno, *Gleanings of Freedom: Free and Slave Labor along the Mason-Dixon Line, 1790–1860* (Urbana: University of Illinois Press, 2011).

6. *Baltimore Patriot,* November 17, 1815, 3.

7. *Niles' Weekly Register,* July 21, 1821, 324 (quotation); Schoen, *Fragile Fabric of Union;* William Calderhead, "The Role of the Professional Slave Trader in a Slave Economy: Austin Woolfolk, a Case Study," *Civil War History* 23 (September 1977): 203–5.

8. Report of November 9, 1820, U.S. Customs Service, Port of Baltimore, MD, Office of the Surveyor of Customs, Orders and Reports concerning Slaves on Ships, Feb.–Dec. 1820, folder February–December 1820, NARA, Mid-Atlantic Branch, Philadelphia; Ahrens, *Design Makes a Difference,* 137; Charles Kennan, *C. Keenan's Baltimore Directory for 1822 and 1823* (Baltimore: J. R. Matchett, 1822), 302; *Baltimore Patriot,* October 3, 1820, 3.

9. Inward Slave Manifest, New Orleans, November 8, 1820 (*Hyperion*), M1895, Roll 1, images 582–83, 626–28, NARA; Inward Manifest, New Orleans, December 5, 1820 (*Hyperion*), NO-151, box 35, folder December 1820, NARA, Southwestern Branch, Fort Worth; Kennan, *Baltimore Directory for 1822 and 1823,* 157; Robert Gudmestad, *Steamboats and the Rise of the Cotton Kingdom* (Baton Rouge: Louisiana State University Press, 2011); Ralph Clayton, *Cash for Blood: The Baltimore to New Orleans Domestic Slave Trade* (Westminster, MD: Heritage Books, 2007), 631.

10. Albion, *Square-Riggers on Schedule,* ch. 1; W. Jeffrey Bolster, *The Mortal Sea: Fishing the Atlantic in the Age of Sail* (Cambridge, MA: Harvard University Press, 2012), ch. 1.

11. Albion, *Square-Riggers on Schedule,* 7–9; Bolster, *Mortal Sea,* chs. 4–5.

12. Albion, *Square-Riggers on Schedule,* 7–9.

13. *Liverpool Mercury,* February 16, 1821, 271; February 23, 1821, 270; Benjamin Silliman, *A Journal of Travels in England, Holland and Scotland* (New Haven, CT: S. Converse, 1820), 1:68–69, cited in John Crosby Brown, *A Hundred Years of Merchant Banking: A History of Brown Brothers and Company* (New York: The author, 1909), 60.

14. Ronald S. Burt, *Neighbor Networks: Competitive Advantage Local and Personal* (New York: Oxford University Press, 2010); Edwin J. Perkins, *Financing Anglo-American Trade: The House of Brown, 1800–1880* (Cambridge, MA: Harvard University Press, 1975).

15. Joseph C. Miller, "Investing in Poverty—Financial Aspects of the Global Historical Dynamics of Commercialization," Conference on "Understanding African Poverty over the Longue Durée," International Institute for the Advanced Study of Cultures, Institutions and Economic Enterprise, Accra, Ghana, July 15–17, 2010; Stanley Chapman, *The Rise of Merchant Banking* (London: George Allen & Unwin, 1984), chs. 2–4; Perkins, *Financing Anglo-American Trade,* 83–113; Leland Hamilton Jenks, *The Migration of British Capital to 1875* (New York: Knopf, 1927), chs. 2–3; Howard Bodenhorn, *State Banking in Early America: A New Economic History* (New York: Oxford University Press, 2003), chs. 3, 10–11; Joseph Inikori, *Africans and the Industrial Revolution in England: A Study in International Trade and Economic Development* (New York: Cambridge University Press, 2002); Brown, *A Hundred Years of Merchant Banking;* Mark Casson, *Information and Organization: A New Perspective on the Theory of the Firm* (New York: Oxford University Press, 1997); Martijn Konings, *The Development of American Finance* (New York: Cambridge University Press, 2011), ch. 3.

16. Perkins, *Financing Anglo-American Trade,* 20; Salvatore Sciascia, Pietro Mazzola, Joseph H. Astrachan, and Torsten M. Pieper, "The Role of Family Ownership in International Entrepreneurship: Exploring Nonlinear Effects," *Small Business Economics* 38 (January 2012): 15–31.

17. Joel Mokyr, *The Enlightened Economy: An Economic History of Britain, 1700–1850* (New Haven, CT: Yale University Press, 2009); Linda Argote and Ella Miron-Spektor, "Organizational Learning: From Experience to Knowledge," *Organization Science* 22 (September–October 2011): 1123–37; Ralph W. Hidy, *The House of Baring in American Trade and Finance: English Merchant Bankers at Work* (Cambridge, MA: Harvard University Press, 1949), 155–58; Bertram Wyatt-Brown, "God and Dun & Bradstreet, 1841–1851," *Business History Review* 40 (Winter 1966): 432–50.

18. Edward E. Baptist, "Toxic Debt, Liar Loans, Collateralized and Securitized Human Beings, and the Panic of 1837," in *Capitalism Takes Command: The Social Transformation of Nineteenth-Century America,* ed. Michael Zakim and Gary J. Kornblith (Chicago: University of Chicago Press, 2012), 69–92; Jonathan Levy, *Freaks of Fortune: The Emerging World of Capitalism and Risk in America* (Cambridge, MA: Harvard University Press, 2012), ch. 2; Robert M. Grant, "The Knowledge-Based View of the Firm," in *The Strategic Management of Intellectual Capital and Organizational Knowledge,* ed. Chun Wei Choo and Nick Bontis (New York: Oxford University Press, 2002), 133–48; Andrew King, "Circular to Bankers (1828–1860)," in *Dictionary of Nineteenth-Century Journalism: In Great Britain and Ireland,* ed. Laurel Brake and Marysa Demoor (Ghent: Academia Press, 2009), 119; Edward J. Balleisen, *Navigating Failure: Bankruptcy and Commercial Society in Antebellum America* (Chapel Hill: University of North Carolina Press, 2001), ch. 1;

Jessica Lepler, *The Many Panics of 1837: People, Politics, and the Creation of a Transatlantic Finan-cial Crisis* (New York: Cambridge University Press, 2013), ch. 1; Larry Neal, "The Financial *Crisis of 1825 and the Restructuring of the British Financial System,"* *Federal Reserve Bank of St. Louis Review* 80 (May–June 1998): 53–76; Cathy D. Matson, "Capitalizing Hope: Economic Thought and the Early National Economy," *Journal of the Early Republic* 16 (Summer 1996): 273–91; Nicholas Onuf and Peter Onuf, *Nations, Markets, and War: Modern History and the Civil War* (Charlottesville: University of Virginia Press, 2006), chs. 6–8.

19. Chris Turner, *The Leap: How to Survive in the Sustainable Economy* (Toronto: Random House of Canada, 2011), prologue, ch. 1; Ele Bowen, *Rambles in the Path of the Steam-Horse* (Philadelphia: William Bromwell and William White Smith, 1855), 32–33. Brown and Tenant also later served on the board of Maryland's first railroad.

20. Alexander Brown and Sons to William and James Brown and Company, May 2, 1822, cited in Brown, *A Hundred Years of Merchant Banking*, 71.

21. *Liverpool Mercury,* May 3, 1822, 348; Frank R. Kent, *The Story of Alexander Brown and Sons* (Baltimore: Alexander Brown and Sons, 1925), 109; Kenichi Ohmae, "The Global Logic of Strategic Alliances," *Harvard Business Review* 67 (March–April 1989): 143–54.

22. David M. Williams, "Liverpool Merchants and the Cotton Trade," in *Merchants and Mariners: Selected Maritime Writings of David M. Williams,* ed. Lars U. Scholl (St. John's, New-foundland: International Maritime Economic History Association, 2000), 23–29; Margaret A. Peteraf, "The Cornerstones of Competitive Advantage: A Resource-Based View," *Strategic Man-agement Journal* 14 (March 1993): 179–91.

23. Hidy, *House of Baring,* 94, 106; Chapman, *Rise of Merchant Banking,* 42; Brown, *A Hundred Years of Merchant Banking,* 64–67.

24. Lynn Willoughby, *Fair to Middlin': The Antebellum Cotton Trade of the Apalachicola/Chat-tahoochee River Valley* (Tuscaloosa: University of Alabama Press, 1993), ch. 1; Johnson, *River of Dark Dreams,* ch. 9.

25. William Chambers, *Things as They Are in America* (Edinburgh: William and Robert Chambers, 1854), 277–78: Walter Johnson, *Soul by Soul: Life inside the Antebellum Slave Market* (Cambridge, MA: Harvard University Press, 1999), ch. 2.

26. Chambers, *Things as They Are in America,* 278.

27. Ibid., 278, 279 (quotations); Johnson, *Soul by Soul,* ch. 1.

28. Chambers, *Things as They Are in America,* 280, 281.

29. Ibid., 281 (quotations); Johnson, *Soul by Soul,* ch. 5.

30. Johnson, *River of Dark Dreams,* 257.

31. Grivno, *Gleanings of Freedom,* ch. 2; David R. MacGregor, *Merchant Sailing Ships, 1815–1850: Supremacy of Sail* (Annapolis: Naval Institute Press, 1984), 163–64: Clayton, *Cash for Blood,* 631.

32. Nelson, *Nation of Deadbeats,* ch. 5; Edward E. Baptist, *The Half Has Never Been Told: Slav-ery and the Making of American Capitalism* (New York: Basic Books, 2014); Nelson Lichtenstein, *The Retail Revolution: How Wal-Mart Created a Brave New World of Business* (New York: Henry Holt, 2009); Joseph C. Miller, *Way of Death: Merchant Capitalism and the Angolan Slave Trade* (Madison: University of Wisconsin Press, 1988), chs. 13, 16–18.

33. Inward Slave Manifest, New Orleans, June 18, 1822 (*Hyperion*), M1895 roll 2, images 283–84, NARA; Marie Jenkins Schwartz, *Birthing a Slave: Motherhood and Medicine in the Antebellum South* (Cambridge, MA: Harvard University Press, 2006), chs. 5–6.

34. Inward Slave Manifest, New Orleans, June 18, 1822 (*Hyperion*), M1895, roll 2, images 290–91, NARA; Calderhead, "Role of the Professional Slave Trader," 195–211.

35. *Baltimore Patriot*, May 21, 1822, 2; *Charleston (SC) City Gazette*, July 29, 1822, 3; Inward Slave Manifests, May 10–14, 1822 (*Hyperion*), M1895, roll 2, images 283–84, 288–91, 298–99, 693–94, NARA; *Baltimore Patriot*, April 30, 1822, 2; Calvin Schermerhorn, *The Business of Slavery and the Rise of American Capitalism, 1815–1860* (New Haven, CT: Yale University Press, 2015), ch. 2.

36. Philippe Pedesclaux, vol. 24, Act 689, June 11, 1822, New Orleans Notarial Archive.

37. Kenneth Morgan, "Remittance Procedures in the Eighteenth-Century British Slave Trade," *Business History Review* 79 (Winter 2005): 715–49.

38. Philippe Pedesclaux, vol. 13, Act 686, April 6, 1820; vol. 13, Act 710, April 10, 1820; vol. 15, Act 1296, July 12, 1820, New Orleans Notarial Archive; Kenneth Morgan, *Slavery, Atlantic Trade and the British Economy, 1660–1800* (Cambridge: Cambridge University Press, 2000); Robin Pearson and David Richardson, "Social Capital, Institutional Innovation and Atlantic Trade before 1800," *Business History* 50 (November 2008): 765–80; Robert Harms, *The Diligent: A Voyage through the Worlds of the Slave Trade* (New York: Basic Books, 2002), ch. 5.

39. *Baltimore Patriot*, January 9, 1823, 2; January 10, 1823, 2.

40. Rowena Olegario, *A Culture of Credit: Embedding Trust and Transparency in American Business* (Cambridge, MA: Harvard University Press, 2006); Stanley Chapman, *Merchant Enterprise in Britain: From the Industrial Revolution to World War I* (Cambridge: Cambridge University Press, 1992), chs. 2, 3, 5–6; Sheryllynne Haggerty, *The British-Atlantic Trading Community, 1760–1810: Men, Women, and the Distribution of Goods* (Leiden: Brill, 2006); R. C. Nash, "The Organization of Trade and Finance in the British Atlantic Economy, 1600–1830," in *The Atlantic Economy during the Seventeenth and Eighteenth Centuries: Organization, Operation, Practice, and Personnel*, ed. Peter A. Coclanis (Columbia: University of South Carolina Press, 2005), 95–151; Terence K. Hopkins and Immanuel Wallerstein, "Commodity Chains in the World-Economy Prior to 1800," *Review* 10 (Summer 1986); Michael Zakim, *Ready-Made Democracy: A History of Men's Dress in the American Republic, 1760–1860* (Chicago: University of Chicago Press, 2003); Ronald Bailey, "The Slave(ry) Trade and the Development of Capitalism in the United States: The Textile Industry in New England," *Social Science History* 14 (Autumn 1990): 373–414.

SILVER BUCKLES AND SLAVES

*Borrowing, Lending, and the Commodification
of Slaves in Virginia Communities*

BONNIE MARTIN

I n May 1772, Nicholas Green sold slaves "Celina, Sith, Tom and Charles[,]
all so four feather beds and furniture and one pair of Shoe Buckles" to
John Green, a gentleman and perhaps a relative, for two hundred pounds.
Or did he? What on its face claimed to be a sale of slaves and other commodities was probably not a pure sale but instead a pledge to secure a loan. Nicholas
Green transferred to John Green symbolic possession of the slaves and personal property "by the delivery of the Buckles in the name of the whole."[1] (See
figure 1.) In other words, Nicholas professed his good faith by performing a
legal ritual that met the expectations of community lending networks on the
British colonial frontier in Virginia. The language and content of the brief
but elegant contract between Nicholas and John Green reflects a transitional
period in an evolving spectrum of legal formalities. This chapter analyzes the
shifts in credit relationships among free Virginians during the seventeenth,
eighteenth, and nineteenth centuries and argues that these changes increased
the commodification of enslaved Virginians.[2]

Evidence for this chapter is drawn from a review of more than thirty-six
hundred transcripts and abstracts recorded in the courthouses of Henrico, Isle
of Wight, Lancaster, Prince William, and Stafford counties in Virginia during the seventeenth and eighteenth centuries and data from approximately
six thousand credit transactions recorded in six Virginia counties during the
eighteenth and nineteenth centuries: Culpeper and Fauquier in northern Virginia, Goochland and Albemarle in the central Piedmont, and Lunenburg and
Halifax in Southside.[3] Three specific debt contracts secured by commodified

FIGURE I.

The Commodification of Celina, Sith, Tom, and Charles
by Nicholas Green and John Green, Virginia, 1772

KNOW all men by these presents that Nicholas Green of Culpeper County for the ~Consideration of two Hundred pounds Current Money to me in hand paid by John Green Gent of the said County the receipt whereof I do hereby acknowledge thereof Acquit and discharge the said John Green Have Bargained and sold and by these presents do Bargain and sell unto the said John Green the following slaves to wit Celina, Sith, Tom and Charles all so four feather beds and furniture and one pair of Shoe Buckles Possession of which said Slaves goods and Chattels was by me this day given to the said John Green by the delivery of the Buckles in the name of the whole and which said Slaves goods and Chattels I do hereby warrant and forever defend to the said John Green Against the Claim of all persons whatsoever as witness my hand and seal this 10th day of May 1772

Teste Nichs Green [his mark]
C Bullitt

At a Court continued and held for the County of Culpeper on Tuesday 19th day of May 1772

slaves, along with supporting contracts and transactions, illustrate how free Virginians experimented with legal debt decorum and human collateral in order to maintain social harmony in community networks of credit. The three major sample contracts reveal a shift from personal promises to pay to more formal mortgage contracts supported by collateral.

Free Virginians used land, tools, and commodities such as crops and slaves as collateral to guarantee the repayment of debts. Lenders were more willing to offer cash and credit loans to borrowers when the promise to repay was backed by valuable property. The use of collateral accelerated economic growth by making capital more freely available and increasing the circulation of resources through Virginia communities. From the seventeenth through the nineteenth century, the number of enslaved Virginians increased dramatically, and they, as human property, became an ideal commodity to use as security. Slaves were the kind of collateral merchants and neighbors preferred when they extended credit or gave cash loans. Both commercial and private lenders easily could seize and transport human property for sale. There were advantages for borrowers as well. They did not have to sell their slaves to raise capital. Owners could promise slaves as collateral for a loan and yet keep them working in homes, fields, and forges.

While the financial advantages grew for free Virginians who used slaves as collateral, so did the disadvantages for the unfree Virginians who were mortgaged. Everyone, including Nicholas Green's slaves Celina, Sith, Tom, and Charles, knew that owners could use slaves to pay or secure their loans and debts. What unfree Virginians could not know was whether they or their friends and family members were mortgaged at any given time. It is unlikely that Celina knew that Nicholas Green had pledged her as security on that day in May. It is even less probable that James, age six; Lewis, age four; and Rachel, "a child," were aware that their owner, William Eatsham, had mortgaged them, along with ten other people, to merchants Hugh Lenox, William Scott & Company to secure a debt of fifty-five pounds.[4] If Celina had children, she ran the same risk: they could be seized to satisfy an unpaid debt. All enslaved Virginians faced the danger of separation. Owners could sell slaves, give them as gifts, distribute them in wills, or lose them to creditors. The potential for the rending of families was always there, but the ability to mortgage the same human property again and again multiplied and reconfigured that risk. While an owner's ability to access the capital stored in enslaved people without selling them undoubtedly prevented some sales of family members, slaves not sold could be mortgaged numerous times in a series of contracts over individual lives and across generations. Each of these mortgages carried a new risk of separation.

Virginia records show that the use of human collateral began to increase in the late 1600s and continued into the early 1800s, as Virginia communities became less isolated and more integrated into the transatlantic marketplace. The growing commercialization of Virginia products triggered a change in legal formalities that made relationships between free neighbors within these communities ever more structured. Virginians began to adopt stricter language, filing rituals, and security requirements. This change was prompted by British merchants such as Lenox, Scott & Company, who demanded legal guarantees that helped reduce the uncertainties and risks involved in extending credit. In the 1740s and 1750s, when Nicholas Green mortgaged his human commodities, the shift from more flexible, neighborly rituals to more formal, mandated procedures was in transition. Courthouse records allow us to observe a number of Virginians still following older community etiquette, the protocols of the late 1600s. They went to the courthouse and recorded simple, personal promises to pay debts. By the 1760s and 1770s, however, most Virginians shifted from short recitations of community commitments unsecured by collateral to longer, more formal debt recitations that guaranteed repayment by pledging valuable property. Micajah Poole's 1750 mortgage on Bacchus, Diana, and Juno, reproduced in figure 2, illustrates these changes.[5] Finally, by the nineteenth century, many free Virginians were repackaging their debts as "deeds of trust." These sophisticated mortgage vehicles had a community ethic all their own, embodying the personal responsibilities for fair dealing found in medieval English law. Chief Justice John Marshall made sure that his 1820 loan to Samuel Hunter, shown in figure 3, followed this legal formula and was protected by a mortgage on five slaves: Ceasar, Lewis, Winney, Bill, and George.[6]

In other words, over the course of about two hundred years, free Virginians modified the debt decorum of small communities of neighbors in order to provide the more rigorous legal safeguards that both commercial and private lenders came to demand. Creditors wanted predictability and security for repayment, and human assets were valuable and fungible. The poetic cadence

---

FIGURE 2.

The Commodification of Bacchus, Diana, and Juno
by Micajah Poole and William Hunter, Virginia, 1750

This Indenture made this twentieth day of June in the Year of our Lord One thousand Seven hundred and fifty **Between Micajah Poole of the County of Culpeper of the one part and William Hunter** of the County of Spotsylvania of the other part Witnesseth That the said Micajah Poole for and in Consideration of the sum of One hundred and fifty four pounds Eight shillings and six pence to him in hand paid by the said William Hunter at and before the Sealing and Delivery of these presents the Receipt whereof the said Micajah

---

FIGURE 2. *(continued)*

Poole doth hereby Acknowledge He the said **Micajah Poole hath Bargained and Sold and by these presents doth Bargain and Sell to the said William Hunter three Negroes named Bacchus, Diana, and Juno, Eight Head of Cattle, two Horses, One Mare, two feather Beds, Six Chairs, and three Iron Potts,** To have and to hold the said negroes, Cattle, Horses, mare, beds &c, above by these presents Bargained and sold unto the said William Hunter as his own proper Negroes Cattle &c ~ from henceforth forever **Provided always and upon Condition That if the said Micajah Poole** his Heirs Executors or Administrators **do well and truly pay or cause to be paid unto the said William Hunter his Heirs Executors or Assigns at or before the first day of December next the Above Mentioned Sum of One hundred and fifty four Pounds Eight Shillings and Six pence with Lawfull Interest** from the Date of these presents without any deduction or abatement whatsoever That **then this present Indenture and every thing herein Contained shall cease determine and be Void** And the said **Micajah Poole** for himself his Executors and Administrators **doth Covenant and Grant to and with the said William Hunter** his Executors and Administrators or **Assigns that the said Micajah Poole** his Executors and Administrators **shall and will well and truly pay** or Cause to be paid unto the said William Hunter his Executors Administrators or Assigns the **said Sum of One Hundred and fifty four pounds Eight Shillings and Six pence** at or before the said first day of December next According to the true intent and meaning of these presents and also that the said **William Hunter** his Executors Administrators or assigns **shall and May at all times after Default** shall be made in accordance with this proviso or Condition herein Contained, **peaceably and quietly have, hold, use, Occupy, possess and enjoy the said Negroes Bacchus, Diana, and Juno, Eight head of Cattle, two Horses, one Mare, two feather Beds, Six Chairs, and, three Iron potts and all and Singular Other the Goods and Chattels Above Mentioned** and every of them to his and their proper use and own uses forever **without the Set Trouble Hinderance Molestation Interception and denial of him the said Micajah Poole** his Executors Administrators assigns or other person or persons whatsoever In Witness Whereof the said Micajah Poole hath hereunto set his hand and Seal The Day and Year first above written

Micajah Poole (LS) [Legal Seal]

FIGURE 3.

The Commodification of Ceasar, Lewis, Winney, Bill, and George by Samuel Hunter, John and James Marshall, Virginia, 1820

This Indenture made and entered into this 27th day of March **1820 between Samuel Hunter of the first part John Marshall Sr and James M Marshall of the second part and John Ashby of the third part,** Witnesseth that the said Samuel Hunter **for and in consideration of the sum of one dollar to him in hand paid by the said John Ashby** at and before the ensealing and delivering of these presents hath granted bargained and sold and by these presents **doth grant bargain and sell unto the said John Ashby and his heirs the following negroes to wit Ceasar Lewis Winney Bill and George** to have and to hold the said Ceasar Lewis Winney Bill and George & unto the said John Ashby and his heirs forever **Upon Trust nevertheless for that the said Samuel Hunter stands indebted to the said John Marshall Sr and James M Marshall** in the sum of **eighty five pounds eight shillings and eight pence half penny with In-terest** from this date and to James M Marshall in the sum of eighteen Pounds fifteen shillings which will be due on the first day of January eighteen hundred and twenty one now **if the said Samuel Hunter shall** at the expiration of Ten months from the date hereof **pay to the said John Marshall Sr & to James M Marshall the sums of money** aforesaid with Interest as aforesaid together with the costs of Drawing and recording this deed **then these presents shall be void** but **if he shall fail therein it shall and may be Lawfull for the said John Ashby** his heirs or assigns **to sell the said Ceasar Lewis Winney Bill and George at Public Auction for cash** and out of the proceeds of such sale pay and satisfy the said sums of money with Interest aforesaid and the Costs aforesaid to the said John Marshall senior and James M Marshall and Return the surplus if any to the said Samuel **Hunter provided that the time and place of such sale shall be advertised at the Front Door of the Court House of Fauquier County and in some public Newspaper** at least one month previous thereto in testimony whereof the said Samuel Hunter hath here unto set his hand and seal the day and year first written

Sealed and delivered in presence of Samuel Hunter (seal)

At a Court held for Fauquier County this 27th Day of March 1820 in the language of the contracts of earlier eras gradually solidified into more pragmatic legal boilerplate. It is important to remember, however, that although the legal formula changed, the goal of community ritual remained fundamentally the same: to encourage borrowing and lending by using land, cash, credit, or commodities like tobacco, wheat, and slaves as collateral to circulate resources safely. Legal ritual evolved to bolster the confidence of borrowers and lenders, increasing stability for the free segment of communities. At the same time, however, the shift to guaranteeing loans with collateral further commodified slaves and destabilized the prospects of unfree populations.

C ourthouse records from the seventeenth century give us a particularly intimate look at the earliest Virginia communities and the way neighbors protected themselves in loan agreements. Today, we generally record wills in one office and land deeds in another. Probate disputes are handled by one set of courts, while civil and criminal trials have their own judges, staffs, and venues. What happens in one sphere of the community occurs in relative isolation from the others. In colonial Virginia, by contrast, the courthouse (along with the church) was a place where everyone came together. At first in private homes and later in buildings built for that purpose, court meetings were where the people of all social and economic levels gathered with their neighbors. They came to vote, to gamble, and to drink. They also came to witness publicly property exchanges, resolutions to disagreements, and reparations for injuries.[7] The court records read like a diary of county life, and it is through these "diaries" that we can follow changes in community relationships and, in particular, the growing commodification of slaves.

The Lancaster County record books provide good examples. A frontier county formed in 1651, Lancaster sat on the peninsula known as the Great Northern Neck. On January 1, 1652, elite members of the community appointed to the county court for Lancaster County met in the house of Colonel Moore Fauntleroy.[8] Their first act was to grant a certificate for two hundred acres to Rice Jones, fifty acres for attracting each of four new colonists to the county—a typical royal reward for encouraging settlement. The second act was a judgment against Thomas Brooks for speaking "coarse words & foule aspersions" on Mary, the wife of David Fox, a member of the court. Brooks was ordered to make a full public apology at the next meeting of the church congregation. Furthermore, Brooks had to provide security that he would make this formal apology by giving a pledge of valuable property. Should he refuse, the court ordered the sheriff to keep Brooks himself in custody.[9] Why did the court take this offense so seriously? Colonists lived on credit, and how much credit a family received was closely tied to its reputation.[10] It was vital, therefore, that such formal apologies be recorded. Some expressly referred to the "wounded Creditt & reputacon" of the aggrieved parties.[11]

Later in the court proceedings, Daniell Howes requested that Mr. Potter, a member of the court, help him collect on accounts owed by William White and others. This entry underscores the importance of book debt in the community. Merchants and tavern keepers provided food, lodging, stabling, and goods on credit tracked by personal paper accounts, not formally executed legal documents. It was only when payments were delayed that businessmen filed an "accon" [action] or lawsuit for debt.[12] These transplanted Englishmen had brought with them expectations of what has been called a "moral economy" or a law of "common sense and consensus."[13] Some debts were secured only by a promise "under seal" or "by Specialtie," that is, by a written promise to pay. At a court meeting on January 10, 1653, Thomas Brice gave the Lancaster court just such a document signed by William Thomas to persuade the court to order Thomas to pay Brice 711 pounds of tobacco.[14] The legal language used in these early contracts for sales and debts was inconsistent. Some parties used "Know ye" or "Know all Men by these presents," and others began simply, "This Bill bindeth mee."[15] The court resolved disagreements over oral debts as well.

A quantitative look at debt entries in Lancaster County shows that only fourteen formal debt contracts were recorded in the years 1652 to 1657. They were vastly outnumbered by adjudications of informal debt contracts. The court settled as many casual debt cases in the eight months between January and August 1653 as the total number of formal debt instruments recorded in the five years 1652 to 1657. In Isle of Wight County, located on the very lightly settled border with North Carolina, court records show an even stronger community norm of relying on oral promises to repay debts. Out of the roughly twenty-five hundred entries from 1688 to 1758 that survive, there were only about two dozen formal debt instruments. The rest were court orders for the payment of informal debts, confessions of judgment (voluntary admissions to the court by the debtors), assignments of debts, and powers of attorney granting the right to pay debts.[16] Nevertheless, it is in those few formal legal documents that we catch the signs of change in legal expectations in Virginia.

O ne Lancaster County Court record clearly shows how slaveholders com-
modified their chattel. On January 1, 1652, the court approved the first formal debt contract of the session, introducing us to Richard Bennett, a major investor and political figure. Bennett owned more than two thousand acres of land in the colony and was part of a family of international merchants prominent in the development of Virginia.[17] The records of the Lancaster County Court for the years 1652 to 1657 are filled with Bennett's transactions: loans, purchases, and sales.[18] In this particular contract, Bennett agreed to serve as surety or guarantor for a debt of forty thousand pounds that Epapraditus Lawson owed to Symon Overzee. Lawson had persuaded Bennett to take this risk by giving him a mortgage on twenty-seven hundred acres. In addition, Lawson pledged his entire stock of cattle and goats, one bill of exchange, and the rights to collect another debt owed to Lawson. Lawson also commodified his human property by giving Bennett a mortgage on eight people. This mortgage contract was drawn up and signed in April 1651, but Lawson died shortly thereafter. Bennett made sure that the next document recorded in the court files was the inventory of Lawson's estate.

The inventory tells us more about Lawson's human collateral. Daniell Dis-
key, John Cooke, Richard Kinge, an Indian woman named Frances, and the "Negroe" Peter were indentured servants. Each had been appraised. "Crom, a Mulatto boy," was probably a slave and was valued at fifteen hundred pounds of tobacco. An "Indian" child who may have been a slave was valued at four hundred pounds sterling. There also were two names that did not appear in the original mortgage, each with a term of years stated. Lawson may have indentured two additional men after making his pledge to Bennett. Nevertheless, Bennett could claim all of these human assets as security for the earlier loan. His argument was that the original mortgage specifically included "all belonging" to Lawson until the debt to Overzee was paid.[19] "All belonging" was construed as all property owned at the time of the contract plus any acquired later. "Property" included all valuable assets, including that of labor owed, whether by slaves or indentured workers. The point is that both groups of unfree Virginians were legal commodities. In merchant Richard Bennett's

contract, we glimpse the beginnings of the shift from oral and private book debts to contracts in the formal British tradition. We also see the commodification of people as collateral.

In 1650 the population of Virginia was close to 19,000, about 400 of whom were black. A century later it had grown to more than 200,000, with nearly half of African descent. As more British settlers arrived with more slaves and settled into larger communities, legal procedures became more complex. Increasing numbers of slaves were commodified. In the decades after those first court meetings in Lancaster, population pressure continued to push people out of the Tidewater counties, while conditions for tobacco cultivation pulled them west.[20] More Virginians began moving to the Piedmont, inland northern Virginia, and the interior of the Southside. Stafford was one of the new counties created. In Stafford County, we find something that is missing in the language of sales, mortgages, and debt in the Lancaster County transactions of the 1650s—something that reveals changes in community attitudes about loan agreements. On September 9, 1686, Henry Peyton confirmed his sale of 150 acres to Thomas Holmes using words that became the standard introduction to a written contract in the late eighteenth century, "This Indenture."[21] Like the Lawson-Bennett mortgage, however, the agreement between Peyton and Holmes still contained the classic formal elements of a modern contract: the duties of the parties, the delivery of property for a stated consideration (value), and the date.[22] This late-seventeenth-century record shows that, while the older, more personal legal decorum still dominated agreements in the 1680s, the shift to a greater formality between neighbors had begun. By the 1740s the majority of contracts read like the Peyton-Holmes contract. They began with "This Indenture," and slaves had replaced indentured servants as laborers and as the prime human commodity used to secure debts.[23]

What the appearance of "This Indenture" signals is that standard British legal literary forms were penetrating Virginia frontiers. This legal formula was quite old, with perhaps the first recorded use around 1304 in England.[24] Reflecting the expectations of the merchants with whom settlers did business, most of the debt contracts they recorded were based on written contracts that followed the established English model.[25] The documents were longer and more sophisticated.[26] The original mortgage on slaves and other personal property given by Culpeper County's Micajah Poole to William Hunter in 1750, shown in figure 2, is an example.

A few comparisons with the Green contract highlight the changes in legal style. By the middle of the eighteenth century, there were two popular drafting styles for debt contracts in Culpeper County and across Virginia. Both used collateral, including slaves. Nicholas Green used a simpler, shorter promise to pay that retained much of the character of legal rituals common in seventeenth-century Virginia. Micajah Poole used a more formal version that was three times longer than Green's and reflected the growing presence of British merchants in the colony. Unlike Green, Poole began with the classic British words used to introduce a contract, "This Indenture." This fourteenth-century ritual phrase became the standard opening used in Virginia contracts by the nineteenth century. In contrast, Green used the less formal, "Know all men"—a generic phrase that had long been used to make any kind of public announcement, including the renunciation of a wife or a change of residence. In Green's words we hear the echoes of those intimate courthouse meetings of the 1680s. Possibly he chose the less commercial-sounding salutation because John Green may have been a relative. Micajah Poole also was publicly acknowledging his promise, but the opening words make it clear that a contract would follow. Another difference is that the Poole agreement stated the terms several times in the document. This repetition was a drafting strategy designed to protect against future complaints that there was confusion or inaccuracy in the parties' expectations. The repeated chants trace their origins from legal ritual recitations pronounced in medieval monasteries and lords' halls, not in communal gatherings in homes on the Virginia frontier.[27] Also missing from Green's promise were the phrases "Provided always" and "upon Condition That." The use of this standard legal jargon removed all doubt about the character of the Poole contract. Micajah Poole was giving Thomas Hunter a mortgage on property in order to secure a debt. This clearly was not a simple sale of Bacchus, Diana, Juno, and other property. In Green's contract, by contrast, we have to search the short recitation to find his intent. We have to look past the statement "[I] . . . Have Bargained and sold and by these presents do Bargain and sell" to the charming but enigmatic phrasing that follows: "by the delivery of the Buckles in the name of the whole and which said Slaves goods and Chattels I do hereby warrant and forever defend." It is only by pondering the meaning of "the delivery of the Buckles in the name of the whole" that we can infer the loan and the mortgage of slaves securing it.

Notice, however, that the more formal eighteenth-century contract still reflected the conscious need to protect community harmony that we saw in the seventeenth-century court records. The language reinforces solemn reciprocal duties. Poole "doth Covenant and Grant to and with the said William Hunter." "Covenant," indicating an exchange of promises, is a legal term dating back to medieval English courts that was retained in contracts for more than five hundred years.[28] The ritual word "covenant" lent an aura of legitimacy and an expectation of fairness. If Poole failed to pay, he promised to behave with the decorum expected by the community. In other words, he pledged to release the slaves and chattels (which probably were the bulk of his material wealth) without resistance. As the mortgage explained, he must relinquish them "peaceably and quietly" and "without the Set Trouble Hinderance Molestation Interception and denial." On the other hand, this language is a foreshadowing. As we will see in the sample contract from the nineteenth century, the goals of such promises not to resist the seizure of property would shift from maintaining community harmony to assuring a creditor quick possession and quick sales of slaves and other collateral.

Both the Poole and the Green mortgages show free Virginians expanding and stabilizing their communities of credit. The records also capture what has been less visible in studies of slavery: the legal creation of financial avatars of the people used as collateral. Bacchus, Diana, and Juno continued to labor for Micajah Poole, and Celina, Sith, Tom, and Charles worked for Nicholas Green. The community saw their bodies there, but their physical presence told only part of their social and economic circumstances. Paper contracts pulled the legally constructed astral bodies of these slaves—and thousands like them— from farm to farm, village to village, county to county, and eventually state to state. These invisible exchanges reduced the personal security of enslaved Virginians and their families. Slaves were endangered when they were promised in lieu of loan repayment, and this insecurity could spread beyond the original contract. Creditors could sell their rights under the mortgages to others, who could sell them to others in turn. Our studies of slavery are incomplete without visualizing the financial manifestations of slaves being dragged in and out of courthouses with little outward indication beyond pens scratching on paper.

The contract on Bacchus, Diana, and Juno in 1750 illustrates the way most Virginia mortgages had swollen since the 1680s. This was followed by further refinement in the nineteenth century. Free Virginians began to use another legal strategy to encourage lending secured by collateral: the "deed of trust."

The term suggests a return to the defense of community harmony, but labels can be deceiving. Our third sample contract, shown in figure 3, is a deed of trust recorded in Fauquier County in 1820, a mortgage given by Samuel Hunter to Chief Justice John Marshall of the U.S. Supreme Court and his brother James. Hunter borrowed a little more than eighty-five pounds from the Marshall brothers, but this nineteenth-century mortgage added a new participant, the "trustee," John Ashby.

This variety of mortgage shared certain components with the Poole-Hunter contract drafted in 1750. The document was introduced with the medieval "This Indenture." It had the choral quality of the twice-chanted "hath bargained and sold" and the repetitions of the amount owed and the property, including enslaved people, pledged as collateral. But significant elements were missing. There was no covenant language and no borrower's promise to give up his property without resistance. In the seventy years separating the Poole-Hunter and the Hunter-Marshall mortgages, significant changes in legal language had come to distinguish mortgages from other deeds. In the 1750 mortgage, we have to search for phrases such as "Provided always" and "upon Condition That," words that identify the document as a debt contract and not a pure sale. By 1820, however, the declarations of debt and mortgage in contracts had become straightforward and formulaic. In this case, the document proclaims, "Samuel Hunter stands indebted" to the Marshall brothers. This is not to say that no nineteenth-century mortgages used the old legal form. What the Virginia deed books reveal is that, over time, most of the lawyers and clerks gravitated toward ritual language that clearly indicated a lending relationship between the parties. Trained lawyers like John Marshall had incorporated and updated another English medieval ritual into Virginia, the deed of trust.

Did the language of the deed of trust reflect Virginians' rededication to the goal of community harmony, a purpose so prominent in the seventeenth and eighteenth centuries? In 1750, Micajah Poole's mortgage had transferred bare legal title to his property directly to his creditor. In 1820, however, Samuel Hunter gave title not to the Marshalls, but "Upon Trust" to John Ashby, appointed by the court. Ashby received a ritual payment of one dollar. As a trustee, the court held John Ashby to a high standard of care in his handling of Hunter's property, the standard required by the law of equity. Many Americans may not be aware that our legal system is not derived from English common law alone, but also from the English law of equity. This is probably because the common law and the law of equity eventually merged in most states. During the colonial and early national periods, however, these two English legal traditions were distinct, with separate courts of law and courts in equity that decided disputes on different theories of damage and recovery. Common law and equity were appeals court creations of the Norman kings in England. Both bodies of law were designed to remedy what ordinary people saw as injustice in the local courts controlled by Anglo-Saxon lords and bishops. Giving subjects the right to appeal to the king gave more legitimacy to the conquerors from France. The common law came first. Over time the common law courts became clogged with lawsuits and cumbersome in operation. In response, the Normans created the Chancery Court to maintain the reputation of the king as the guarantor of fairness or "equity." These royal judges held the trustees whom they appointed to high standards of fairness.[29]

Admittedly, the Normans were trying to gain authority and popular support at the expense of local leaders, but the medieval law of equity was also a conscious attempt to redress power imbalances between rulers and the people they ruled. A deed of trust was supposed to shift control over the collateral away from both the borrower and the lender and into the hands of an impartial trustee. Ideally, this "trusted one" acted in the interests of community justice. This was not the spirit of the deed of trust in nineteenth-century Virginia, however. Trustees like John Ashby were often business partners and relatives chosen by the lender. Notice, too, that the Marshalls built in conditions to streamline the seizure and sale of Ceasar, Lewis, Winney, Bill, George, and the other property if Hunter did not meet the payment dates and terms.[30] Once Ashby determined there was a default on the deed, he was empowered to arrange for the seizure and sale of the collateral. Hunter still had the right to protest, but we get the sense that these legal rituals were designed by powerful creditors and fellow elites to accelerate debt recovery. John Ashby had to publicize the sale of the slaves in a newspaper as well as at the front steps of the courthouse. Advertising the sale was likely to increase the number of bidders at the public auction, thereby maximizing the chances that lenders like the Marshall brothers would benefit from higher prices for the slaves. Although not necessarily the goal of creditors, deeds of trust also protected borrowers like Samuel Hunter. If the slaves sold for more than the debt amount, Hunter received the difference. If the slaves sold for less than the debt, a higher price reduced what Hunter still owed the Marshalls.[31]

John and James Marshall were elite members of the Fauquier County community. The Marshalls were creating interest income for themselves and giving neighbor Samuel Hunter a chance to use some of the savings stored in his human property. The financial avatars of Ceasar, Lewis, Winney, Bill, and George were moved to the Fauquier County courthouse. If Hunter did not pay, trustee John Ashby would reunite the avatars and the physical bodies of the slaves on the steps of the courthouse. There they would be sold to the highest bidder. Ashby would pay the Marshalls, giving any surplus to Hunter. Ceasar, Lewis, Winney, Bill, and George would be sent to new living places and quite possibly completely new communities, where they would continue to face the physical, psychological, and financial uncertainties of living in a slave society.

E ighteenth-century Virginia neighbors blended community ritual with a more commercial standard of legal language and collateral. This was because British merchants, now established in the backcountry, were using formal documents, lawyers, and lawsuits to protect their advances of cash, credit, and goods.[32] For example, on July 21, 1768, in the Southside county of Halifax, John Sanders gave merchants Thomas Yuille and James Murdoch a mortgage on Lucy, Sall, and Jack to secure a loan of £115.[33] In the central Piedmont county of Goochland, Robert Cawthon reassured Alexander McCaul that his debt of £218 would be paid, giving McCaul a mortgage in 1769 on 170 acres and six slaves: Hitee and her child, Roger, Ned, Priss, and Nancy.[34] Farther north, in Fauquier County, George Boswell placed a mortgage, dated March 26, 1770, on eight men and ten women in favor of Glasgow merchants Andrew Cochrane, William Cunningham & Company to secure the payment of £200.[35] While the style of debt contracts spread in popularity, so did the number of people mortgaged and the uncertainty about their future. Like Bacchus, Diana, and Juno, the twenty-seven people pledged to these merchants joined thousands of other slaves used as collateral in colonial Virginia. From 1740 to 1780, the number of counties in Virginia grew from about forty to about sixty. More than one thousand enslaved Virginians were mortgaged in six counties alone during just twenty-two years of the colonial period (1745–55 and 1765–75). Free Virginians not only forced enslaved Virginians to do much of the labor needed to grow the colonial economy but also used slaves' bodies to raise and circulate capital in that economy. Measured in January 2014 U.S. dollars, mortgages using slaves as all or part of the collateral raised more than 50 million dollars, more than double the amount of capital raised by mortgages secured without human collateral.[36] Certainly not everyone who needed a loan owned slaves. In Culpeper County, Robert Frogit, a neighbor of Micajah Poole and William Hunter, borrowed £24 from James Turner in 1751, using his blacksmith's tools and future crops as security.[37] Yet slaves had become a common medium in the transaction of neighborhood business. In 1769 James Dunn lent John Almond £153, backed by a mortgage on Roger, Sarah, Cate, and Bess.[38] At times, the number of slaves pledged was quite large, as when Tarlton Fleming listed fifty-one slaves as security for a loan of 74 pounds, 16 shillings, 8 pence from Thomas Mann Randolph, George Webb, and Neill Campbell in July 1773.[39]

The Virginia data reveal that, in the seventeenth century, Virginians tended not to record personal debt. There were scattered documents, but the bulk of the records showed neighbors coming to the court meeting to get a ruling on overdue book debts or oral contracts for goods and services. By the second half of the eighteenth century, many more Virginians were recording formal mortgage contracts, now secured by slaves, land, chattels, or combinations thereof. Tables 1 and 2 display the data collected and indicate the types of collateral used by borrowers to secure equity mortgages, that is, mortgages using property, such as slaves, already fully owned by the borrower, as security for a debt. They also show how much capital was raised by unsecured promises to pay, identifying these promises as personal debt.[40] The amount of capital raised by unsecured promises to pay dropped from 18 percent in the 1745–55 sample to 2 percent in the years 1765–75 (table 1). In contrast, the amount raised by loans secured by slaves only rose from 6 to 16 percent, and those using a mix of slaves and chattels jumped from 2 to 22 percent. Finally, the amount raised by loans where slaves were a part of the collateral (the four categories of slaves only; land and slaves; land, slaves, and chattels; and slaves and chattels) jumped from 23 to 71 percent.

From 1775 to 1860, expectations among neighbors in Virginia counties continued to change. By 1820, both free and enslaved populations had grown in most counties.[41] In the years 1817 to 1821, unsecured promises still accounted for 12 percent of the capital raised by debt instruments recorded in the six counties sampled. In the two later sample periods, 1835 to 1839 and 1855 to 1859, unsecured personal debt had essentially disappeared from the records, making the total for the fifteen years sampled in the nineteenth century just 5 percent

TABLE 1. Equity Mortgages in Six Sample Virginia Counties, Colonial Era
(Albemarle, Culpeper, Fauquier, Goochland, Halifax, and Lunenburg): Capital
Raised in January 2014 US$ Equivalents.

| | 1745–1755 | | 1765–1775 | |
COLLATERAL CATEGORY	TOTAL $	PERCENT	TOTAL $	PERCENT
Chattels Only	1,244,000	20	2,115,000	3
Land Only	1,704,000	27	13,839,000	20
Slaves Only	362,000	6	10,595,000	16
Land and Chattels	751,000	12	2,354,000	3
Land and Slaves	937,000	15	10,992,000	16
Land, Slaves, and Chattels	—	—	11,878,000	17
Slaves and Chattels	114,000	2	15,266,000	22
Personal Debt	1,095,000	18	1,035,000	2
Unidentified Property	—	—	—	—

TABLE 2. Equity Mortgages in Six Sample Virginia Counties, National Era
(Albemarle, Culpeper, Fauquier, Goochland, Halifax, and Lunenburg): Capital
Raised in January 2014 US$ Equivalents.

| | 1817–1821 | | 15-YEAR CUMULATIVE SAMPLE (1817–21, 1835–39, & 1855–59) | |
COLLATERAL CATEGORY	TOTAL $	PERCENT	TOTAL $	PERCENT
Chattels Only	4,039,000	6	19,837,000	12
Land Only	22,640,000	33	67,454,000	40
Slaves Only	8,440,000	12	14,520,000	9
Land and Chattels	2,304,000	3	10,298,000	6
Land and Slaves	7,934,000	11	14,161,000	8
Land, Slaves, and Chattels	12,129,000	18	23,925,000	14
Slaves and Chattels	3,104,000	4	7,863,000	5
Personal Debt	8,245,000	12	8,245,000	5
Unidentified Property	416,000	1	1,412,000	1

of the capital raised (see table 2). While the amounts raised using slaves as a part of the security dropped from 45 percent in the 1817–21 period to 36 percent over the entire fifteen years, the Virginia data show that slaves were often used as commodities and were still a key source of collateral.

Gradually the legal rituals and written memorials that Virginians used and expected changed. Rather than congregating in private homes on lightly settled frontiers, nineteenth-century Virginians in more populated districts recorded their transactions in less communal courthouses. Deeds, wills, and other court proceedings were "performed" less publicly before separate clerks in separate courts and then were filed in separate books. There was no longer a one-volume diary of county life. The fines for disturbing the peace and investigations of sudden deaths no longer mingled with will contests and loans exchanged for mortgages on slaves. The Marshall mortgage document covered only two of the more than sixty-four equity mortgages recorded in Fauquier County between 1817 and 1821 that, combined, used 345 people as human collateral. More than 2,500 slaves became security in the six Virginia counties sampled in the same five-year period. Over the fifteen-year sample, almost 5,500 slaves were commodified as collateral for recorded equity mortgages (the mortgages on property the borrower already owned).[42] The records also document purchase-money mortgages—those used to buy slaves, land, and other property. The Virginia sample did not collect data from these mortgages, but extensive review of the Virginia records suggests that the loans arranged to buy slaves as commodities (purchase-money mortgages) could easily have outnumbered equity mortgages by more than three to one.

V irginia courthouse records show that people of the most exalted and the most humble economic circumstances participated in local credit networks. Some recorded their debts in formal legal documents, listing enslaved people and other property as collateral. Others made oral promises to pay or placed a simple written acknowledgment in the public record. In the thirty-seven years sampled in the quantitative study from before the American Revolution to the eve of the Civil War, borrowers in Virginia pledged more than seven thousand slaves whom they already owned as security for loans. It was common practice to commodify slave property to get the cash and credit needed to create personal wealth and support regional economic development.

Public rituals of exchange, including the solemn language of promises, shifted as populations grew and modern commercial links were established. In the eighteenth century, medieval legal poetry replaced less formal, though still solemn, declarations in debt contracts. Underneath, there was a disturbing quantitative and qualitative baseline. Human beings were commodified: They were subject to legal rules designed to sell land, livestock, featherbeds, and iron pots, or used to secure loans. With these undertones, refrains of legal lyricism seem harsh and discordant to twenty-first-century ears. Nicholas Green's ritual offer of silver shoe buckles becomes less chivalric and more shrill as we perceive the increased risks these rituals created for Celina, Sith, Tom, and Charles. Thousands of slaves like them were turned into commodities in the surge of borrowing and lending in Virginia communities.

NOTES

1. Culpeper County, Virginia, Land Records, Deed Book (LRDB) F, 485, LVA. The work of Richard Kilbourne inspired this and a wider project on the use of slaves as collateral across Virginia, Louisiana, and South Carolina. See Richard Holcombe Kilbourne Jr., *Debt, Investment, Slaves: Credit Relations in East Feliciana Parish, Louisiana, 1825–1885* (Tuscaloosa: University of Alabama Press, 1995); and Richard Holcombe Kilbourne Jr., *Slave Agriculture and Financial Markets in Antebellum America: The Bank of the United States in Mississippi 1831–1852* (London: Pickering & Chatto, 2006).

2. There is a large literature on the expansion of the Virginia economy and slavery in the eighteenth century, including the following classics in the field: Ira Berlin, *Many Thousands Gone: The First Two Centuries of Slavery in North America* (Cambridge, MA: Harvard University Press, 1998); Philip D. Morgan, *Slave Counterpoint: Black Culture in the Eighteenth-Century Chesapeake and Lowcountry* (Chapel Hill: University of North Carolina Press, 1998); Allan Kulikoff, *Tobacco and Slaves: The Development of Southern Cultures in the Chesapeake, 1680–1800* (Chapel Hill: University of North Carolina Press, 1986); and T. H. Breen, *Tobacco Culture: The Mentality of the Great Tidewater Planters on the Eve of Revolution* (Princeton, NJ: Princeton University Press, 1985).

3. Ruth Sparacio and Sam Sparacio, eds., *Virginia County Court Records: Deed and Will Abstracts Lancaster County, Virginia, 1652–1657* (McLean, VA: R. & S. Sparacio, 1991); and Ruth Sparacio and Sam Sparacio, eds., *Virginia County Court Records: Deed and Will Abstracts Stafford County, Virginia, 1686–1689* (McLean, VA: R. & S. Sparacio, 1991); Benjamin B. Weisiger III., ed., *Henrico County, Virginia: Deeds, 1677–1705* (Richmond, VA: B. B. Weisiger, 1986). William Lindsay Hopkins, ed., *Isle of Wight County, Virginia, Deeds 1647–1719, Court Orders 1693–1695, and Guardian Accounts 1740–1767* (Richmond, VA: Gem-N-Dex, 1993); William Lindsay Hopkins, ed., *Isle of Wight County, Virginia, Deeds 1720–1736, 1741–1749* (Athens, GA: Iberian, 1994); William Lindsay Hopkins, ed., *Isle of Wight County, Virginia, Deeds, 1750–1782* (Athens, GA: Iberian,

1995); William Lindsay Hopkins, ed., *Isle of Wight County, Virginia, Deeds, 1736–1741* (Miami Beach, FL: T. L.C. Genealogy, 1992). John Anderson Brayton, ed., *Colonial Families of Surry and Isle of Wight Counties, Virginia*, vol. 5, *Isle of Wight County, Virginia Deeds, Wills, Conveyances, Book A* (Memphis: J. A. Brayton, 2001). The sampling method in the larger, quantitative study of Virginia debt instruments was as follows. The first study analyzed more than six thousand equity mortgages of land, slaves, and personal property filed in more than sixty thousand pages of public records in Virginia and South Carolina. The Virginia samples were from both colonial and national eras: twenty-two years in the colonial period (1745 through 1755 and 1765 through 1775) and fifteen years in the national period (1817 through 1821, 1835 through 1839, and 1855 through 1859). In other words, the nineteenth-century samples were centered on the years of the panics before the Civil War, framed by the two years before and the two years following each panic. Data were collected from all the equity mortgages recorded in the deed books of six counties selected in three geographical regions: in northern Virginia, Culpeper and Fauquier counties; in the Piedmont, Albemarle and Goochland counties; and in Southside, Halifax and Lunenburg counties. Albemarle County, LRDB, vols. 1, 4, 5, 6, 20, 21, 22, 32, 33, 34, 35, 36, 37, 53, 54, 55, 56, 57, 58; Culpeper County, LRDB, vols. A, B, D, E, F, G, HH, II, KK, LL, MM, NN, 2, 3, 4, 12, 13, 14; Fauquier County, LRDB, vols. 2, 3, 4, 5, 6, 21, 22, 23, 24, 25, 26, 34, 35, 36, 37, 38, 39, 54, 55, 56, 57, 58; Goochland County, LRDB, vols. 4, 5, 6, 7, 8, 9, 10, 11, 22, 23, 24, 30, 31, 32, 37, 38, 39; Halifax County, LRDB, vols. 1, 2, 3, 4, 5, 6, 7, 8, 9, 10, 12, 13, 26, 27, 28, 29, 30, 42, 43, 44, 45, 46, 55, 56, 57, 58; Lunenburg County, LRDB, vols. 1, 2, 3, 4, 10, 11, 12, 13, 14, 15, 24, 25, 30, 31, 35, 36, all LVA. For maps of the sampled regions and a detailed discussion of the results, see Bonnie Martin, "Slavery's Invisible Engine: Mortgaging Human Property," *Journal of Southern History* 76 (November 2010): 817–66.

4. William Eastham to Hugh Lenox, May 16, 1765, Culpeper County, LRDB, D:605. Eastham's collateral included livestock and other personal property in addition to the thirteen slaves.

5. Culpeper County, LRDB, A:268, author's emphasis in bold.

6. Fauquier County, LRDB, 24:31, author's emphasis in bold.

7. A. G. Roeber, *Faithful Magistrates and Republican Lawyers: Creators of Virginia Legal Culture, 1680–1810* (Chapel Hill: University of North Carolina Press, 1981), 78–79. On the treatment of the transition from this kind of society in early Virginia, see Rhys Isaac, *The Transformation of Virginia, 1740–1790* (Chapel Hill: University of North Carolina Press, 1982).

8. Maurice Duke, *The Land between Waters: Virginia's Lancaster County* (Lancaster, VA: Mary Ball Washington Museum and Library, 2001), 29–30.

9. Sparacio and Sparacio, *Virginia County Court Records: Lancaster, 1652–1657*, 1.

10. On the potential for slander accusations to affect reputation and credit, see Kathleen M. Brown, *Good Wives, Nasty Wenches, and Anxious Patriarchs: Gender, Race, and Power in Colonial Virginia* (Chapel Hill: University of North Carolina Press, 1999), 99–100.

11. Apology of John Edgecombe to court member Maier [Moore] Fauntleroy, recorded in June 1655. Sparacio and Sparacio, *Virginia County Court Records: Lancaster, 1652–1657*, 98. So grievous was the slander that the court ordered a protective bond of twenty thousand pounds of tobacco should Edgecombe make future slanderous statements.

12. For examples of book debts recorded in Stafford County, see Sparacio and Sparacio, *Virginia County Court Records: Stafford, 1686–1689*, 64, 65, 91, 112.

13. For E. P. Thompson's classic use of the term "moral economy," see Thompson, *Customs in Common: Studies in Traditional Popular Culture* (New York: New Press, 1993), 185–351. On "common sense and consensus," see F. Thornton Miller, *Juries and Judges versus the Law: Virginia's Provincial Legal Perspective, 1783–1828* (Charlottesville: University of Virginia Press, 1994), 5.

14. Sparacio and Sparacio, *Virginia County Court Records: Lancaster, 1652–1657*, 10.

15. Miller, *Juries and Judges versus the Law*, 16, 17, 20. Also see the variations in the debt acknowledgments by Herd, Carter, and Lambertson (49, 51).

16. Hopkins, *Isle of Wight County, Deeds 1647–1719*; Hopkins, *Isle of Wight County, Deeds 1720–1736, 1741–1749*; Hopkins, *Isle of Wight County, Deeds, 1750–1782*. Hopkins, *Isle of Wight County, Deeds, 1736–1741*. Brayton, *Isle of Wight County, Book A*. On book debt and collection in Southside, see Charles J. Farmer, *In the Absence of Towns: Settlement and Country Trade in Southside, Virginia, 1730–1800* (Lanham, MD: Rowman & Littlefield, 1993), 174–77.

17. Robert Brenner, *Merchants and Revolution: Commercial Change, Political Conflict, and London's Overseas Traders, 1550–1653* (Princeton, NJ: Princeton University Press, 1993), 143, 145; W. G. Stanard, ed., "Abstracts of Virginia Land Patents," *Virginia Magazine of History and Biography* 3 (July 1895): 53–56.

18. For examples, see Sparacio and Sparacio, *Virginia County Court Records: Lancaster, 1652–1657*, 12, 13, 17, 20, 56, 125, 139.

19. Sparacio and Sparacio, *Virginia County Court Records: Lancaster, 1652–1657*, 4.

20. Philip D. Morgan and Michael L. Nicholls, "Slaves in Piedmont Virginia, 1720–1790," *William and Mary Quarterly*, 3rd ser., 46 (April 1989): 215–16.

21. Sparacio and Sparacio, *Virginia County Court Records: Stafford, 1686–1689*, 1.

22. For the elements of a consensual sale, see Daniel R. Coquillette, *The Anglo-American Legal Heritage: Introductory Materials* (Durham, NC: Carolina Academic Press, 1999), 36.

23. Estimated Population of American Colonies, 1630–1780, Bureau of the Census, U.S. Dept. of Commerce, 1998 World Almanac and Book of Facts, 378, http://web.viu.ca/davies/h320/population.colonies.html; Morgan, *Slave Counterpoint*, 1.

24. "This Indenture" meant "this Contract." In the Middle Ages, "to indent" came to mean to enter into an agreement, and an "endenture" or "edenteure" was a deed with mutual covenants. The first extant example is from 1304. The origins of indenture lay in an early technique for preventing fraud in written documents, in which "to indent" meant "to snip" or "to create notched edges." Indentures were "originally . . . written on one piece of parchment or paper, and then cut asunder in a serrated or sinuous line, so that when brought together again at any time, the two edges exactly tallied and showed that they were parts of one and the same original document." *Oxford English Dictionary*, compact ed. (London: Oxford University Press, 1971), 1:1412–13.

25. Most contracts are in Deed Book E, 1740–1741, recorded in Prince William County, which was carved from Stafford's northern half in 1731. Ruth Sparacio and Sam Sparacio, eds., *Virginia County Court Records: Prince William County, Virginia (1740–1741), Deed Book E* (McLean, VA: R. & S. Sparacio, 1989); Roeber, *Faithful Magistrates*, 77, 112–15.

26. Sparacio and Sparacio, *Virginia County Court Records: Stafford, 1686–1689*, 3.

27. In medieval European societies, as in colonial Virginia, oral agreements were the bases of exchange, and there was a suspicion of those using the "secret" language of legal phrases. Roeber,

Faithful Magistrates, 113. This tension persisted into nineteenth-century America. For example, see Miller, *Juries and Judges versus the Law*, 5–8. For an in-depth treatment, see Charles M. Cook, *The American Codification Movement: A Study of Antebellum Legal Reform* (Westport, CT: Greenwood Press, 1981). As in the Middle Ages, the Virginia courthouse documents "not only record agreements, transactions, or donations (gifts). They are also records of performances." Alice Rio, *Legal Practice and the Written Word in the Early Middle Ages: Frankish Formulae, c. 500–1000* (New York: Cambridge University Press, 2009), 9–11 (quotations on 14, 15). This was public theater, a recitation of traditional legal poetry using the words and phrases that people came to know as binding the parties in expected ways. Wendy Davies and Paul Fouracre, eds., *The Settlement of Disputes in Early Medieval Europe* (Cambridge: Cambridge University Press, 1992), 217, 240.

28. J. H. Baker, *An Introduction to English Legal History*, 4th ed. (London: Butterworths, 2002), 321–28.

29. For general treatments on the development of the common law and equity, see R. C. Van Caenegem, *The Birth of the English Common Law*, 2nd ed. (Cambridge: Cambridge University Press, 1988); and S. F. C. Milsom, *Historical Foundations of the Common Law*, 2nd ed. (Toronto: Lexis Law, 1981).

30. Joseph Story, *Commentaries on Equity Jurisprudence*, 5th ed. (Boston: Charles C. Little & James Brown, 1849), 1:67–375, esp. 341–75; 2:293–315.

31. Roeber, *Faithful Magistrates*, 84–85.

32. Culpeper County, LRDB, vols. A, B, D, E, F, G, HH, II, KK, LL, MM, NN. On British merchants in the backcountry in the 1740s, see Marc Egnal and Joseph A. Ernst, "An Economic Interpretation of the American Revolution," *William and Mary Quarterly*, 3rd ser., 29 (January 1972): 3–32, reprinted in *Historical Perspectives on the American Economy: Selected Readings*, ed. Robert Whaples and Diane C. Betts (New York: Cambridge University Press, 1995), 52–54. On the increase of lawyers and formal British legal traditions, see Roeber, *Faithful Magistrates*, xvii, xix, 129–35.

33. Halifax, LRDB, 7:176.

34. Goochland, LRDB, 9:192.

35. Fauquier, LRDB, 3:535.

36. Amounts have been converted to January 2014 U.S. dollars, using John J. McCusker's conversion tables and the U.S. Department of Labor, Bureau of Labor Statistics Consumer Price Indexes. John J. McCusker, *How Much Is That in Real Money? A Historical Commodity Price Index for Use as a Deflator of Money Values in the Economy of the United States*, 2nd ed. (Worcester, MA: American Antiquarian Society, 2001), 49–60. See the U.S. Department of Labor, Bureau of Labor Statistics, Consumer Price Index History Table, www.bls.gov/cpi/tables.htm (accessed February 25, 2014).

37. Culpeper, LRDB, A:307.

38. Goochland, LRDB, 9:188.

39. Goochland, LRDB, 10:370.

40. The amounts are in U.S. dollar equivalents because in the larger study of Virginia, South Carolina, and Louisiana, across both the colonial and national periods, many kinds of currencies had to be converted to a standard measure to make comparison possible.

41. Historical Census Browser, University of Virginia, Geospatial and Statistical Data Center (2004): http://fisher.lib.virginia.edu/collections/stats/histcensus/index.html.

42. See Martin, "Slavery's Invisible Engine," 836–40; and the discussion in Bonnie Martin, "Mortgaging Slaves in North America and South Africa: Parallels in Funding Slavery and Slave Societies," presented at Bridging Two Oceans: Slavery in Indian and Atlantic Worlds, conference organized by the Wilberforce Institute for the Study of Slavery and Emancipation in Cape Town, South Africa, November 2009.

"TO REALIZE MONEY FACILITIES"

Slave Life Insurance, the Slave Trade, and Credit in the Old South

KAREN RYDER

I n the popular imagination, the term "slave trade" evokes images of Africans chained together in transit, the auction block, and unspeakably painful separations of families in consequence of the legal sale of human beings as property. Such powerful emotional imagery can have the unintended effect of obscuring the extent of the domestic slave trade. Many slaveholders engaged in financial transactions involving bondpeople that lacked the finality of sale but nonetheless proved as potentially disruptive to the enslaved. Masters had a variety of options short of outright sale that converted the market value of bondpeople into cash. These activities must be included in estimations of the extent of the domestic slave trade, broadly defined.[1]

At least sixty-one companies insured the lives of slaves in the antebellum South.[2] Slave life insurance supported the growth of industries such as coal mining, railroad building, iron manufacturing, and brickmaking in the South's emerging towns and cities.[3] Some industrialists purchased enslaved workers, but many relied on hiring bondpeople on an annual basis. This phenomenon led to the appearance of the hiring agent, an entrepreneur who connected people seeking enslaved laborers with owners who wished to hire them out. Hiring agents provided a multitude of services in addition to arranging slave hiring contracts. Some also sold slaves, sold or rented real estate, collected rents, and secured the earnings of hired bondpeople. By the 1840s, many hiring agents also made arrangements to obtain slave life insurance, a process complicated by the increasing complexity of life insurance underwriting.

Slave life insurance also supported the growth of credit networks based in part or entirely on the value of bondpeople. Slave life insurance policies could be transferred as the "interest" in slaves changed, sometimes resulting in long chains of credit that facilitated slave sales and protected creditors' pocketbooks. But each paper transfer had potentially devastating effects on the enslaved. Moreover, insurance corporations held financial interests in bondpeople that resulted directly in slave sales. Thus, slave life insurance had a far-reaching impact well beyond providing financial protection for some slaveholders; it was also an integral part of the slave trade.

The first part of this chapter briefly traces the development of slave life insurance in the Old South. With deep roots in the Atlantic slave trade, slave life insurance during the antebellum era continued a very old idea—insuring bondpeople under marine insurance contracts—that many slaveholders found familiar. But it was not until the development of actuarial science in the early nineteenth century that the modern life insurance industry began to emerge in the United States. Compared to marine insurance, life insurance operated upon different principles and suggested new possibilities for insuring slaves. Business historian Sharon Murphy, in her study of life insurance, found that sales of life insurance among "white male northeasterners by the mid-1850s" roughly equaled sales of slave life insurance to southern slaveholders. Sales of life insurance among whites in the South, however, lagged behind sales in the Northeast.[4] Murphy suggested that perhaps the more rapid urbanization of the Northeast caused this disparity. The South's overwhelmingly rural character may partially explain why southerners lacked interest in insuring their own lives, but it does not explain why they displayed so much greater interest in insuring slaves.

In fact, life insurance developed in the South on two separate tracks, one for the free and one for the enslaved. Certainly, as Murphy has shown, the American life insurance business developed in the Northeast and expanded around the nation as it sought new markets. But a much older precedent for insuring slaves existed in the South. Slave life insurance developed not only because of the expansion of nonsouthern life insurers into southern states but also because it continued an old practice originating in the Atlantic slave trade, made more sophisticated and flexible by the invention of actuarial science. By the time northeastern life insurers began expanding into southern markets, marine and fire insurance were well established in the South. Slaveholders were accustomed to insuring property, both human and inanimate. Thus, they readily understood and accepted slave life insurance. Yet many southerners found the idea of placing a monetary value on their own lives, for insurance purposes, repugnant. They clung to an old-fashioned view of life insurance, holding that the lives of free people could not be quantified as a dollar value.

The second part of the chapter concerns the role of slave life insurance in the expansion of credit networks. Slave life insurance encouraged the growth of credit in the slave South and, in turn, fed off southern credit systems. Individuals and institutions lent money against the market value of slaves and other property. In a variation on the old custom of creditor-debtor insurance, slave owners insured slaves to make themselves more creditworthy, and creditors insured slaves belonging to their debtors. Slave life insurance thus helped to sustain a growing credit system collateralized by the bodies of the enslaved. As the practice of insuring slaves grew in the late antebellum years, it began to play a crucial role in the expansion of credit networks in southern financial centers such as Richmond, Charleston, and New Orleans.

S lave life insurance in the antebellum South grew out of the Atlantic slave trade. Centuries before life insurance became commonplace or even legal in many places, merchants insured the lives of enslaved Africans under marine insurance policies covering ships and cargoes.[5] Yet markets for life insurance grew slowly until the nineteenth century. Insurance involves commodification, the reduction of the intrinsic value of the object being insured, whether a building, a ship, or a life, to a monetary value. As Samuel Marshall noted in 1802, many European countries restricted or banned life insurance on the grounds that it represented "an offence against public decency, to set a price upon the life of man, particularly the life of a freeman, which is above all valuation." Since the law regarded the enslaved as "an article of commerce," however, "and capable of valuation," they could lawfully "be the subject of insurance."[6]

Many lawsuits arose over the interpretation of marine insurance contracts involving slaves.[7] When slaves escaped, revolted, or died of despair, marine insurers often refused to pay insurance benefits on the grounds that such losses were excluded from coverage. Marine insurance contracts covered only losses caused directly by uncontrollable conditions at sea, such as storms, shipwrecks, and running aground. By the early nineteenth century, insurance law on both sides of the Atlantic held that "no loss or damage shall be recoverable on account of the mortality of slaves by natural death or ill treatment,"[8] but the legal definition of "natural death" often remained elusive.

After the American Revolution removed British constraints on American business, marine insurance began to grow in the United States, where the insurance business also grew alongside the slave trade. Merchants in Charleston, South Carolina, often sold slaves as well as insurance and other products. As early as 1800, and possibly earlier, "insurance broker" David Denoon sold marine insurance out of an office in Charleston's central business district, where he also sold "Houses, Lands, Negroes, Vessels, or any part of Cargoes upon the wharves." Edward Ainger, an "insurance broker" and a "commission broker," operated, like Denoon, in close proximity to the waterfront, selling "Lands, Negroes, &c. at Private Sale."[9] When vessels wrecked offshore, insurers on both sides of the Atlantic employed agents to handle the disposition of retrieved cargoes. John Maynard Davis advertised to "merchants and captains whose vessels have suffered . . . losses" that he would, for a small fee, negotiate with their insurers to obtain the best settlement, quickly and without litigation. Part of his service included the sale of insured slaves and the settlement of claims for slaves lost at sea.[10] His experience with Lloyd's and other insurers made Davis a local insurance expert. He helped to found and direct the South Carolina Insurance Company, one of the first marine insurance companies chartered in the United States.[11]

In the early years of the American republic, any marine insurance corporation could insure slaves. In 1798 the Virginia legislature chartered the Marine Insurance Company of Alexandria. The charter granted powers to insure vessels, merchandise, "or other personal property gone or going by land or water."[12] Although the charter contained no explicit mention of slaves, its inclusion of broad powers to insure "other personal property" enabled Alexandria Marine and similarly chartered companies to insure slaves as chattel. After the United States banned the African slave trade in 1808, marine insurers throughout the new nation continued to insure slaves being shipped coastwise or in inland waters as part of the burgeoning domestic slave trade. Alexandria Marine, for instance, insured, as cargo, thirty slaves being sent from Alexandria, Virginia, to New Orleans.[13]

To eschew lawsuits, marine insurers inserted special exceptions in contracts insuring slaves. The Alexandria Marine underwriters "warranted" slaves to be "free of loss by mutiny, escapes, deaths accidental or natural, unless the Vessel be lost."[14] General Mutual Insurance Company of New York insured slaves "solely against loss by drowning in consequence of the stranding or shipwreck otherwise of the vessel."[15] Such language was neither necessary nor present in marine insurance contracts covering shipments of nonslave property.

Life insurance contracts, in contrast, offered the possibility of insuring slaves against risks that lay beyond the scope of marine insurance. Using the methods of actuarial science, a new field of statistics emerging in the nineteenth century, underwriters considered health, family history, occupational risks, and age in issuing life insurance contracts on slaves.[16] These methods enabled them to insure slaves in occupational situations not covered by marine insurance. Furthermore, marine insurance contracts endured only for the duration of a voyage, while life insurance contracts could last for a term of years or for life. These characteristics made life insurance attractive to slave masters.

In commercial regions throughout the South, marine and fire insurers embraced the new "science" of life insurance as a means of satisfying the regional demand for insuring slaves. In February 1820, the officers of the Charleston Fire & Marine Insurance Company of South Carolina placed an advertisement offering insurance on "healthy persons, accustomed to this climate, residing in the city, and 21 years old." After a lengthy explanation of the uses of life insurance, aimed at the commercial men of Charleston, the advertisement continued: "The lives of Negroes may also be insured, and the advantages of such insurance to owners, deriving profit from their labor, [are] strikingly obvious."[17] This is the earliest known advertisement for slave life insurance. Clearly, masters understood the principle of insuring slaves and would need no extensive marketing to persuade them to purchase the product. And because life insurance, unlike marine insurance, held the potential to insure the enslaved over long periods of time, it promised that "persons owning slaves may secure a perpetuity of income by insuring their lives."[18]

The spread of cotton agriculture fueled the growth of the domestic slave trade. Slaveholders forcibly moved more than one-quarter of a million of the enslaved in the 1830s.[19] Thus, it is no coincidence that the number of companies advertising slave life insurance also began to grow during the decade. The directors of the St. Louis Insurance Company, a marine and fire insurer in business by the mid-1830s, advertised insurance on "THE LIVES OF SLAVES whether working on shore or on boats navigating the rivers. To persons owning slaves who hire them on steamboats, this affords advantages of security too palpable to need insisting on."[20] As Jonathan Martin observed in his study of slave hiring markets, slaveholders perceived the enslaved as not only agricultural laborers "but also a cash crop in themselves."[21] Protecting themselves from financial loss by means of slave life insurance became especially important to slaveholders when they sent bondpeople to work on steamships or transported them upriver from the New Orleans slave market. Commercial Insurance Company of Charleston, South Carolina, sold marine and fire insurance from Charleston to Boston. Its St. Louis agent advertised insurance "on the hulls of steamboats, on bank notes by the United States Mail, on the lives of slaves, and on cargoes."[22] Readers of such advertisements may also have read sensationalistic accounts of steamboat explosions. Slave traders and slave owners hiring slaves to work on steamboats were among the most avid purchasers of slave life insurance. By the early 1850s, St. Louis was home to some thirty slave traders and seven life insurance agencies, six of which insured slaves.[23]

Clearly, southern property insurers expanded into life insurance primarily to satisfy the demand for insuring the enslaved. Some of these insurers had little interest in expanding life insurance sales among the free white population of the South. The directors of Charleston's Commercial Insurance Company expected "limited demand for Insurance on the Lives of White Persons." They predicted that such a practice would be primarily "for the purpose of securing a debt, or for some other special object."[24] Other companies did not insure free people at all. Under the heading "Life Insurance," William Willis Jr., agent for the Lynchburg (Virginia) Fire, Life & Marine Insurance Company, advertised insurance against "Fire, Life (Slave) and Marine Risks."[25] The James River Insurance Company of Richmond, Virginia, likewise advertised "Fire, Marine and Slave Life Insurance." Neither of these companies insured free people.[26]

In contrast to property insurers, some life insurers declined to insure bondpeople. In February 1852, Charles Beynroth, a longtime agent in Louisville, Kentucky, for Girard Life of Philadelphia, sent information on slave life insurance, together with rates charged by a competitor, to Girard's actuary, Jonathan F. James.[27] Beynroth wanted to supply customer demand for slave life insurance, but, as he explained in a later letter to Richard B. Dorsey, the secretary of the Baltimore Life Insurance Company, the Girard directors refused to consider "that class of Risks." Perhaps he reasoned that the directors of a company domiciled in Baltimore, Maryland, a major slave-trading city, might be more amenable to insuring slaves. Thus Beynroth proposed a dual agency. He would continue as Girard agent for any insurance on free lives that he happened to sell. But in addition, he proposed that Baltimore Life grant him an agency "*restricted* to Negro Risks," which, he assured Dorsey, "could be made profitable."[28] Although the directors of both companies agreed to accept some slave life insurance business from Beynroth, they did so on a limited basis. Neither company was focusing on insuring slaves. As James explained to Beynroth, they would need to investigate "the character of the owner for integrity and good Standing" and to obtain "particulars as to identity, . . . marks &c and weight, besides the particulars asked in the usual examining physician's certificate."[29]

The long association of "slave" with "property" suggested to some life insurers, northern and southern alike, that slaves should not be insured under life insurance contracts. The directors of Baltimore Life received far more requests for slave insurance than they approved in the company's early decades, because they did not consider slaves "desirable risks."[30] Girard and Baltimore Life focused on increasing sales among the free population, but in the South, the demand to insure slaves dramatically outpaced that to insure free people. In the early years of the company, Baltimore Life directors flatly declined to insure slaves being traded to the Deep South. They cautiously insured slaves living and working with their owners but did not want "to be answerable for them should they be sold & dispersed in different directions & owned by men that we know nothing of."[31] Facing continual demand, the directors gradually relaxed their rules regarding slave life insurance. By the mid-1850s, the company was insuring gangs of enslaved miners and railroad workers, and the directors no longer declined risks on slaves being transported to the Deep South by slave traders. Antebellum life insurers domiciled in southern states insured far more slaves than free people. Even northern companies insured more slaves than free people in the South. Of the policies sold in southern states by New York Life in its early years, 66 percent covered slaves.[32]

Since the law treated the enslaved as both persons and property, slave life insurance combined the functions and the principles of both property and life insurance in one product. Charles Beynroth's description of slave life insurance in Louisville illustrates how such policies drew on principles of fire, marine, and life insurance underwriting. Following accepted fire insurance practice, insurers underwrote slaves as they did buildings, insuring no more than two-thirds to three-fourths of full market value. Additionally, slave life insurance policies became effective immediately, "it being customary here to issue the Policy on Slaves at the time of application, as we do on term Policies in Fire & Marine Risks." A typical slaveholding customer would "bring in a gang of ½ a dozen or more Slaves, whom he has hired for one trip, or a season on our Steam Boats or in Manufactories and expects the risk taken at once, on the Paym[en]t of the Premium."[33] Waiting for policies to be approved and returned by underwriters in distant home offices meant extra costs boarding slaves and extra risks that slaves might escape. Yet, to demonstrate that slave insurance was, in fact, life insurance, Beynroth made clear that "each case would undergo a Separate and Strict Medical Examination by an Authorized and competent Physician." Beynroth wanted to reassure the Baltimore Life directors that such examinations would certify slaves sound enough to survive being "hired for one trip"—working off passage costs to the New Orleans slave market—or hired to work on a steamboat or in a waterfront factory.[34]

In one sense, all life insurance is a form of property insurance, since it quantifies the value of human life by approximating the amount of money a person may be expected to earn during an average lifetime. Thus, the primary function of life insurance is to protect a beneficiary against the sudden and untimely loss of the earning power of the insured. Slave life insurance, however, combined the risk of loss of earning power with the risk of loss of property value, as an 1852 advertising circular revealed. J. Leander Starr, general agent in New York City for the National Loan Fund, explained that, if an insured slave died, "the owner, although deprived of the revenue of his *labour* . . . will still not be unrecompensed for his loss." Here, Starr emphasized the promise of life insurance to replace earning power. But slave life insurance also fulfilled a basic function of property insurance, the replacement of all or most of the monetary value of lost or destroyed property. A slave owner would still have "not his Slave—but the $500 which constituted his value, which sum he can invest to replace the revenue the death of the Slave would have deprived him of if *uninsured*."[35] Slave life insurance, as Starr presented it, promised slave owners a way to preserve both the earning power and the property value of slaves.

Thus, slave life insurance both resembled and differed from both life and property insurance. The uniqueness of slave life insurance was reflected in underwriting, accounting, and marketing practices. Except in very rare cases, no company insured slaves for life, although some insurers underwrote slaves for terms as long as twelve years. All insurers charged more to insure slaves than free people of the same ages, largely owing to the lack of mortality statistics on enslaved populations. Some agents placed separate advertisements for "life insurance" and "insurance on Negroes," sometimes on the same newspaper page.[36] In accounting, some insurers separated slave life insurance premium income from that derived from other insurance. Aetna's directors apparently considered insuring the enslaved far riskier than insuring the free. From its inception in 1850 through 1853, the Aetna Annuity Fund insured both free and enslaved people. After 1853 the life insurance portion of the business was spun off into a new company, Aetna Life Insurance Company.[37] The Annuity Fund continued to insure slaves. Aetna's directors clearly treated slave life insurance as a form of life insurance, requiring medical examinations and setting premium rates according to the ages of slaves. Yet they also considered it a form of property insurance inappropriate for their life insurance subsidiary.

Reflecting the dual designation of slaves as people and property, slave life insurance stood midway between life and property insurance, as an 1859 advertisement illustrates. The St. Louis Mutual Life and Health Insurance Company offered insurance on "the *Lives* of persons of both sexes, the *Health* of persons, . . . the life of *Live Stock,* and upon *Negroes.*"[38] This company, like others, combined the insurance of property and people under one roof, but few so clearly identified slave insurance as a separate product.

I n the absence of widespread banking facilities in rural areas, individuals contracted credit arrangements, often by mortgaging slaves.[39] Slave owners and their creditors helped to create demand for slave life insurance, which minimized risk for both creditor and debtor. In August 1835, a Georgetown creditor named Mattingly sought to insure an enslaved man "on whom he has a lien to secure a debt due from E.D. Withers."[40] The directors of Baltimore Life recognized this arrangement as a form of creditor-debtor insurance—a longstanding use of life insurance—and approved the risk.[41] Edward Reynolds extended loans to various slave owners in Calvert and Anne Arundel counties, Maryland, during the early 1850s. In return, Reynolds accepted mortgages along with insurance on slaves belonging to these farmers.[42] In all of these cases, creditors could have insured the slave owners rather than the slaves. Slave owners accustomed to commodifying enslaved individuals as property easily accepted slave life insurance; they remained "ignorant and prejudicial" about insuring themselves.[43]

Slave owners also insured slaves to make themselves more creditworthy. Slave life insurance helped to facilitate a credit arrangement between Henry Mandeville and John McDonnell, from whom Mandeville wanted to purchase slaves. Mandeville agreed to pay McDonnell $900, $700, and $550, respectively, for Alfred, Rachael, and Jane, for a total purchase price of $2,150. But Mandeville did not pay the full purchase price in cash. Instead, he gave McDonnell $1,500 in cash and his note at 8 percent interest for the remaining $650. Mandeville immediately insured Alfred and Rachael, Alfred's wife, for $500 each. He then separated them, hiring each on different steamboats. The insurance, with a total death benefit of $1,000 at an annual cost of $56, must have eased the minds of both Mandeville and McDonnell.[44] Although McDonnell sold Alfred and Rachael "fully guaranteed," meaning that he could demonstrate clear legal ownership and certify the health of both slaves, the medical examinations required to insure Alfred and Rachael provided Mandeville a second medical opinion of their soundness. For McDonnell, the promise of a $500 cash payment in the event of either slave's death meant an extra guarantee, above and beyond Mandeville's reputation, that the $650 loan he extended to Mandeville would be repaid. Separated, Alfred and Rachael faced the distinct possibility of being burned, scalded, blown up, or drowned on their respective steamboats, *Princess* and *Natchez*. Would Mandeville have employed them in less hazardous work in the absence of insurance? This question cannot be answered. But insurance enabled Mandeville and many other slaveholders to participate in a relatively risk-free system of slave-based credit, with potentially devastating effects for the enslaved.

Some slave traders insured slaves not only to protect their own pocketbooks but also to create credit opportunities. The New Orleans slave trader Bernard Kendig had a reputation as a ruthless salesman, stemming from the numerous lawsuits he faced for selling slaves with "known defects." Kendig also extended "liberal credit" to customers, closing out most of his paper transactions quickly.[45] In February 1854, Thomas Murphy purchased three men from Kendig. William Miles and two others known only by their first names, Reuben and John, worked as draymen, or cart drivers, on the streets of New Orleans. Murphy insured the men through the New Orleans broker C. C. Lathrop, an agent for the Aetna Annuity Fund. On February 15, the day the insurance went into force, Murphy transferred "all my right and interest to the within policy" back to Kendig. Five days later, Kendig transferred the insurance to a Wilson Davis. Thus, Wilson Davis, a man unknown to William Miles, Reuben, or John, became beneficiary of an insurance policy worth \$2,900 on their lives.[46]

Kendig no doubt knew of the business periodical the *Commercial Review*, published in New Orleans. In an 1851 article announcing the intention of the British Commercial Life Insurance Company to begin insuring slaves, editor J. D. B. DeBow had alerted his readers to the possibilities of raising credit using slave life insurance. DeBow had suggested to readers that "by hypothecating the policies of the Company, our planters will be able to realize money facilities with their merchants upon negroes, as well as any other description of property."[47] Insuring slaves would make their owners more creditworthy. The medical examinations required to insure slaves served as an extra warranty of their health, reassuring debtors and creditors about dealing with traders of dubious reputation. The flexibility of insurance policies, as paper financial instruments standing in for the sale value of slaves, made them potentially better and more liquid collateral than actual human bodies. The insurance policy on William Miles, Reuben, and John could easily be transferred in a chain of credit extending from Murphy to creditors unknown to him. Murphy and Kendig used the slave life insurance policy as a way of obtaining credit in much the same way that automobile dealers and purchasers use insurance today. The slave insurance policy removed some of the uncertainty of extending a loan by promising to replace all or part of the value of the collateral, should it be destroyed. Just as most present-day car buyers are required to do in order to obtain credit, Murphy had to show evidence of insurance on the slaves before Kendig extended the credit. The slave life insurance then assisted Kendig in extending the chain of credit to his creditor, Wilson Davis.

Insurance lowered the financial risk of investing in slaves for individual slave owners and traders but raised risks for slaves. If any of the slaves insured by Murphy showed "defects" that had escaped the notice of physicians, the insurance potentially posed a grave threat. The monetary value of insured slaves who became injured or too ill to work could drop below the value of the insurance, creating an incentive for a creditor to destroy enslaved "property" to recoup debts. The level of the potential threat is suggested by the language inserted into slave policies by insurers in response to various losses. As marine insurers had done earlier, life insurers exempted some types of losses from benefits. The wording of these policy exceptions indicates that some slave life insurers suspected intentional mistreatment of insured bondpeople. For instance, one company's slave insurance policy form asked purchasers to attest "that I will always, and promptly, call a physician, in case of sickness."[48] Most slave life insurance policies also contained language intended to control policy transfers. While these efforts may have represented paternalistic efforts to protect slaves from harm, the insurers who wrote them also surely had their eyes firmly fixed on company profits. In any case, insured slaves became unwitting participants in credit networks far removed from concerned directors in distant home offices.

Virginian Bickerton Lyle Winston speculated in slaves as a young man before inheriting a plantation in Hanover County, where he farmed until his death in 1902.[49] Winston liked to purchase young, male slaves cheaply, insure them, hire them out to area industries, and watch his human investments grow. Winston purchased Beverley, a nine-year-old male slave, in 1853 and sent him to work on the Virginia and Tennessee Railroad. In 1854, Winston insured him with Baltimore Life, along with two other railroad laborers: nine-year-old Henry Jr. and John, age eleven. Winston took out policies on Frederick, an eleven-year-old brickyard laborer, and twelve-year-old Dandridge as well.[50]

The Baltimore Life underwriters firmly insisted on insuring no slave for more than two-thirds of market value.[51] They did not require a bill of sale, but simply asked applicants to affirm the value of slaves they wished to insure. Since slave prices were not hard and fast, the underwriters must have accepted that the insurance amounts that Winston requested fell within the normal range of values for slaves of similar age. Altogether, Winston insured seven of the slaves listed in his account book for more than he had paid for them. In 1854, Winston insured Dandridge for $700, making Dandridge's market value $1,050 by the two-thirds rule. Winston had bought Dandridge, then eight years old, for $400 in 1850. In four years, Dandridge's market value appreciated by more than 250 percent. Dandridge's annual earnings climbed from $45 in 1850 to $90 by 1854. The insurance policy, with a term of seven years, cost Winston $11.34 annually. By 1855, when the entries for Dandridge in Winston's account book end, Winston had almost recouped his initial investment in Dandridge, plus interest. If Dandridge died, Winston would receive $700, or roughly 1.75 times his investment in Dandridge. Winston bought George and John Jr. on December 31, 1853, paying $500 and $465, respectively. The following spring, he insured both for $500 each.[52] Thus, Winston purchased young slaves with the expectation that they would increase in value. He insured them, sometimes for more than their market value, and collected the earnings from their labor. When they died, Winston received insurance benefits. Indeed, insurance provided Winston a "perpetuity of income" from his bondpeople.

Winston's investment portfolio consisting of enslaved children offered him multiple ways to profit. If slave investments did not earn, Winston sold them. He bought Joshua for $450 in January 1850. Having earned only $20 from Joshua's hire by July, Winston sold him for $700, a profit of more than 150 percent.[53] Winston purchased Travis in 1847, hiring him at an annual rate of $100. By April 1852, Travis had worked off his purchase price plus interest. In 1854, Winston insured Travis with Baltimore Life for $500 at an annual cost of $17.80. The relatively high cost of the insurance indicates that the underwriters viewed Travis as a higher-than-average risk, due perhaps to advanced age, poor health, or occupational hazards. In any case, Travis died on May 28, 1857. Winston received a $500 death benefit check a few days later.[54]

In addition to insuring slaves for speculators, insurance corporations themselves became slave traders. Their investment activities magnified the risks slaves faced. First, the charter language of many insurance corporations empowered them to own slaves. The charters of both Virginia Slave Insurance Company and Kanawha Slave Insurance Company authorized them to insure "against risks upon the interests they [the company owners] may have in any slaves in virtue of any loan or loans."[55] That is, the charters of both these companies empowered their directors to lend money on slave collateral and to insure the resulting financial "interests" against the risk of loss of any collateralized slaves during the term of a loan. The South Carolina legislature authorized Commercial Insurance Company of Charleston to "lend money on the security of real and personal property," including slaves.[56] Southern Life Insurance & Trust invested in the southern slave plantation system by extending loans secured by slaves. When debtors defaulted on such loans, courts often ordered their slaves sold. An 1849 lawsuit against the estate of Archibald Hunter resulted in the sale of five enslaved families—twenty-seven people in all, ranging in age from infancy to fifty-five—to repay Hunter's creditor, the Southern Life Insurance & Trust Company. An 1850 lawsuit awarded the company proceeds of the sale of six enslaved adults and approximately 240 acres of land in Florida. Again in 1853, Southern Life won a mortgage foreclosure on the property of Augustus Lanier that resulted in the sale of twenty-five enslaved individuals.[57]

Overcommitment to slave-based credit could affect insurers negatively as well. Arranging slave-based credit may have been one of the primary functions of the New Orleans branch of the United States Insurance, Annuity and Trust Company. Based in Philadelphia, this company sold life insurance products in Pennsylvania and throughout the Northeast. Its agencies in New Orleans, St. Louis, Richmond, and perhaps other southern urban locations, sold slave life insurance as well. By 1855 "a prominent source of revenue" for the company "was 8 per cent on collateral loans at New Orleans."[58] The company failed in 1862 largely owing to "losses on collateral loans in the savings-fund department and speculation with the funds."[59] Richard Holcombe Kilbourne Jr. found that in antebellum East Feliciana Parish, "slaves accounted for most of the collateral for both short-term and long-term credit arrangements." [60] Given the probable extent of loans collateralized by slaves in Louisiana, some portion of the "speculative" loans extended by United States Insurance would have been collateralized by enslaved individuals. The outbreak of war would certainly have severely affected the viability of such loans.

Southern insurance companies amassed capital from premium income and invested it in other enterprises such as industrial development, internal improvements, and real estate, all of which supported the slave system. Slave life insurance sales accounted for approximately 22 percent of the premium income of the Southern Mutual Life Insurance Company in 1858. The bulk of this company's assets was invested in Georgia and South Carolina state bonds.[61] The Virginia Life Insurance Company, chartered in 1860, appealed to southern customers to stop insuring through northern and British companies, which "ARE NOT PERMITTED TO INVEST their funds . . . in the STOCKS OF SLAVEHOLDING STATES."[62] The company's charter required that its premium income be invested in mortgages or bonds in slaveholding states and that its directors be "citizens of Virginia, or some other slaveholding State."[63]

I n the slave South, a culture that philosophically, if not practically, rejected capitalism, slaveholders selectively adapted one of capitalism's most important financial tools—insurance—to insure slave property. Insurers responding to customer demand to insure slaves combined characteristics of various types of property and life insurance to create a unique product. The practice of insuring slaves thus continued a centuries-long tradition of underwriting slaves as part of marine cargoes. Combining principles of life insurance with that old tradition simply made slave life insurance all the more marketable. By the 1850s, two separate markets for life insurance existed in the South. The market for life insurance of "persons" grew sluggishly, but that for the enslaved grew along with the expansion of the domestic slave trade after 1808. Most companies used separate "Slave Policy" forms designed to insure multiple slaves under one policy, reflecting the demand from slave traders. Southern insurers relaxed rules on acclimation in order to serve the huge slave markets in the Deep South. Insurance agents placed separate advertisements for "life insurance" and "slave life insurance." Some companies combined insurance of slaves with insurance of livestock, boats, bank notes, specie, and buildings, while issuing life insurance for "whites" through a separate department.

Many of the southern companies that committed heavily to insuring slaves were short-lived. Evidence of their activities is scattered, and the full extent to which they supported the southern credit system may never be known. It is clear, however, based on available evidence, that both life and property insurers—southern, northern, and international—insured and maintained a financial interest in the enslaved. These insurers must be included when considering the full extent of the slave trade.

Looming over all of this is the unanswered question: What risk did slave life insurance create for slaves? Not until the late nineteenth century did insurers give a name—"moral hazard"—to the risk posed to the insured by the existence of insurance. Clearly, though, the existence of slave life insurance affected the lives of many slaves by supporting the slave trade and the use of slave-based credit arrangements.

NOTES

1. Our understanding of the extent of the domestic slave trade has undergone revision over the past twenty-five years, thanks to the work of Michael Tadman, *Speculators and Slaves: Masters, Traders, and Slaves in the Old South* (Madison: University of Wisconsin Press, 1989); Walter Johnson, *Soul by Soul: Life inside the Antebellum Slave Market* (Cambridge, MA: Harvard University Press, 1999); Robert H. Gudmestad, *A Troublesome Commerce: The Transformation of the Interstate Slave Trade* (Baton Rouge: Louisiana State University Press, 2003); Steven Deyle, *Carry Me Back:*

The Domestic Slave Trade in American Life (New York: Oxford University Press, 2005); and Jonathan D. Martin, *Divided Mastery: Slave Hiring in the American South* (Cambridge, MA: Harvard University Press, 2004).

2. Karen Kotzuk Ryder, "'Permanent Property': Slave Life Insurance in the Antebellum Southern United States, 1820–1866" (PhD diss., University of Delaware, 2012), 205–6.

3. Robert S. Starobin, *Industrial Slavery in the Old South* (New York: Oxford University Press, 1970), 72; Ronald L. Lewis, *Coal, Iron, and Slaves: Industrial Slavery in Maryland and Virginia, 1715–1865* (Westport, CT: Greenwood Press, 1979), 95; Sharon Ann Murphy, "Securing Human Property: Slavery, Life Insurance, and Industrialization in the Upper South," *Journal of the Early Republic* 25 (Winter 2005): 615–52; Sharon Ann Murphy, *Investing in Life: Insurance in Antebellum America* (Baltimore: Johns Hopkins University Press, 2010), 184–206; Todd L. Savitt, "Slave Life Insurance in Virginia and North Carolina," *Journal of Southern History* 43 (November 1977): 583–600.

4. Murphy, *Investing in Life,* 184.

5. Geoffrey Clark, *Betting on Lives: The Culture of Life Insurance in England, 1695–1775* (New York: Manchester University Press, 1999), 13–18.

6. Samuel Marshall, *A Treatise on the Law of Insurance, Book I* (1802; reprint, Boston: Manning and Loring, 1805), 132. Marshall quoted two French jurists, Valin and Pothier.

7. James C. Oldham, "Insurance Litigation Involving the *Zong* and Other British Slave Ships, 1780–1807," *Journal of Legal History* 28 (December 2007): 299–318; Ryder, "'Permanent Property,'" 28–29.

8. Marshall, *Treatise,* 134.

9. *Charleston (SC) City Gazette and Daily Advertiser,* July 8, 1800; January 18, 1800; and July 9, 1803.

10. *Charleston (SC) Courier,* December 31, 1804.

11. *Charleston (SC) Times,* May 26, 1804.

12. Act of Incorporation of the Marine Insurance Company of Alexandria, reprinted in *Alexandria (VA) Advertiser,* February 8, 1798.

13. Policy 2157, June 21, 1809, Policy Books, Marine Insurance Company of Alexandria, Insurance Policies, May 18, 1807–November 8, 1810, Mss3M3387a, VHS. This policy is reproduced in A. Glenn Crothers, "Commercial Risk and Capital Formation in Early America: Virginia Merchants and the Rise of American Marine Insurance, 1750–1815," *Business History Review* 78 (Winter 2004): 626.

14. Policy 2157, Marine Insurance Company of Alexandria.

15. *Hunter, Murphy & Talbot v. The General Mutual Insurance Company of New York,* 11 La. Ann. 139, http://web2.westlaw.com/.

16. On the history of actuarial science, see E. J. Moorhead, *Our Yesterdays: The History of the Actuarial Profession in North America, 1809–1979* (Schaumburg, IL: Society of Actuaries, 1989).

17. *Charleston (SC) City Gazette and Daily Advertiser,* February 17, 1820.

18. Ibid., January 18, 1831.

19. Tadman, *Speculators and Slaves,* 12.

20. *St. Louis Daily Commercial Bulletin,* December 16, 1837.

21. Martin, *Divided Mastery,* 19.

22. *St. Louis Daily Missouri Republican,* December 19, 1853.

23. Ryder, "Permanent Property,'" 91. On enslaved steamboat workers, see Thomas C. Buchanan, *Black Life on the Mississippi: Slaves, Free Blacks, and the Western Steamboat World* (Chapel Hill: University of North Carolina Press, 2004).

24. Commercial Insurance Company, *Charter of the Commercial Insurance Company, of Charleston, SC . . . Also By-Laws and Regulations of the Company; Rates of Insurance on Lives, Table of Annuities, and Semi-Annual Statements of the Company's Affairs* (Charleston: A. J. Burke, 1853), 4–6.

25. *Richmond Daily Dispatch,* July 2, 1860.

26. James River Insurance Company, Howardsville, Albemarle County, VA, *Fire, Marine and Slave Life Insurance* (Howardsville, VA: N.p., 1860?), 7–8.

27. Jonathan F. James to Charles E. Beynroth, October 26, 1852, Beynroth Papers, MSS A/B 573/37, Filson Historical Society Special Collections Department, Louisville, KY. This letter indicates that Beynroth had sent rates used by the Louisville agent of Mutual Benefit Life and Fire Insurance Company of Louisiana to James in February 1852.

28. Charles E. Beynroth to Richard B. Dorsey, June 22, 1852, correspondence, BLIC; *Records, 1831–1867,* MS175, correspondence, H. Furlong Baldwin Library, MHS (emphasis in original).

29. James to Beynroth, October 26, 1852, Beynroth Papers. For Baltimore Life's arrangement with Beynroth, see Dorsey to Beynroth, July 2, 1852, correspondence, BLIC.

30. John Donaldson to Robertson and Branda, October 31, 1846, Letter Book, April 1833–March 1841, BLIC. Baltimore Life correspondence contains many inquiries for slave life insurance that are not matched in policy books, indicating that the company declined many requests to insure slaves.

31. Donaldson to Jonathan O. Lay, July 12, 1839, Letter Book, April 1833–March 1841, BLIC.

32. Ryder, "Permanent Property,'" 165.

33. Beynroth to Dorsey, August 10, 1852, correspondence, BLIC. Life insurance policies typically did not become valid until they were approved and signed by company officers. When a customer made application for insurance and paid the initial premium, local agents forwarded all application materials to company directors, who reviewed each application for approval. The process could take weeks.

34. Beynroth to Dorsey, August 10, 1852, correspondence, BLIC.

35. National Loan Fund Life Assurance Company, of London, "A Method by Which Slave Owners May Be Protected from Loss," March 1, 1852, copy attached to Thomas Pollard to Henry F. Thompson, January 11, 1855, correspondence, BLIC (emphasis in original).

36. See, for example, advertisements for Union Mutual Life of Boston in the *Hannibal Missouri Courier,* October 7, 1852.

37. Hooker, *Aetna Life Insurance Company,* 11–15.

38. *Liberty (MO) Weekly Tribune,* May 13, 1859.

39. Bonnie Martin, "Slavery's Invisible Engine: Mortgaging Human Property," *Journal of Southern History* 76 (November 2010): 817–66.

40. James Causten to John Donaldson, August 10, 1835, correspondence, BLIC.

41. Donaldson to Causten, August 11, 1835, Letter Book, April 1833–March 1841, BLIC.

42. Applications 2164 and 2168, applications; policies 2164, September 4, 1850, on John and Richard, and 2168, September 20, 1850, on James, Wesley, and Nat, policies, BLIC.

43. Donaldson to John Mosby, August 12, 1837, Letter Book, April 1833–March 1841, BLIC.

44. Henry D. Mandeville Account Book, 1842–52, Henry D. Mandeville and Family Papers, 1815–1865, *Records of Ante-bellum Southern Plantations on Microfilm*, ed. Kenneth M. Stampp, Series I, Selections from Louisiana State University, Part 3, The Natchez Area, reel 5, frames 840–73. See also Martin, *Divided Mastery*, 80.

45. Judith Kelleher Schafer, *Slavery, the Civil Law, and the Supreme Court of Louisiana* (Baton Rouge: Louisiana State University Press, 1994), 140–42 (first quotation 140); Deyle, *Carry Me Back*, 129 (second quotation). See also Gudmestad, *Troublesome Commerce*, 97; and Johnson, *Soul by Soul*, 50–51.

46. Policy 158, February 10, 1854, in Hooker, *Aetna Life Insurance Company*, 14–15.

47. "Insurance on Negroes," *DeBow's Review* 10 (February 1851): 241. Hypothecation means the use of a paper financial instrument as loan collateral.

48. Application 3158, April 2, 1861, Albemarle Insurance Company, box 17, BLIC.

49. By 1860, Winston lived at Signal Hill plantation in Hanover County, Virginia, with twenty-two slaves in addition to those he hired out. Eighth Census of the United States, 1860, St. Paul's Parish, Hanover County, Virginia, accessed through Ancestry Library Edition.

50. Bickerton Lyle Winston, Ledger 1846–1859, Mss5:3 W7334:1, VHS; Application 2505 on Beverley, applications; policies 2503–5, April 18, 1854; 2568, October 25, 1854; 2571, November 7, 1854, policies, BLIC.

51. This rule remained in effect from 1839 through 1857. See Donaldson to Lay, July 12, 1839, Letter Book, April 1833–March 1841; A. B. Coulter to Philip Price, February 5, 1857, Letter Book, January 1852–June 1867, BLIC.

52. Winston Ledger, pages headed "Dandridge"; policies 2504 (John Jr.), April 18, 1854; and 2569 (George), October 25, 1854, policies, BLIC.

53. Winston Ledger, pages headed "Joshua."

54. Winston Ledger, pages headed "Travis"; policy 2567, policies; ledger "Policies Cancelled," BLIC. The rate to insure Travis was 3.56 percent.

55. "An Act to Incorporate the Virginia Slave Insurance Company," March 10, 1835, *Acts of the General Assembly of Virginia, Passed at the Session of 1835–36* (Richmond: Thomas Ritchie, 1836), 161–64 (quotation 162); "An Act to Incorporate the Kanawha Slave Insurance Company," February 18, 1836, *Acts of the General Assembly of Virginia, Passed at the Session of 1835–36* (Richmond: Thomas Ritchie, 1836), 268.

56. Commercial Insurance Company, *Charter*, 7.

57. *Tallahassee Floridian and Journal*, January 27, 1849; May 11, 1850; April 9, 1853.

58. J. A. Fowler, *History of Insurance in Philadelphia for Two Centuries (1683–1882)* (Philadelphia: Review, 1888), 688.

59. Ibid., 819.

60. Richard Holcombe Kilbourne Jr., *Debt, Investment, Slaves: Credit Relations in East Feliciana Parish, Louisiana, 1825–1885* (Tuscaloosa: University of Alabama Press, 1995), 49.

61. Southern Mutual Life Insurance Company, 1858 Annual Report, *Charleston Mercury,* October 5, 1858.

62. Virginia Life Insurance Company, *Virginia Life Insurance Company, Incorporated January 1860, Brochure and Rates Booklet* (Richmond: Virginia Life Insurance Company, 1860), 6 (emphasis in original).

63. Virginia Life Insurance Company, *Charter and By-Laws of the Virginia Life Insurance Company* (Richmond: H. K. Ellyson, 1860), 5–6.

NAT TURNER IN PRINT AND ON FILM

KENNETH S. GREENBERG

etween 1998 and 2003, I worked with two filmmakers to write and produce *Nat Turner: A Troublesome Property*. Ultimately, the National Endowment for the Humanities supported completion of the film with a substantial grant, and PBS broadcast it nationally. It has since been shown in scores of locations throughout the world, including universities, academic conferences, film festivals, and in venues such as the Museum of Modern Art, the Louvre, and the Getty Museum. Both before and after making this film I also wrote about Nat Turner, discussing the rebellious slave briefly in *Honor and Slavery*, more extensively in the introduction to *The Confessions of Nat Turner and Related Documents*, and most extensively in the edited volume *Nat Turner: A Slave Rebellion in History and Memory*.[1] It is rare that a historian gets the opportunity to explore the same subject in print and in film. The experience forced me to reflect on the similarities and differences between presenting historical stories in these two very different types of media. This chapter describes some of what I learned from that experience and reflects on its meaning for my work as a historian as well as for the larger community of historians.

Many historians consider the Nat Turner slave rebellion to be the most significant slave rebellion in American history. They see it that way not because of its size or scope but because it loomed so large as an event and as a memory in the minds and imaginations of those who lived through it, as well as those who thought about it during the years after the rebellion. The uprising broke out in Southampton County, Virginia, on August 22, 1831. The organizer was Nat Turner, an extraordinary man inspired by religious visions to lead his people in a violent attempt to overthrow slavery. On the evening of August 21, he met with six fellow conspirators for a dinner in the woods to plan the attack. Then, early the next morning, the seven rebels killed Turner's master and his family and moved swiftly from farm to farm, killing nearly every white man, woman, and child they encountered and gathering recruits as they went. In the end, they visited eleven farms, enlisted somewhere between 50 and 60 rebels and killed between 57 and 60 whites. Within twenty-four hours of the outbreak, the local militia captured or summarily executed all of the rebels except Nat Turner. Turner eluded his pursuers for more than two months, until October 30. He was tried a week later, convicted of insurrection, and hanged on November 11.[2]

By many measures the Nat Turner rebellion was a small and relatively insignificant uprising. It was very quickly suppressed. It involved a tiny group of rebels who killed a small number of masters. In comparative terms, it contrasts dramatically in size and scope with large uprisings such as the Haitian slave rebellion of the early nineteenth century that overthrew the regime of the master class and created an independent nation led by former enslaved people, or the Russian peasant rebellions of the seventeenth and eighteenth centuries involving hundreds of thousands of serfs.[3]

Yet the Nat Turner rebellion had significance for Americans that went well beyond its comparatively small scale, short duration, and narrowly circumscribed geographic location. Most immediately, the rebellion created a fear among the master class that had significant consequences. Masters could not be certain whether Virginia and other slave communities harbored large numbers of other enslaved people who, like Nat Turner, might not appear threatening until the moment they rose up in rebellion. In this kind of atmosphere, masters reacted and overreacted in ways that dramatically demonstrated their fear to themselves and to their enemies. The initial mobilization of military power to suppress the rebellion involved more than three thousand armed men. False rumors of other impending rebellions spread throughout neighboring counties and beyond. Militia members and other enraged citizens summarily executed scores of suspected rebels—many more than could possibly have participated in the rebellion. Witnesses reported that several members of the militia carried with them the severed heads of rebels. They displayed some of the heads publicly, as a warning to the black population. In addition, Virginia passed new legislation to prevent enslaved people from preaching and from gathering in groups to hold religious meetings. Most significantly, the members of the Virginia legislature were so frightened by the threat of future rebellions that they engaged in extended debate about the possibility of abolishing slavery. While they ultimately rejected this idea, that the political leaders of the state gave the matter such serious consideration stood as an extraordinary immediate consequence of the rebellion.[4]

In the years after 1831, the Nat Turner rebellion occupied an important place in the memory and imagination of many Americans. Before the Civil War, northern abolitionists pointed to the rebellion as an example of what would happen on a grander scale if the South failed to abolish slavery. Whereas some abolitionists were pacifists who rejected insurrection as a possible way to end slavery, others began to portray Turner as a heroic freedom fighter whose example should be followed. At the same time, a powerful African American folk tradition began to include Nat Turner stories, portraying him as a clever trickster who knew just the right ways to mock and to manipulate the master class. Not surprisingly, white southerners invoked a different set of images associated with Nat Turner, repeatedly vilifying him as an insane fanatic who killed innocent women and children. For many whites in the South, the Turner rebellion became a warning of what would happen on a grander scale should the forces of abolition triumph.[5]

The contrasting images of Nat Turner as hero and Nat Turner as insane fanatic, along with a broad range of variations on those themes, reappeared over and over again in American memory. Mention of Turner can be found in fugitive slave narratives, in abolitionist and proslavery speeches, in conversations about John Brown's 1859 raid at Harpers Ferry, during debates about emancipation and Reconstruction, and in writings and speeches during the development and triumph of the Jim Crow South. Images of Turner continued to be invoked repeatedly in the twentieth century, during the era of the "New Negro," in the records of the Federal Writers' Project interviews with people who had once been slaves, and during the civil rights movement, as well as in more than a century of debates among historians about the nature of slave resistance.

Numerous prominent American political leaders, activists, novelists, historians, playwrights, and poets spoke or wrote about Nat Turner in works devoted wholly or partially to him. During the nineteenth century, William Lloyd Garrison, Henry Highland Garnet, Martin Delany, Frederick Douglass, Harriett Beecher Stowe, G. P. R. James, William Wells Brown, Thomas Wentworth Higginson, and scores of less prominent figures invoked the slave rebel. In the twentieth century, Turner received attention from W. E. B. Du Bois, Randolph Edmunds, Herbert Aptheker, Sterling Brown, and Stephen B. Oates, among others.

The single most influential work devoted to Nat Turner in the twentieth century was William Styron's novel *The Confessions of Nat Turner,* published in 1967. In a brief introductory note, Styron explained his intention to "re-create a man and his era, and to produce a work that is less an 'historical novel,' in conventional terms than a meditation on history."[6] Styron claimed he wrote a novel that was completely true to the known historical facts of the rebellion, but also one in which he used his literary imagination to fill in many of the blank areas not covered by the documentary record. Initially, the novel won extraordinary critical acclaim. It was awarded the Pulitzer Prize, and Styron rose to celebratory status, appearing on the covers of *Newsweek* and of *Time* magazines. But the late 1960s was a period of sharp racial division in America. Black critics and others soon attacked the novel for its lack of historical accuracy, for what some described as its racist stereotypes, for its denigration of a black hero, for the expropriation of a black voice by a white novelist, and, most significantly, for its evocation of a long racist tradition by inventing Nat Turner's lust for a young white female teenager.[7]

My first serious exposure to Nat Turner as a major historical figure was during graduate school in the 1970s as a student of Peter Kolchin at the University of Wisconsin. Like many other students of slavery, Kolchin's students read William Styron's novel, the responses of the critics, and the original 1831 *Confessions of Nat Turner.* Young scholars hotly debated the Styron novel in the context of the era's racial politics. My research focus at the time did not allow me to linger on Turner and his rebellion, but I recognized the importance of the topic for the history of slavery and hoped one day to return to work on the many unanswered questions about the historical Nat Turner.

During the 1990s, I turned my attention directly to Nat Turner as a historical subject, beginning with a series of extended visits to archives in Washington, D.C., and Virginia. I was well into research in preparation for a book about the historical Nat Turner when I first met California film producer Frank Christopher. By the late 1990s Christopher had established himself as a major documentary film producer, director, and writer. *In the Name of the People* (1985) had been his most important work. Narrated by Martin Sheen, it was a film focused on the rebellion in El Salvador. Christopher had risked his life to travel with the rebels, and his film was nominated for an Academy Award in the category of Best Feature Length Documentary. Christopher had also written and produced *Fei Hu: The Story of the Flying Tigers* (1999), a film that told the story of the American airmen who fought in China during World War II, making skillful and powerful use of home movies taken by the airmen themselves.

The controversy surrounding the Styron novel attracted Christopher's attention. He believed that a film about the rebel leader could open a conversation about race in the United States. In preparation for a Turner film, Christopher contacted every historian who had ever written about Nat Turner, seeking a scholar-collaborator who could join him in the project. At the same time, he contacted the African American film director Charles Burnett. Burnett had first become famous for *Killer of Sheep* (1979), a feature film written and produced for his master's thesis at UCLA. The film portrayed the difficult life of an African American family living in the Watts neighborhood of Los Angeles. Working in a slaughterhouse, the father in the household struggled to earn enough money to preserve his family. The film became a rarely seen but widely admired instant classic, standing in stark contrast to the "blaxploitation" films of the period, an era when films about African Americans rarely attempted to portray real characters struggling through the problems of real life. Ultimately, *Killer of Sheep* was recognized as a national treasure and became one of the first films entered into the National Film Registry of the Library of Congress.

Killer of Sheep marked the beginning of Burnett's extraordinary film career. Later highlights included *To Sleep with Anger* (1990), starring Danny Glover, a film about a south-central Los Angeles family struggling with its relationship to a southern past; *The Glass Shield* (1994), with Ice Cube, which told a story of racism and corruption in a Los Angeles police department; and *The Wedding* (1998), a made-for-television film based on a Dorothy West story about an interracial union, starring Halle Berry. During his career, aside from many major film prizes, Burnett was awarded Guggenheim and MacArthur fellowships as well as Ford Foundation, National Endowment for the Arts, and Rockefeller Foundation grants. Burnett became a much admired director known especially for his ability to offer realistic depictions of black family life, always treating his story and characters with a simple directness, respect, and honesty rarely seen among successful filmmakers. It was not a formula for commercial success, but it generated the kind of quiet admiration that marked him as a major

American director. The *New York Times* succinctly summed up his career when it described Burnett as "the nation's least-known great filmmaker and most gifted black director."[8] Burnett joined the Nat Turner film project because he was fascinated by the story of a man who, for more than 170 years, had been such a key figure in America's racial memory.

Given Burnett's background in film, he early on suggested that we tell the "real" Nat Turner story as a feature film in a simple and straightforward way. Given my background as a historian, I immediately noted that this would be extremely difficult, if not impossible. First, the very spare documentary record presented a serious problem. The central source for the life of Nat Turner was the original *Confessions of Nat Turner*, published shortly after his execution in 1831. But that document was problematic. For one thing, there was the issue of the "double voice." The "author" of the *Confessions* was not Nat Turner but Thomas R. Gray, a white lawyer who met with Turner in his jail cell shortly before his trial and execution. Gray assumed Turner's voice in the *Confessions*, but it is very difficult for a reader to sort out the places where Turner ends and Gray begins. Moreover, the *Confessions* largely described the movement of the rebels from farm to farm, offering only some tantalizing but very brief glimpses of the rest of Turner's life before the rebellion. For example, in describing the chain of events that motivated him to lead the revolt, Turner/Gray explains, "Being at play with other children, when three or four years old, I was telling them something, which my mother overhearing said . . . had happened before I was born," causing the community to believe "I surely would be a prophet." The *Confessions* offers a few other fleeting glimpses of Turner's early life. His mother and father, for example, believed he "was intended for some great purpose." His religious grandmother "remarked I had too much sense to be raised . . . as a slave." And he learned to read and to write without anyone teaching him.[9]

These glimpses into the life of Turner are suggestive, but they could not become the basis of a simple, straightforward, realistic historical film portrait without the addition of a great deal of invention. The documentary record offered an occasional snapshot of a life, but a full-length feature film would have required the creation of invented dialogue and full characters we knew little or nothing about. A few other original sources contain similar hints of Turner's life, but they are only hints. For example, the author of one newspaper account notes, "I have in my possession, some papers given up by his wife, under the lash."[10] This seems like good evidence that Turner had a wife, but it does not tell us anything about her character, physical appearance, or the kind of relationship she had with her husband. A feature filmmaker (and even a documentary filmmaker) telling the story of Nat Turner and his wife would have to invent much of that story. This would require clearly crossing the line from history into fiction, admittedly a blurry line in modern times, but a line that still retains meaning. It was a line that William Styron had clearly crossed, and we did not want to duplicate his approach and trigger again the anger it had generated.

At the time, my own research forced me even to question some of the few apparently well-known facts about Nat Turner's life. For example, I had come to wonder whether Nat Turner's name was really "Nat Turner." Legally, enslaved people in Virginia had no surname. Hence, in the few legal documents that mention Nat Turner before 1831, he was referred to as "Nat," and he most probably was called "Nat" by the white people of the community. Sometimes, because first names were not always a sufficient identifier of an enslaved person, whites commonly linked an enslaved person's first name to the name of a master. Hence, the name "Nat" could have been linked in conversation to a surname in a form such as "Nat, slave of Benjamin Turner" or "Turner's Nat." But we have no record of this usage specifically for Nat Turner. Moreover, Benjamin Turner was only Nat Turner's master for the early years of his life. He was sold to Thomas Moore in 1822 and then became the property of Moore's son Putnam Moore in 1828. But no records indicate that "Nat" was ever referred to as "Moore's Nat" or "Nat, slave of Putnam Moore." Shortly before the rebellion, Putnam Moore's mother married Joseph Travis, but we have no record of the name "Travis" ever being associated with Nat Turner. More importantly, no records indicate that anyone called the rebel leader "Nat Turner" before the rebellion. During the trials of other slaves accused of insurrection, no African American ever referred to Nat Turner as "Nat Turner." Sometimes he was called "Nat," but more often he was "Captain Nat" or "General Nat." It is in newspaper accounts of the rebellion and in the *Confessions of Nat Turner,* documents all written by whites, that scholars encounter Nat Turner as "Nat Turner" for the first time. We do not know, and we will *never* know, what Nat Turner called himself, and we do not know what his mother or his wife may have called him.[11]

This kind of thinking does not generally lead to a blockbuster feature film, and probably not even to a minor documentary film. A film requires Nat

Turner to be called something, and this kind of complicated, speculative, and probabilistic historical analysis is extremely difficult to depict on screen. There may be "truth" in this type of analysis, but there is definitely no drama. Looking back, I marvel at the patience and tolerance of filmmakers Charles Burnett and Frank Christopher as I explained this issue and similar historical matters to them. These were filmmakers of integrity and honesty who wanted to tell a Nat Turner story that was "true" but also dramatically engaging. Grappling with these kinds of complex problems and the difficulty of translating such ideas into film formed the basis of our collaboration.

Eventually, after many conversations, including a weeklong retreat in a remote mountain cabin, we agreed on an approach to create a Nat Turner film that could be defended as "historically accurate" while maintaining a dramatic flow and power. We rejected as impossible the idea of telling a single, simple "true" story of the historical Nat Turner. Instead, we embraced the notion that we should portray Nat Turner just as we, in fact, had encountered him in multiple forms in a variety of documents, including newspaper accounts, the original *Confessions*, novels, plays, paintings, and memory. We would tell "Nat Turner stories" and not a single and unified "Nat Turner story." Instead of attempting to transcend historical interpretation, we would embrace it; historical interpretation would become our subject matter. We would tell the dramatic story of a nation divided by race, unable to tell a coherent story about a critical episode in its history. Moreover, although our film would assume many of the features common to contemporary documentary films, including scholars and other experts talking about Nat Turner and Nat Turner imagery, it would also include dramatic recreations of different descriptions contained in the sources. For example, instead of just listening on screen to the critics of novelist William Styron's *Confessions of Nat Turner,* the film would also dramatically recreate the passages in the novel that had generated the most intense comment. Our audience would be able to see on film what had generated so much anger in print and at the same time listen to the voices of critics and defenders of the imagery. This approach was essential if we wanted to avoid a film that consisted only of what might prove to be relatively unexciting "talking heads." Hence, we would need several actors to portray the different images of Nat Turner that were at the heart of our story. Appropriately, we decided to title our film *Nat Turner: A Troublesome Property,* a simultaneous reference to the original enslaved Nat Turner and to the multiple images of Nat Turner created by our culture. Working within this structure, I learned a great deal about the special problems associated with telling a historical story on film.

One central constraining factor involved cost. The Nat Turner film we intended to create would never make money at the box office. The best venue for broadcast would be PBS, but public television had little money to invest in filmmaking and certainly not in a single project with a limited audience such as the one we proposed. A film like *Nat Turner* could only be funded through grant support or through the generosity of a major philanthropist. This required us to engage in years of fund-raising work, first raising money through small grants and then through an ultimate production grant from the National Endowment for the Humanities. This meant that we would have a relatively small pool of money to invest in the film (just over $1 million, a tiny amount for a film with dramatic recreations). Hence, as with all films, budget considerations played a significant role in every decision we made. This was quite different from producing history in print. On the issue of costumes, we could not afford to design and make our own; we had to rely on renting costumes already created for other films by designers with other purposes. In scouting locations, each scene might have benefited from a unique location, but given the high cost of moving trucks and equipment, we had to find a location that could serve multiple functions simultaneously and efficiently. Cost also determined whom we could hire as actors as well as in all the support roles required in a film. Moreover, if we wanted to depict a decapitated head, we could not seek out the very best maker of severed heads, but only the best maker we could afford.

Another key feature of filmmaking is that it is a group activity. Burnett, Christopher, and I were all very different people who brought radically different sensibilities and experiences to the film. But, given our commitment to producing a collaborative film, we had to agree on everything before we could move forward. Luckily, we did share a common set of core values, which made it possible for us to work together. Otherwise the project would have broken apart immediately. For example, we believed that everyone who spoke to us on camera had to be treated with full dignity and respect. The camera is a powerful weapon, and it can be misused to make anyone look foolish. The first time we filmed William Styron, we mistakenly positioned the camera to create the illusion of an elongated body. Once we viewed it, we instantly agreed to jettison the footage. Similarly, we interviewed one unusual man spouting unconventional ideas whose hair flew back from his head in a wild and unkempt manner. We stopped the camera every few minutes to comb his hair.

We also shared a commitment to creating a film that would not simply unleash in a modern audience the passionate disagreements of the past. For example, in depicting the William Styron controversy, our goal was not to create new supporters and opponents of the novel, but to explain the nature of the controversy and to point an audience toward understanding and transcendence rather than hatred. We hoped that viewers would treat Turner and those who wrote about him with the same respect that Burnett, Christopher, and I developed for one another. I marvel at the infinite patience of my collaborators toward the one member of the trio who had never before made a film. I came to understand why historians rarely play a central role in the making of films and how lucky I was to collaborate with colleagues who respected my profession.

Even though we worked well together, we came to the project with very different ideas that often clashed. Inherently, film tends to be a group and not an individual creation, quite different from the solitary work of historical research and writing.[12] Ultimately, each of us needed to compromise. For example, at one point I argued that, in the spirit of dealing with the subject of interpretation, we had to break the frame of the film and turn the camera on ourselves, identifying us as interpreters creating a film about interpretation. This was a far different approach than the simple and straightforward storytelling that was characteristic of the previous work of my colleagues. Despite Burnett's initial reluctance, in the end he appreciated the value of the suggestion and embraced it as a key element of the film. Similarly, Frank Christopher convinced us that the best title for the film would be *Nat Turner: A Troublesome Property,* even though Burnett and I were initially skeptical that an audience would understand the reference. Meanwhile, Christopher and I repeatedly learned to respect and to follow the judgments of Burnett as a great director who knew how to tell a moving story on film as well as how to best direct actors.

But the *Nat Turner* film was a group production involving far more than three collaborators. Even this relatively inexpensive film drew on the talents of hundreds of people—actors, set designers, truckers, animal wranglers, casting agents, production assistants, camera crews, and scores of other people performing an array of jobs. While Burnett, Christopher, and I collectively created the script and then organized, hired, and directed everyone, many people made contributions to the film under their own direction. The actors drew upon their past experiences as actors. Similarly, we could tell the set designers generally what we had in mind, but in the end the designers did most of the creative work themselves. Film is often experienced by its creators as a series of surprises, because it rarely has a single "author" in full control, at least not to the extent that the author of a book can maintain control.

Some of the most fascinating differences between depicting a historical story in writing and in film became evident because so many parts of the film were rooted in particular historical documents. Consider the filming of the original *Confessions of Nat Turner*. As with all the written documents we recreated on film, we committed ourselves to treating the *Confessions* as an interpretation. Our goal was not to present a historian's vision of the "real" moment of the *Confessions* but to depict a document created by Thomas R. Gray and to give modern audiences the sense that it was, in fact, a document created by Thomas R. Gray. This was a complex undertaking. The double voice of the *Confessions* proved challenging to translate on film.[13] The original written document was largely in Turner's voice as created by Gray, but occasionally Gray addressed readers in his own voice. We decided to portray such moments by having Gray turn to the camera and directly talk to the film audience, in exactly the way he sometimes spoke directly to readers of the original *Confessions*. Such an approach gave these scenes a strange quality that was true to the document and yet also quite odd, with Gray sometimes speaking to a camera and to a modern audience while Turner sits across from him in a jail cell apparently unaware of Gray's words and unaware of the audience Gray is addressing. Another problem of trying to portray the double voice of the *Confessions* was that it required us to give viewers a sense that Turner's voice might have been largely no more than Gray's voice in disguise. How could we accomplish that? As a possible solution to this problem, Charles Burnett at one point suggested that we should portray Turner as a white man in blackface—rather bluntly and startlingly making the point that in the *Confessions*, Turner was no more than Gray. In the end, we decided that such an approach would be too extreme, closing off the possibility that, at least at some moments, when Turner spoke, it might actually have been Turner speaking. Instead, we attempted to solve the problem in a simpler and more straightforward manner by having a narrator and modern commentators explain this complex aspect of the double voice problem.

Ultimately, our approach proved only partially successful. Since I have shown this film to hundreds of students and talked to many other viewers in different venues, it is clear to me that many viewers do not understand our point about the double voice. Our approach relied heavily on making the visual images of the *Confessions* problematic by having the narrator and academic commentators speak in the film about the double-voice issue. But visual images often have a power that resists the ability of words to make them problematic. In the same way that most people, when presented with the picture of a horse that is labeled "dog," would react by believing they were looking at a mislabeled picture rather than a "mispictured" label, our viewers often experienced the visual image as more convincing than the words that attempted to make the image more complex. When Nat Turner spoke on our screen, most viewers experienced Nat Turner speaking and not Thomas R. Gray possibly speaking through a Nat Turner he created. Perhaps more skillful filmmakers could have found a better way to depict the problem of the double voice. But my own experience in writing about this topic is that it is a subject far more easily dealt with in writing than on film.

Another difference between telling historical stories in print and in film is illustrated by our portrayal of Nat Turner's death by hanging. The main historical document that describes the hanging of Nat Turner is an article published in the *Norfolk Herald* on November 14, 1831.[14] Within a very spare description, the account includes the following key detail about the execution: "There were but a few people to see him hanged." As a historian familiar with many other features of the capture, trial, and execution of Nat Turner, I knew it was implausible that few people came to watch Nat Turner's execution. During the two months prior to his capture, the entire state of Virginia had been mobilized to apprehend the man they considered the most notorious fugitive in the history of the nation. Once he was captured, the public took an intense interest in the man. Wherever he appeared, he attracted large crowds. The *Petersburg Intelligencer* reported on November 4 that after Benjamin Phipps captured Turner, he "took Nat to his own residence, where he kept him until Monday morning—and having appraised his neighbors of his success, a considerable party accompanied him and his prisoner to Jerusalem," the county seat.[15] Similarly, Nat Turner's trial attracted a substantial group of angry white people, enough of a mob for the trial record to mention, "For reasons appearing to the Court it is ordered that the Sheriff summon a sufficient additional guard to repel any attempt that may be made to remove Nat alias Nat Turner from the custody of the Sheriff."[16] Moreover, the very short news article that described the small crowd at the execution included another "fact" that could not possibly have been true. It claimed that "General Nat sold his body for dissection, and spent the money on ginger cakes." While it was almost certainly the case that Nat Turner's body was dissected, it is inconceivable that anyone would have paid him for the right of dissection. Turner did not own his body while alive; no one would have paid him for the use of his body after death. It is very likely that the claims that Turner sold his body to purchase ginger cakes and that few people witnessed his execution were both invented stories designed to serve the same purpose. Both were ways of making Turner seem unimportant and trivial.

If we had been making a film that required a historian's vision of the likely scene of Turner's execution, we certainly would have depicted a large and angry crowd. But our focus was to treat documents as interpretations, and in that spirit we portrayed the image contained in the words of the *Petersburg Intelligencer* article of November 14, showing that "there were but a few people to see him hanged." Just as in our *Confessions* scene, we attempted to undercut this image on the screen by having the narrator note, "We know very little about the hanging of Nat Turner. The only contemporary account appeared in a local newspaper and as with all Nat Turner stories we are left with more questions than facts." And just as in our *Confessions* scene, we later discovered that the visual image of the hanging often proved more compelling to viewers than the words the narrator used to undermine that image.

But the depiction of the hanging of Nat Turner also illustrates another complicating factor in moving from words on a page to images on a screen. Historians in writing can confine their descriptions to areas that can be supported by documentary evidence. But history on film must fill in many of the blank spaces left out in writing. To portray the hanging of Nat Turner required us to ask and answer questions using sources other than the November 14 *Petersburg Intelligencer* article, questions that were sometimes not answerable using any sources. What did people in the crowd wear? Were white women present? How was the militia dressed? What was the weather at the moment of execution? Was Turner hanged from a scaffold? If there was a hanging tree, what did it look like? Was there a coffin, and did Turner sit on it on his way to execution?

Describing the thought process that went into handling just two of these questions illustrates the more general difficulty of telling historical stories on film. In both cases, readers of this chapter should note my progression as a print historian from naïvely attempting to work on film using the conventions of written history to recognizing that film requires movement away from those conventions. First, consider the issue of the hanging tree. When my film colleagues first came to me with the question of how to stage the hanging of Nat Turner, I immediately told them I knew nothing about such matters, but I would do what I could to answer the question. I learned that Richmond had a permanent scaffold, but I reasoned that was only because it was a larger city with frequent hangings. I decided that a small, rural town like Jerusalem was not likely to have had a permanent scaffold. This reasoning was confirmed by the discovery of a folk-tradition reference to a sweet gum tree commonly used for hangings in the town and by a photograph of an old, dead tree published in 1898 and reported to be the tree from which Nat Turner was hanged.[17] So I told my colleagues we needed to find a hanging tree, and in particular a sweet gum tree. We had chosen northern Virginia as our film location, and so we embarked on a search of the area for an appropriate tree, but to no avail. This was painful, since the sweet gum tree was the one "fact" I knew about the hanging and now, for very practical reasons, we had to abandon that "fact." We had become compelled to engage in the kind of invention I had hoped to avoid as much as possible in a history film. Ultimately, we settled on an old plantation location for most of our scenes and moved several large trucks adjacent to areas where we intended to film. It was only after all the trucks had parked and unloaded that I noticed in their midst a sweet gum tree appropriate for our purposes. I excitedly ran to my colleagues and told them about the discovery. As experienced filmmakers, they immediately noted that if we were to use the sweet gum tree, we would have to pack up all the trucks and move them—causing the loss of at least a day in our schedule and adding thousands of dollars to the costs of production. They wondered if this was really necessary, and I told them I would take the night to think about it.

That evening, I mulled over my response. Did I *really* know that Turner hanged from a sweet gum tree? The reference only appeared as a folk tradition. The photograph of the old dead tree was indecipherable. Moreover, if we were to use this sweet gum tree it would still be an invention, since it was not the original sweet gum tree anyway. In addition, we were filming in June and Nat Turner was hanged in November, so the leaves on the tree would all be wrong. Finally, I asked myself the question I should have asked at the beginning: Who really cares whether or not we use a sweet gum tree in this film? No viewers would notice, and even if they did, what difference would it make? I realized I had fallen into a way of thinking that had fetishized a fact for no good reason. I told my colleagues the next morning to forget about the sweet gum tree. Now, only the readers of this chapter will know that we did not use a sweet gum for the hanging. And I had learned an important lesson. Filmmakers must engage in invention all the time. There is no way to avoid it. Historians working on films need to move away from a narrowly defined, impossible-to-achieve notion of historical accuracy. The world of film is a world of approximation. Other species of trees often replace sweet gum trees in historical films.

The problem of the coffin in the hanging scene illustrates a similar point. The demands of the film required me to make hundreds of choices, and the coffin problem was one of many I had not anticipated. In a higher-budget film, every scene would have been worked out in advance in every detail, but in our planning we had done only a rough sketch of the hanging, with many details to be filled in later. A few days before we were scheduled to film this scene, a set designer came to me and asked what kind of coffin I wanted Nat Turner to sit on as he was carted to the hanging. He had seen other hangings depicted on film and knew that in the nineteenth century the condemned often sat on a coffin on the final trip to the gallows. Moreover, he noted, a condemned man sitting on a coffin added to the drama of the scene. He wanted me to make a choice. Did I want to use the tapered coffin common in western movies or did I prefer a simpler rectangular box? In anticipation of this moment, he had constructed both, and he was now asking me to make a choice.

I knew that Nat Turner most definitely did not have a coffin. His body was given to the surgeons for dissection. A coffin was just the kind of sign of respect for a dead body that no one would have offered the corpse of Turner. So I told the set designer to forget the coffins and to throw away both models. But filmmaking is full of unanticipated surprises, and we faced one the day we were to film the execution. The cart we had rented to carry Turner to his execution had rotted in several places, and the floorboards were weakened by decay. If Turner were to stand up in the back of the cart, as we now had planned, he would have fallen through one of the rotted planks. So we chose the quickest and easiest solution. The set designer had not yet followed through on my directions to destroy the coffins. A coffin, we realized, would redistribute the weight in the back of the cart. If Turner simply sat on a coffin on his way to execution he would not fall through the rotted planks. And so I consented to what I knew to be a fiction. Had I abandoned my ethical obligations as a historian by consenting to the coffin in the cart? Consider the context. It was part of a scene grounded in a newspaper article that I knew to be false and about which a narrator was going to tell the audience they would be left "with more questions than facts." It was a scene in which Turner would be hanged from a fictional tree in June rather than the real sweet gum tree in November. Moreover, in the end, no viewer has ever noticed the coffin in this scene. The coffin, mandated by an unanticipated contingency during the making of the film, was just one among scores of fictions that became part of this film—as fictions must invariably become part of any historical film. The most we can expect from historical films is that they get the big things right. If we demand the kind of detailed accuracy in film that we seek in print, we will always be disappointed.

A final point worthy of note in a consideration of the differences between the process of producing history on film and in print is that the act of filmmaking reveals aspects of the relation between past and present that writing does not. Although a dialogue between past and present is always a part of producing history in any form, the nature and content of that dialogue differs between history in print and in film. Consider some examples. The great actor Carl Lumbly portrayed in our film the Nat Turner of the original *Confessions*. Hence, all his lines were "written" by Thomas R. Gray. At one point I asked him if he thought he was mostly speaking in the voice of Gray or in the voice of Turner. Without hesitation he reported that he believed he was largely speaking in the voice of Turner. This fact taken alone means little, but it does stand as suggestive corroboration for the work of those print historians who have also reached the same conclusion, while using a radically different method. Another example of the way filmmaking can reveal surprising connections between past and present occurred during one of our visits to Southampton County. On one occasion we met with the leadership of the Historical Society, a group of local white residents who were the keepers of artifacts of the rebellion. At some point during our meeting, they showed us Nat Turner's sword, allowing us to hand it from one member of our group to another. When the sword finally reached Charles Burnett, he hesitated a moment before passing it on. As he later revealed to us, he understood this was a historic moment. He was very likely the first black man to hold Nat Turner's sword since Turner himself had held it in 1831. It was the kind of moment when past and present became powerfully linked in a way not available to more conventional print historians. Burnett even briefly considered "liberating" the sword.

A final example of the unique way in which film can link past and present occurred during our filming of the hanging scene. We filmed this moment several different times, and each time I noticed a ritual repeated by our prop person and the actor who portrayed Nat Turner. The prop person was white and Turner, of course, was black. The scene required Turner to be in shackles, and each time, just before the prop person was about to place the shackles around Turner's legs, he asked, "Sir, may I shackle you?" Turner responded, "Yes you may." When I asked the prop person why he asked permission in the same form each time, he replied, "When a white man places shackles around the legs of a black man in Virginia, even in a film, he carries with him the heritage of the past—and this is a dangerous moment which must be handled with great care."

The best way to summarize the lessons learned about the differences between producing history on film and in print is to note that these are two different enterprises that cannot be measured by the same set of standards. While clever film producers probably can make films about any subject matter, some subjects—such as the issue of Nat Turner's name—are better discussed in print than on film. Statements that require significant qualification or must be expressed in probabilistic language are much more difficult to depict on film. Moreover, films are shaped by issues of cost, chance contingencies, and the group nature of the activity in ways that rarely confront print historians. Films also demand invention to a degree that print historians can largely avoid. A historical scene on film must fill up the screen with characters, dialogue, and images that go beyond the documentary record. It is unfair to judge the success of such work with reference to the conventions of print history. In addition, the world of film is a world of visual images, and the complex relation between words and pictures is a problem rarely encountered by those who write history. Finally, as Charles Burnett discovered while holding the sword of Nat Turner, the process of filmmaking reveals aspects of the relation between past and present that historians in print rarely encounter.[18]

NOTES

1. Kenneth S. Greenberg, *Honor and Slavery: Lies, Duels, Noses, Masks, Dressing as a Woman, Gifts, Strangers, Humanitarianism, Death, Slave Rebellions, the Proslavery Argument, Baseball, Hunting, and Gambling in the Old South* (Princeton, NJ: Princeton University Press, 1996), 105–7; Kenneth S. Greenberg, ed., *The Confessions of Nat Turner and Related Documents* (Boston: Bedford Books of St. Martin's Press, 1996), 1–35; Kenneth S. Greenberg, ed., *Nat Turner: A Slave Rebellion in History and Memory* (Oxford: Oxford University Press, 2003), xi–xix, 3–23, 243–49.

2. A brief narrative of the rebellion can be found in Greenberg, *Confessions of Nat Turner.*

3. Peter Kolchin, *American Slavery, 1619–1877* (New York: Hill and Wang, 1993), 156.

4. Greenberg, *Confessions of Nat Turner,* 1–35.

5. Greenberg, *Nat Turner: A Slave Rebellion,* 26–31.

6. William Styron, *The Confessions of Nat Turner* (New York: Vintage, 1967), xi.

7. John Henrik Clarke, ed., *William Styron's Nat Turner: Ten Black Writers Respond* (Boston: Beacon Press, 1968).

8. Bernard Weinraub, "A Director Who Collects Honors, Not Millions," *New York Times,* January 30, 1997, C13.

9. Greenberg, *Confessions of Nat Turner,* 44–45.

10. *Richmond Constitutional Whig,* September 26, 1831, reprinted in Greenberg, *Confessions of Nat Turner,* 81.

11. A full discussion of the problem of Nat Turner's name can be found in Kenneth S. Greenberg, "Name, Face, Body," in Greenberg, *Nat Turner: A Slave Rebellion,* 3–14.

12. One influential theory of film criticism, known as "auteur" theory, maintains that for certain films, the director is the author of the film and is the equivalent to the author of a book. While it is certainly the case that some directors have a distinct style and technique that is recognizable across their body of work, even the few directors who have been identified as "auteurs" could never exercise the degree of control characteristic of the authors of books. Even the most controlling film auteurs, like any master on a plantation, must work with groups of people they cannot fully control. Some classic essays on auteur theory can be found in Barry Keith Grant, ed., *Auteurs and Authorship: A Film Reader* (Oxford: Blackwell, 2008).

13. For a discussion of the "double voice" in the "Confessions," see Greenberg, *Confessions of Nat Turner,* 7–10; David F. Allmendinger Jr., "The Construction of *The Confessions of Nat Turner,*" in Greenberg, *Nat Turner: A Slave Rebellion,* 14–42.

14. Reprinted in Henry Irving Tragle, ed., *The Southampton Slave Revolt of 1831* (New York: Vintage, 1973), 140.

15. Reprinted in ibid., 135.

16. Nat Turner's trial record reprinted in ibid., 221.

17. For the reference to the sweet gum tree, see F. Roy Johnson, *The Nat Turner Story* (Murfreesboro, NC: Johnson, 1970), 179. On the reproduction of the image of the old, dead hanging tree, see Tragle, *Southampton Slave Revolt,* 169.

18. Many of the insights of this essay can be seen as particular examples of points made by others who have thought about the relation between history on film and in print. The modern

conversation about film and history dates from a 1988 forum published in the *American Historical Review*. In that issue, Robert A. Rosenstone wrote the lead essay, "History in Images / History in Words: Reflections on the Possibility of Really Putting History on Film," and four prominent historians—Hayden White, David Herlihy, John E. O'Connor, and Robert Brent Toplin—responded. In the forum, Rosenstone first argued that history on film and history in print are different genres and needed to be judged by different standards. See *"AHR* Forum," *American Historical Review* 93 (December 1988): 1173–1227. Since then Rosenstone has elaborated this idea in several places, including Robert A. Rosenstone, *History on Film / Film on History* (Harlow, UK: Pearson, 2006). Natalie Zemon Davis, *Slaves on Screen: Film and Historical Vision* (Cambridge, MA: Harvard University Press, 2000), also makes some, but not all, of the points noted here.

II

THE SLAVE COMMUNITY

TAKING LIBERTIES

Saint Dominguan Slaves and the Formation
of Community in Philadelphia, 1791–1805

JOHN DAVIES

Jean Baptiste Reynaud de Barbarin, having fled from the French Caribbean colony of Saint Domingue, arrived in Philadelphia responsible for eight children, twelve adolescents, and three young adults. His relationship with his twenty-three charges was troubled at best and coercive and exploitative at worst. Barbarin was a planter from the Saint Domingue western district of Saint-Marc, and he manumitted twenty-three slaves, of ages three months to nineteen years, between December 1794 and July 1795: sixteen males and seven females.[1] In liberating them, Barbarin was observing Pennsylvania law. To bring about the gradual end of slavery in the commonwealth, a Pennsylvania statute of 1788 held that "slaves . . . brought into this state by persons . . . intending to inhabit or reside therein shall be immediately considered, deemed and taken to be free to all intents and purposes."[2] Freedom came with strings attached, however, complicating relationships between ex-slaves and their former masters. In October 1796, for example, Toussaint, one of Barbarin's former slaves, by then tied to him only through an indenture, was incarcerated for "being disobedient and [quitting] the service he [was] put to."[3] Toussaint was one of dozens of bound Dominguans who, in challenging their onetime masters, were redefining social relationships in their new home in the United States.[4]

The Philadelphia that Barbarin, Toussaint, and some four thousand other refugees entered was the capital of the United States in the 1790s and an essential part of social and economic networks that connected the new nation with Europe and the Caribbean. French émigrés made use of those networks in coming to Philadelphia during the French Revolution.[5] There were reasons enough for many Dominguan planters to choose the city as a refuge from the events we know as the Haitian Revolution: the slave revolt that began in the colony in August 1791; the shifting antagonisms and alliances between whites and free people of color; the burning of the northern city of Cap Français in June 1793; the general slave emancipation of that same year; the attempted British conquest of Saint Domingue (which many planters supported) that was repulsed by the summer of 1798; French efforts to assert control over its colony through military force in 1802 and 1803; and the establishment of an independent republic of Haiti on January 1, 1804.[6] Philadelphia was also already the center of abolitionist activity in the United States, but this did not deter white planters from seeking refuge there.[7]

At least 25,000 Dominguan refugees arrived in the United States between 1791 and 1809. Members of all of Saint Domingue's social groups were caught up in the exodus: approximately 15,000 white refugees; 4,000 free people of color; and 6,000 slaves. The 4,000 refugees arriving in the Delaware Valley included at least 700 enslaved Dominguans and perhaps 100 free people of color.[8] The last mass migration to the North American mainland occurred in 1809, when roughly 10,000 Dominguan refugees arrived in Louisiana via Cuba.[9]

Migration did not mean a complete break with the past. In Saint Domingue, both flight and "creative tinkering" with established law were employed by Dominguans resisting the conditions of slavery. *Marronage*— short- or long-term escape from one's master—was one form of resistance and simultaneously a form of community building. Escaped slaves gathered in the mountainous regions of the colony, establishing autonomous settlements in many cases. Slaves and free people of color in Saint Domingue also used the courts to contest their status and treatment, attempting to take full advantage of the few protections that French colonial law allowed them. Similar methods of resistance and community formation were replicated by enslaved Dominguans in Philadelphia and assisted them in creating new relationships there.[10]

Enslaved Dominguans most likely contested their social conditions in Philadelphia because they could not do so in Saint Domingue. Slaves were rarely carried to Philadelphia in intact family units. Fewer than 200 of some 650 Dominguans manumitted between the summer of 1791 and July 1798— including the eight children whom Barbarin brought to Philadelphia—were age twelve or younger. Direct relations between enslaved parents (generally mothers, but on one occasion a father) and children are indicated in only five cases. In a small number of other instances, enslaved women were likely the mothers of the infants or very young children whom they accompanied. All of this suggests that many bound Dominguans had little say in their leaving Saint Domingue.

Although few enslaved Dominguans arrived in Philadelphia as part of a family, they may have been involved in more complicated attachments. Some women made the voyage to the North American mainland while pregnant. This was apparently the case for two of the women brought by Barbarin, Marion and Agathe. When granted their freedom—in January and July of 1795, respectively—Marion, age fifteen and a half, had a three-month old son, Victoire. Agathe, nineteen, had a six-month-old daughter, Rose (as well as a four-year-old daughter, Claire). The names of these children's fathers were not recorded.[11]

Elsewhere in the United States, enslaved domestics and caregivers who "may have been genuinely reluctant to abandon their young white charges" were reported as accompanying white families.[12] Records do not indicate the extent of such relationships for Dominguan migrants and refugees in Philadelphia. The ages of enslaved Dominguans brought to Philadelphia suggest that a fictive kinship may have existed, among slaves as well as between some slaves and masters. The majority of enslaved Dominguans brought to Philadelphia were most likely domestics. Source limitations make it difficult to know their specific roles or their attachments to their masters. But it seems likely that, through their service to their masters, some sort of personal connection existed.

Real and fictive kinship among black and white Dominguans was tested in Philadelphia. As Dominguans of African descent asserted their autonomy, some broke the law, while others displayed a keen understanding of its protections. Regardless, they joined with one another and with both black and white Philadelphians in creating new social bonds and networks. Relocation to Philadelphia provided paths to freedom and opportunities for social connections for bound Dominguans and led in a number of directions: a return to the Caribbean, assimilation into larger African American communities, and the creation of community based on a French-speaking, Roman Catholic ethnic identity.

P ennsylvania's Act for the Gradual Abolition of Slavery of 1780 stipulated that all slave owners must register their slaves by November 1 of that year. Those not registered were to be freed. A number of factors contributed to the creation of the abolition act. Members of the Society of Friends, or Quakers, had been advancing moral and religious arguments against slavery in Pennsylvania since the late 1600s. The formation in 1775 of the Society for the Relief of Free Negroes Unlawfully Held in Bondage illustrated how revolutionary sentiments, rooted in natural rights ideology, expanded the abolitionist cause. The society withered during the American Revolution but reformed in 1784 as the Pennsylvania Society for Promoting the Abolition of Slavery, or Pennsylvania Abolition Society. War, the decline of slavery in Philadelphia but not elsewhere in Pennsylvania, a concern for property rights, and the objections of slaveholders all influenced the final language of the act.[13]

As a result of the many interests that helped shape it, the law curtailed certain slaveholder rights even as it reinforced the socioeconomic advantages of the master class. In the case of Dominguan masters, the abolition act instructed that, after a period of six months' residence, slaves brought into the state were to be freed. Further revisions in 1788 attempted to close a number of loopholes in the existing legislation, prohibiting the movement of slaves out of Pennsylvania in order to evade the six-month-residency provision.[14] Slave-owning Dominguans living in Pennsylvania longer than six months were therefore required to free their slaves. Most manumitted Dominguans were then indentured to their former owners.

The abolition act upheld the existing social order through the mechanism of indentures. Children born to registered slaves after March 1, 1780, were free yet bound to the service of their master "until such child shall attain unto the age of twenty-eight years, in the manner and on the conditions whereon servants bound by indenture . . . are or may be retained and holden," or for seven years if over age twenty-one.[15] The requirement of indenture reflected practice in Pennsylvania dating to the late 1770s, modeled after similar customs relating to the indenture of poor white children throughout the British Atlantic. A key difference was the length of indentures: terms of indenture for white servants were generally four to seven years. A Pennsylvania Abolition Society challenge to lengthy indentures met with failure in 1794, just as many enslaved Dominguans were entering the state.[16]

The practice of indentures may have eased the shock of abolition for Dominguan slave owners, as they generally contracted the labor of their former slaves for the longest duration possible. In January 1795 Barbarin manumitted his youngest charges—Victoire, the three-month-old daughter of Marion; and

Rose, the six-month-old daughter of Agathe—indenturing both for the full twenty-eight years.[17] Although enslaved Dominguans had to give their consent in court to indentures, the young ages of so many suggest that compulsion was more often the rule; or perhaps enslaved Dominguans "viewed an indenture as an unwelcome but unavoidable transition from bondage to freedom."[18]

The work that many indentured Dominguans performed required close, ongoing contact with their masters. In Philadelphia, both male and female Dominguans fulfilling indentures were often employed as domestic servants. For domestics, who were "simultaneously workers to be controlled and extended members of the family to be disciplined," work was arduous and constant. Caring for children, tending to the needs of the house, attending to sick family members, and waking in the cold and dark to start and tend fires were but a few of the many duties of the domestic servant, who was always on call.[19] It seems likely that white Dominguans, like many well-to-do native Philadelphian families, "employed small staffs who executed a combination of domestic duties. In all probability, a single maid did most of the cleaning and cooking in the households that employed domestic help."[20] While a few white Dominguans indentured large numbers of former slaves, most held only one or two.[21] The responsibilities of these domestics would easily have brought them into contact with neighbors, shopkeepers, and other servants, communications through which they could have gained some knowledge of English and some sense of Philadelphia customs.

Indentured Dominguans joined a servant population in Philadelphia that was also relatively young and largely African in descent.[22] After 1780, many formerly enslaved African Americans found domestic service to be the only path of employment open to them, whether indentured on release from slavery or paid wages. A majority of the African American domestics were young: "During its first five years of existence, the Pennsylvania Abolition Society's Committee for Improving the Condition of Free Blacks recorded one hundred and seventy-nine indentures for black minors. Of these boys and girls, 85 percent were bound out as domestics." In terms of age, then, the majority of indentured Dominguans were similar to Philadelphia's domestic servant population.[23]

Just as for other Philadelphia servants, life and work for Dominguan domestics were not easy. Yet economic circumstances provided reasons to remain in the employ of their masters and mistresses. Between 1793 and 1804,

twenty-one black Dominguans—fifteen men and six women—resided for
varying periods of time in Philadelphia's almshouse.[24] This was a relatively
small number. Several factors may account for the limited numbers of refugees
found in almshouse records. Applicants for relief needed recommendations
for admittance to the almshouse, and furthermore, the oppressive conditions
found there likely deterred black Dominguans from seeking shelter.[25] Thus,
as with free African Americans, indentured Dominguans may have chosen to
"[remain] within white households where their opportunities were severely
restricted but shelter, food, and clothing were assured."[26] If so, relations with
masters and mistresses would have often tested pragmatic considerations.

As more free and enslaved Dominguans arrived in Philadelphia, they increasingly challenged their subordinate status. For some Dominguans who
originally felt a sense of duty or loyalty to their masters and mistresses, such
sentiments were "severely compromised by the nature of the flight" from Saint
Domingue or eroded by the combination of untenable treatment and the opportunities that life in Philadelphia seemed to present.[27] The adolescence of
many of these servants might also suggest motivations for their behavior, with
rebellion against authority taking a number of forms.

The presence of black Dominguans in the city's criminal justice records
reveals a pattern of disobedience, theft, assault, or flight among those enslaved
or indentured. Between 1792 and 1797, some ninety black Dominguans were
charged with attempting to escape from their masters. Numerous other black
Dominguans were alleged to have stolen from, conspired against, or disobeyed
their masters. In some cases, two or three Dominguans might be charged for
offenses against the same master.[28] Disobedience lay in the eye of the beholder,
as seen in descriptions of black Dominguans as "audacious" or "ill tempered."
Calypso, manumitted by and then indentured to Joseph Antoine in November
1793, was charged in May 1795 "with being very ill tempered & of behaving
very insolent toward her mistress . . . and others." She would have been roughly
eighteen years old at the time. In October of that same year, Hillaire, a male
also about eighteen, was charged with running away from his master, Benjamin Nones, "and other misconduct."[29] Hillaire had been manumitted by Jean
Baptiste LaSalle in August 1793 and then immediately indentured to Nones
for two hundred dollars.[30]

In Philadelphia, charges of flight and disobedience were classified as
vagrancy, separate from misdemeanors or capital crimes. Regardless of the

charge, vagrants, suspects, and convicts alike were held in the Walnut Street jail. Through the mid-1790s, bound Dominguans would have encountered one another in the jail and would have had opportunities for contact with other incarcerated Philadelphians, whether black or white, as well as with escaped slaves from rural Pennsylvania, from the mid-Atlantic, and from ships docked in Philadelphia's harbor. Through such contacts, bonds between masters and servants would have been further eroded, as Dominguans learned more of the strange new world they found themselves in. At the very least, incarceration did not necessarily teach lessons of submission and obedience; it was not unusual for "disorderly" Dominguans to be placed in jail on more than one occasion.[31]

Other enslaved and indentured Dominguans attempted to use the law to their advantage. To that end, they developed connections with some white Philadelphians, as seen in a willingness to work with the Acting Committee of the Pennsylvania Abolition Society. With a number of lawyers among its membership, the Acting Committee sought cases that violated Pennsylvania law regarding slavery, often creatively interpreting the law in their efforts to free enslaved blacks. Meeting regularly "to receive reports of suspected violations," the Acting Committee received information "by various means: word of mouth, a rumor of suspected or potential evasion of the law, letter, or through its own routine inspection of the jail."[32] The committee pressed suits against white Dominguans believed to be violating the abolition act, often for not manumitting slaves after residing in state for longer than six months.[33]

The vigilance of the Acting Committee was the difference between enslavement and freedom for many Dominguans, and even then, members of the committee did not win every case they pursued.[34] Given the law's limited protections in Pennsylvania, it is little wonder that enslaved and indentured Dominguans took liberties with it, disobeying or running away from their masters. Yet gradual emancipation did provide opportunities unavailable elsewhere in the United States during the 1790s, and the successes of the Pennsylvania Abolition Society reveal the limits the abolition act placed on former masters.

One white Dominguan, Maffron, had fled to Philadelphia in June 1793 on the ship *Fair Lady*. He brought with him five enslaved Dominguans, the males Podie and Noel and the females Orsul, Marinett, and Betegal, whose ages ranged from twelve to about thirty. In the spring of 1794, Podie claimed to city authorities that he and his fellow slaves had not been manumitted and were about to be returned to the Caribbean. After a certificate from Philadelphia mayor Clarkson was offered in support of Podie's claim, a judge ruled in favor of the Acting Committee, freeing the five slaves. Podie's case was not unique; other black Dominguans also took a leading role in securing their rights under Pennsylvania law.[35]

The Pennsylvania Abolition Society Acting Committee minutes contain the stories of Dominguan men, women, and children seeking their freedom. Some entries describe journeys over vast distances of time and space, such as that of Ann Josephine Charlotte, "formerly an inhabitant of Pondicherry," then a French possession in what is today southeastern India. Charlotte had been enslaved when eight years old and taken to France, then sent to Cap Français before being brought to Philadelphia. Imprisoned there in a dispute between two men who claimed ownership over her, Charlotte was bailed out by the Pennsylvania Abolition Society in April 1794, after which she disappeared from the attention of the committee.[36]

Charlotte's story reflects a common thread in the committee's reports: enslaved and indentured people on the move, whether from Saint Domingue to the mainland, from city to city on the eastern seaboard of the United States, or even within Philadelphia. "In the time of the great sickness" (most likely the yellow-fever epidemic in the summer of 1793, which killed more than five thousand people in Philadelphia), John Dickey had arrived in the city from Cap Français, via New Providence in the Bahamas. Reporting in December 1794, Dickey told the committee how he "first lived at Francis's Hotel [South Fourth Street], next at Mrs. Clinton's, next in Walnut Street—in the house the French Consul now lives—and then with Madam Clarence in Third Street near Church Alley [now Church Street]."[37] Although Dickey's moves covered only a few city blocks, they illustrate the uncertainty and instability that so many enslaved and indentured Dominguans experienced.

Dickey's case also reveals the extent of Francophone communities in Philadelphia. Free and enslaved Dominguans in Philadelphia settled with other French-speaking exiles along Second, Third, and Fourth streets, "[gathering] together on Front Street and out Spruce and Pine as far as Eighth Street" and often taking lodging in boarding houses. This placed them in close proximity to the French consulate, as well as to Roman Catholic churches such as St. Joseph's on Willings Alley just off of Fourth Street and St. Mary's at Fourth between

Locust and Spruce. Oellers Hotel, on Chestnut near Sixth, became a meeting place for white refugees.[38] This general area was also where many black migrants could be found, as Dickey's comments to the Pennsylvania Abolition Society Acting Committee indicated, given that enslaved and indentured Dominguans often lived with their owners.

Within these communities, both former slaves and masters attempted to take advantage of the opportunities presented or to escape from the limits imposed by refugee life in the United States. One way of doing this was by giving careful attention to developments in the larger world. Free and enslaved Dominguans, public officials, and members of the Pennsylvania Abolition Society could follow developments in Saint Domingue closely. News of battles or new pieces of legislation were reported in personal correspondence, reports of sailors and merchants, and Philadelphia newspapers. These events mattered in a variety of ways. After France abolished slavery in its colonies in February 1794, Pennsylvania Abolition Society officials worked to receive a translation of the decree. They then consulted with other abolition societies and French officials in an effort to understand how best to apply the legislation when dealing with Dominguan refugees in the United States.[39] In Pennsylvania, fourteen enslaved Dominguans sued for their freedom on the basis of abolitionist decrees in Saint Domingue and France.[40]

Many Dominguans in Philadelphia still considered return to Saint Domingue, which was a source of concern for the Pennsylvania Abolition Society, given the possibility that Dominguan masters would take freed people out of state without legal claim. Numerous refugees and migrants did make the voyage back to Saint Domingue, aided by their knowledge of current events in the colony. Throughout the 1790s, whites, free people of African descent, and even enslaved Dominguans might travel to reunite with family members or conduct business. Others made the trip to resettle, whether at the invitation of authorities in Saint Domingue in 1798 or because of the French invasion of 1802. Many whites fled the colony in 1803. When, with French defeat imminent, the rebel general Dessalines called for the massacre of white French colonists, some returned to Philadelphia.[41]

During this period, though, many indentured Dominguans in Philadelphia must have considered their prospects with some ambivalence. Though freed from slavery, a majority faced a term of servitude until twenty-eight years of age, often with their former masters and mistresses. This provided some protection against the worst economic conditions, but it also resulted in limited freedom of action. The creation of an independent Haiti in January 1804 and the creation of the "empire of Hayti" with the constitution of 1805 meant that many Dominguans had new choices to make. Some white and free Dominguans of color left Philadelphia for France. Others remained in the city, where a portion of the whites and presumably a few blacks quickly assimilated into American life.[42]

This meant that once-enslaved Dominguans of African descent had more opportunities to chart their own futures. Although the fate of many is unknown because they passed out of the historical record, some apparently chose to return to the Caribbean. As French diplomatic officials in the United States worked to curtail American economic and military assistance to Haiti during the early 1800s, they claimed that black Dominguans were returning to help defend Haiti. At least two cases involved Philadelphia directly: one in May 1804, when French chargè d'affaires Louis-André Pichon claimed that the *Betsey,* based in Philadelphia, was "[carrying] arms and ammunition, twelve cannons, and a crew largely composed of Negroes who were returning to Haiti." In June 1804, Pichon claimed that Dessalines, now ruler of Haiti, was offering forty dollars per person for black refugees returning to Haiti. In June 1805, a vice consul stationed in Philadelphia reported another case of black "recruits" leaving for Haiti. One ship, the *Louisiana,* reportedly had ninety would-be soldiers on board.[43] After the forced separations that marked the flight of many black Dominguans to the United States, it seems likely that some would return to Haiti out of a sense of identification with either their family or the new nation.

Many more seem to have remained in Philadelphia. By 1805, many bound Dominguans were experiencing transitions to personal freedom; perhaps as many as five hundred lived in the city during the early 1800s.[44] The average age for an enslaved migrant arriving in 1793 was fourteen or fifteen.[45] If manumitted and remaining in Philadelphia for the length of his or her indenture, generally until age twenty-eight, the migrant would have been freed of that obligation by about 1807. Others would have gained full freedom earlier, by at least 1800. If city directories of the period are any indication, circumstances for some black Saint-Dominguans had improved by this time.

A number of black Dominguans appear in an 1811 city directory, representing various trades and occupations. Among five individuals with variations on the name Jean Baptiste, three were hairdressers, one a laborer, and the other a cigarmaker. These men illustrate how Dominguans were beginning to move out of the French refugee communities and mix with white and black Philadelphians. One lived in a northern section of the city proper, on what is today Race Street; another in the heart of the city, near present-day Society Hill; two others in the southern section; and the last in Southwark, just outside of the city boundaries as they stood, in what is today Queen Village.[46]

Yet residential proximity to other Philadelphians did not always mean assimilation. Even before indentures ended, ties of family and friendship, language, and religion connected black migrants with one another. For many, religious community seemed especially important. By 1800, Catholics in Philadelphia worshipped at three locations: a large number of Irish Catholics attended St. Mary's, German Catholics attended Holy Trinity, white refugees from Saint Domingue attended both churches, and black Dominguans worshipped at St. Joseph's and participated in sacramental rites at Holy Trinity.[47]

Black Dominguans attended separate Masses in the parish of St. Joseph's beginning in the 1790s. More than one hundred baptisms were recorded in St. Joseph's Roman Catholic Church registers between 1793 and 1805, and black Dominguans were increasingly listed as sponsors by 1801.[48] Only a few marriages were registered there during the same period. By comparison, at least seventeen marriages involving formerly enslaved Dominguans took place at Holy Trinity between 1796 and 1803. Seventy-five baptisms of children born to black Dominguan parents were also recorded at Holy Trinity between 1803 and 1806.[49]

Religious community among black Dominguans extended beyond the neighborhoods of Philadelphia. In 1812 two groups of women from the city were listed as participating in the Confraire de Notre Dame du Rosaire, a Catholic confraternity, one group in May, and the other in October.[50] The confraternity met in Baltimore at the religious seminary of St. Mary's, founded in 1791.[51] In this environment, black Dominguans played a role of supporting Catholic institutions and practices as well as practicing their faith. Confraternities, with roots in medieval Europe, were devotional associations that served many purposes throughout the early modern Catholic world. At St. Mary's, the groups were led in their devotions by clergy. Most likely, they said the Rosary, with the "recitation of prayers and meditation on the mysteries of the life of the Virgin and Christ" the focus of their activities.[52]

By participating in the Confraire de Notre Dame du Rosaire, black Dominguan women also became more familiar with the practices and teachings of Roman Catholicism.[53] This marked another way in which formerly enslaved Dominguans were transforming their lives. After 1801, the godparents of black Dominguans were, increasingly, black Dominguan men and women. This suggests that they were both gaining familiarity with the teachings of the Church and moving away from the influence of their former masters.[54]

Women from both groups of Confraire de Notre Dame du Rosaire participants appear in the sacramental registers for St. Joseph's. Marie Claude witnessed the August 1811 wedding of Sylvain Valere and Emilie Lewis, the January 1813 marriage of Nicholas and Anisette Laupair, and the October 1813 wedding of Jean Le Brun and Marie Françoise Le Roy. Marie Fortuneè Charlotte witnessed a number of weddings between 1813 and 1824. The presence of these women suggests a dedication to the religious and community-building aspects of these sacraments.[55]

For black Dominguans in Philadelphia, then, community was defined in a number of ways through overlapping identities: a "Dominguan" identity, defined by kinship, culture, and investment in the Roman Catholic faith; and a Roman Catholic identity, in which support for the orders, institutions, and mission of the Church guided individuals and placed them in religious community with other believers. Assuming these identities meant exchanging one master for another, since newly free Dominguan communicants within the Catholic Church had to accept their place with respect to the Church hierarchy. Both identities involved direct experience of the limits of social boundaries defined by race, class, and gender.

B y 1799, Jean-Baptiste Reynaud Barbarin was living in Trenton, New Jersey, where he and his wife Margaret Charlotte D'aquin presented their daughter Caroline Jacqueline Margaret Alexandra for baptism into the Roman Catholic Church on February 17 of that year.[56] After that, Barbarin may have returned to military service in Saint-Marc, participating as an inspector in the unsuccessful French attempt to reinstate full (white) control over the colony. If so, he apparently survived, since an official French publication lists him as a retired captain in 1819.[57] By contrast, further research in the Pennsylvania Abolition Society records is needed, because much less is known about Barbarin's former slaves. Whether they remained in Philadelphia and lived to experience their full freedom is yet to be determined.

Relations between masters and slaves changed dramatically with flight from Saint Domingue to Philadelphia. Old relationships, built on legal, social, and political foundations formed in a Caribbean colonial context, were transformed. While stopping far short of armed rebellion in Philadelphia, many bound Dominguans came together in disavowing the authority of their masters and in seeking the protection of Pennsylvania law. Their new legal status often meant living in close contact with their masters, but enslaved and indentured Dominguans interacted with one another, and increasingly with white and black Philadelphians, over the course of the 1790s.

Changing historical circumstances further weakened the social structures brought from Saint Domingue. Once-enslaved Dominguans created even closer ties with one another by living, working, and worshipping together. Many disappeared from the historical record, whether by returning to Haiti or by assimilating into Philadelphia's emerging African American communities. Yet others found—or created—meaning in the assumption of a French Roman Catholic identity that emphasized familial and cultural connections, ties that remained vital for many black Dominguans and their descendants into the 1850s.[58] In Philadelphia, formerly enslaved Dominguans took the liberty of creating lives and communities of their own.

NOTES

The author wishes to thank Tricia Davies for reading earlier versions of this chapter.

1. Papers of the Pennsylvania Abolition Society, Series IV: Manumissions, Indentures, and other Legal Papers, Manumission Book (hereinafter cited as PAS Manumission Book) B, reel 20, PASC-HSP, 137, 261–64; PAS Manumission Book C, PASC-HSP, 28–31.

2. James T. Mitchell and Henry Flanders, comps., *The Statutes at Large of Pennsylvania from 1682 to 1801*, vol. 10, *1779–1781* ([Harrisburg, PA?]: Wm. Stanley Ray, 1904), 71; and vol. 13, *1787–1790* (Harrisburg: Harrisburg, 1908), 52–53.

3. Prison Vagrant Docket, May 31, 1790–December 29, 1797 (RG 38.44, P83), 368, PCA.

4. Gary B. Nash, "Reverberations of Haiti in the American North: Black Saint Dominguans in Philadelphia," *Pennsylvania History* 65, no. 5 (1998): 52, 69n32, 69n36.

5. See François Furstenberg, *When the United States Spoke French: Five Refugees Who Shaped a Nation* (New York: Penguin Press, 2014).

6. Recent works dealing with the events of the Haitian Revolution include Laurent Dubois, *Avengers of the New World: The Story of the Haitian Revolution* (Cambridge, MA: Belknap Press of Harvard University Press, 2004); Madison Smartt Bell, *Toussaint Louverture: A Biography* (New York: Pantheon Books, 2007); Jeremy D. Popkin, *You Are All Free: The Haitian Revolution and the Abolition of Slavery* (Cambridge: Cambridge University Press, 2010); and Philippe R. Girard, *The Slaves Who Defeated Napoleon: Toussaint L'Ouverture and the Haitian War of Independence, 1801–1804* (Tuscaloosa: University of Alabama Press, 2011).

7. For the impact of the Haitian Revolution in Philadelphia, see Susan Branson, "St. Dominguan Refugees in the Philadelphia Community in the 1790s," in *Amerindians/Africans/Americans: Three Papers in Caribbean History* (Mona, Jamaica: Canoe Press, University of the West Indies, 1996); Nash, "Reverberations of Haiti," 44–73; Susan Branson and Leslie Patrick, "Etrangers dans un Pays Etrange: Saint-Dominguan Refugees of Color in Philadelphia," in *The Impact of the Haitian Revolution in the Atlantic World*, ed. David P. Geggus (Columbia: University of South Carolina Press, 2001), 193–208; John Davies, "Saint-Dominguan Refugees of African Descent and the Forging of Ethnic Identity in Early National Philadelphia," *Pennsylvania Magazine of History and Biography* 133 (April 2010): 5–22.

8. Catherine A. Hebert, "The French Element in Pennsylvania in the 1790s: The Francophone Immigrants' Impact," *Pennsylvania Magazine of History and Biography* 108 (October 1984): 452; Nash, "Reverberations of Haiti," 50, 55.

9. Winston C. Babb, "French Refugees from Saint Domingue to the United States, 1791–1810" (PhD diss., University of Virginia, 1954), 370, 375; Thomas Fiehrer, "From La Tortue to La Louisiane: An Unfathomed Legacy," in *The Road to Louisiana: The Saint-Domingue Refugees, 1792–1809*, ed. Carl A. Brasseux and Glenn R. Conrad (Lafayette, LA: Center for Louisiana Studies, 1992), 21, 23. Ashli White discusses the range of estimates of refugee numbers made by contemporaries and later scholars. See Ashli White, "'A Flood of Impure Lava': Saint Dominguan Refugees in the United States, 1790–1820" (PhD diss., Columbia University, 2003), 37.

10. Malick W. Ghachem, *The Old Regime and the Haitian Revolution* (New York: Cambridge University Press, 2012), 97–100, 102, 106–11, 131–44, 156, 167–206. Ghachem uses the term "creative tinkering" to describe the involvement of colonial officials, masters, slaves, and free people of color in shaping the French slave code—the *Code Noir*—over the course of the eighteenth century (6).

11. Gary B. Nash commented on the small number of enslaved families among Dominguan migrants to Philadelphia as part of his larger argument that bound Dominguans generally did not accompany their masters out of loyalty. Nash, "Reverberations of Haiti," 50–52. Manumission numbers for 1791–98 were compiled from PAS Manumission Books A, B, C, D, PASC-HSP. Marion's and Agathe's conditions are discussed in Nash, "Reverberations of Haiti," 69n32, and recorded in PAS Manumission Book B, PASC-HSP, 262–64, and PAS Manumission Book C, PASC-HSP, 31–32.

12. Popkin, *You Are All Free*, 231–32.

13. Gary B. Nash and Jean R. Soderlund, *Freedom by Degrees: Emancipation in Pennsylvania and Its Aftermath* (New York: Oxford University Press, 1991), 41–56, 74–77, 79–80, 99–111, 115. For an analysis of the promise and the limits of abolitionist sentiment as embodied by the PAS in the context of the Haitian Revolution, see James Alexander Dun, "Philadelphia Not Philanthropolis:

The Limits of Pennsylvanian Antislavery in the Era of the Haitian Revolution," *Pennsylvania Magazine of History and Biography* 135 (January 2011): 73–102.

14. Mitchell and Flanders, *Statutes at Large of Pennsylvania,* 10:69–71; 13:53. An extension for registering slaves was granted to slave owners living in territory disputed by Pennsylvania and Virginia. See Arthur Zilversmit, *The First Emancipation: The Abolition of Slavery in the North* (Chicago: University of Chicago Press, 1967), 136–37.

15. Mitchell and Flanders, *Statutes at Large of Pennsylvania,* 10:69–71 (quotation 69).

16. Wayne J. Eberly, "The Pennsylvania Abolition Society, 1775–1830" (PhD diss., Pennsylvania State University, 1973), 56–57, 61; Jasper Yeates, *Reports of Cases Adjudged in the Supreme Court of Pennsylvania: With Some Select Cases at Nisi Prius, and in the Circuit Courts* (Philadelphia: John Bioren, 1817), 1:368; Nash and Soderlund, *Freedom by Degrees,* 177, 194–95, 201–4; Edward Raymond Turner, *The Negro in Pennsylvania: Slavery—Servitude—Freedom, 1639–1861* (Washington, DC: American Historical Association, 1911), 93–94; Stanley I. Kutler, "Pennsylvania Courts, the Abolition Act, and Negro Rights," *Pennsylvania History* 30 (January 1963): 23.

17. Manumission Book A, PASC-HSP, 197; Manumission Book B, PASC-HSP, 261–62; Branson, "St. Dominguan Refugees," 27–29; Nash, "Reverberations of Haiti," 55–56. Most enslaved Dominguans brought to Philadelphia were young, with an average age of fifteen for females and fourteen for males. Females slightly outnumbered males. See Nash, "Reverberations of Haiti," 50–52; Branson and Patrick, "Etrangers dans un Pays Etrange," 199–200.

18. Nash, "Reverberations of Haiti," 55–57 (quotation 57).

19. Sharon V. Salinger, *"To Serve Well and Faithfully": Labor and Indentured Servants in Pennsylvania, 1682–1800* (Cambridge: Cambridge University Press, 1987), 100–101.

20. Katie Diethorn, "Domestic Servants in Philadelphia, 1780–1830," research paper, Division of Museum Operations, Independence National Park, Philadelphia, 1986, 18.

21. The estimate of the number of slaves held was taken from a count of manumissions entered in PAS Manumission Books A, B, C (PASC-HSP). With roughly 246 slaveholders counted, 149 manumitted one slave, 47 manumitted two slaves, 32 manumitted three slaves, and 18 manumitted four or more slaves.

22. Diethorn, "Domestic Servants," 8–15; Salinger, *"To Serve Well and Faithfully,"* 150–52. For a fuller analysis of the historical development of indentured labor in the eighteenth century, see Salinger, *"To Serve Well and Faithfully,"* 47–81.

23. Diethorn, "Domestic Servants," 23–27 (quotation 25, 27); Salinger, *"To Serve Well and Faithfully,"* 146–48. Like indentured Saint-Dominguans, black Philadelphia women had traditionally filled domestic roles as slaves. See Jean Soderlund, "Black Women in Colonial Pennsylvania," in *African Americans in Pennsylvania: Shifting Historical Perspectives,* ed. Joe William Trotter Jr. and Eric Ledell Smith (University Park: Pennsylvania State University Press, 1997), 82.

24. Branson and Patrick, "Etrangers dans un Pays Etrange," 197; Guardians of the Poor, Admissions, 1785–1805 (RG 35.110), PCA. The name "John Baptist" is recorded three times between February 1801 and March 1803.

25. *Philadelphia Independent Gazetteer,* January 3, 1797, 3; Branson and Patrick, "Etrangers dans un Pays Etrange," 197. See also Billy G. Smith and Cynthia Shelton, "The Daily Occurrence Docket of the Philadelphia Almshouse, 1800," *Pennsylvania History* 52 (April 1985): 87.

26. Nash and Soderlund, *Freedom by Degrees*, 173.

27. Nash, "Reverberations of Haiti," 52 (quotation), 55–57; Nash and Soderlund, *Freedom by Degrees*, 180.

28. Nash, "Reverberations of Haiti," 56–57, 71nn54–58, nn60–62. Nash enumerated 17 cases of theft in the Prisoners for Trial Dockets of 1795 and 1796, currently held in the PCA. Susan Branson counted the names of 128 Dominguans in the Vagrancy Dockets for the period between 1790 and 1798. See Branson, "St. Dominguan Refugees," 29.

29. Prison Vagrant Docket, May 31, 1790–December 29, 1797 (RG 38.44), 294, 311, PCA.

30. PAS Manumission Book A, PASC-HSP, 206, 207. An "M. LaSalle & wife" are recorded as landing in Philadelphia on July 12, 1793. Although no slaves are directly associated with them, eighteen unnamed black servants are recorded as arriving on the same ship. See "Registers of the Names of Passengers and Servants Arrived in the Port of Philadelphia . . . from Oct. 25, 1792 to April 28, 1794," Captain's Reports to Health Officer, September 30, 1789–May 3, 1794, Philadelphia Port Records, Pennsylvania State Archives, Harrisburg, PA.

31. Simon P. Newman, *Embodied History: The Lives of the Poor in Early Philadelphia* (Philadelphia: University of Pennsylvania Press, 2003), 1–10, 43–45; LeRoy B. DePuy, "The Walnut Street Prison: Pennsylvania's First Penitentiary," *Pennsylvania History* 18 (April 1951): 134; Prison Vagrant Docket, May 31, 1790–December 29, 1797 (RG 38.44, P83), 71, 263, 304, 404, 406, PCA.

32. Eberly, "Pennsylvania Abolition Society," 56–57. See also Nash and Soderlund, *Freedom by Degrees*, 130–31; Richard A. Newman, *The Transformation of American Abolitionism: Fighting Slavery in the Early Republic* (Chapel Hill: University of North Carolina Press, 2002), 28–30.

33. PAS Acting Committee Minutes, vol. 2, 1789–1797, PASC-HSP, 286, 288, 294–96; Dun, "Philadelphia Not Philanthropolis," 90–91.

34. PAS Acting Committee Minutes, vol. 2, 1789–1797, PASC-HSP, 310–17, 320, 325; Nash and Soderlund, *Freedom by Degrees*, 127–28.

35. PAS Acting Committee Minutes, vol. 2, 1789–1797, PASC-HSP, 286, 288; Branson, "St. Dominguan Refugees," 31–32; Nash, "Reverberations of Haiti," 57–58.

36. PAS Acting Committee Minutes, vol. 2, 1789–1797, PASC-HSP, 294–95.

37. Loose Minutes of the Acting Committee, PASC-HSP, December 31, 1794.

38. Frances Sergeant Childs, *French Refugee Life in the United States, 1790–1800: An American Chapter of the French Revolution* (Baltimore: Johns Hopkins Press, 1940), 103–4, 110.

39. Popkin, *You Are All Free*, 246–88; PAS Acting Committee Minutes, vol. 2, 1789–1797, PASC-HSP, 315, 321; PAS General Meeting Minute Book, vol. 1, 1787–1800, PASC-HSP, April 6, 1795, April 11, 1796; PAS Committee of Correspondence Letterbook, PASC-HSP, 51–52; Dun, "Philadelphia Not Philanthropolis," 91.

40. Sue Peabody, "Free upon Higher Ground: Saint-Domingue Slaves' Suits for Freedom in U.S. Courts, 1792–1830," in *The World of the Haitian Revolution*, ed. David Patrick Geggus and Norman Fiering (Bloomington: Indiana University Press, 2009), 261–83.

41. Hebert, "French Element," 466; Ashli White, *Encountering Revolution: Haiti and the Making of the Early Republic* (Baltimore: Johns Hopkins University Press, 2010), 140–41; Girard, *Slaves Who Defeated Napoleon*, 303.

42. "In the Name of the People of Hayti," *Aurora (PA) General Advertiser,* March 27, 1804;

"Translated for the Mercantile Advertiser: Constitution of Hayti," *Aurora (PA) General Advertiser,* July 17, 1805; Hebert, "French Element," 466, 468–69; Davies, "Saint-Dominguan Refugees," 10–11.

43. Rayford W. Logan, *The Diplomatic Relations of the United States with Haiti, 1776–1891* (Chapel Hill: University of North Carolina Press, 1941), 162–63, 164, 173–74. Further research is needed to verify these reports and to determine whether migrants from Philadelphia were involved. Given the amount of travel by Dominguans between Philadelphia and the Caribbean, though, the accounts seem plausible.

44. Taking the estimate of seven hundred enslaved migrants arriving in the 1790s, I further speculate that births and immigration would not have offset population loss due to deaths and migration elsewhere. Roughly one hundred infant baptisms were recorded at St. Joseph's between 1793 and 1805. Another seventy-five were recorded at Holy Trinity between 1803 and 1806. See notes 49 and 50.

45. Nash, "Reverberations of Haiti," 50.

46. Ibid., 59–60; Nash, *Forging Freedom: The Formation of Philadelphia's Black Community, 1720–1840* (Cambridge, MA: Harvard University Press, 1988), 158–63; James Robinson, *The Philadelphia Directory for 1811* (Philadelphia: James Robinson, 1811). In Robinson's directory, race is generally indicated for individuals, but determining whether these individuals were from Saint Domingue and whether the Dominguans were former slaves or free people of color is difficult, given inconsistencies in recording names, possible name changes, and continued migrations to Philadelphia from the French Caribbean. If formerly enslaved, these individuals had developed skills such as hairdressing, basic carpentry, and gourmet cooking.

47. The Augustinians dedicated St. Augustine's in 1801, incorporating it in 1804. Altogether, it and the three Catholic churches identified in the text were home to roughly two thousand white and black parishioners in the first years of the nineteenth century. Joseph L. J. Kirlin, *Catholicity in Philadelphia: From the Earliest Missionaries down to the Present Time* (Philadelphia: John Jos. McVey, 1909), 34–35, 91, 93, 122–24, 128, 159–62, 166–67, 171; Thomas B. Falls, "Development of the Diocese and Province of Philadelphia," *Records of the American Catholic Historical Society of Philadelphia* 64 (March 1953): 51 (hereinafter cited as *RACHS*).

48. "Sacramental Registers at St. Joseph's Church, Philadelphia, Pa., of the Eighteenth Century," *RACHS* 15 (1904), 16 (1905), 17 (1906); "The Baptismal Registers at St. Joseph's Church, Philadelphia, Pa.," *RACHS* 18 (1907); "Old St. Joseph's Baptismal Registers for the Year 1805," *RACHS* 19 (1908); "Marriage Registers at St. Joseph's Church, Philadelphia, Pa., from December 1799, to December 1808," *RACHS* 20 (1909).

49. My counts made use only of published or transcribed records. "Baptismal Registers of Holy Trinity Church, Philadelphia, for 1793-4-5," *RACHS* 22 (January 1911): 1–20; "Marriage Registers of Holy Trinity Church, Philadelphia, Pa., A.D. 1791–1799," *RACHS* 24 (June 1913): 160; Barbara Brady O'Keefe, *Holy Trinity Catholic Church, Philadelphia, Pa.: Marriages, 1796–1803; Baptisms, 1803–1806* (Miami: B. B. O'Keefe, 1983), 1–2, 25–64. At the Old St. Joseph's Church Archives, Mary Jane Green and the late Bobbye Burke were generous in sharing a list of Dominguan baptisms and marriages at that church, taken from the information found in the *RACHS*.

50. "Registre des noms des Personnes . . . dans la Confraire de N.D. du Rosaire," Baltimore Record of Confraternities, SAB RG 1, box 17, Sulpician Archives, St. Mary's Seminary, Baltimore.

My thanks to Alison M. Foley of the Associated Archives at St. Mary's Seminary and University for providing me with a copy of the document and additional information on St. Mary's.

51. John Gilmary Shea, *Life and Times of the Most Rev. John Carroll, Bishop and First Archbishop of Baltimore* (New York: John G. Shea, 1888), 348–51; Charles G. Herbermann, *The Sulpicians in the United States* (New York: Encyclopedia Press, 1916), 14–15, 17, 22.

52. Diane Batts Morrow, *Persons of Color and Religious at the Same Time: The Oblate Sisters of Providence, 1828–1860* (Chapel Hill: University of North Carolina Press, 2002), 20; Christopher Black, "Introduction: The Confraternity Context," in *Early Modern Confraternities in Europe and the Americas: International and Interdisciplinary Perspectives,* ed. Christopher Black and Pamela Gravestock (Burlington, VT: Ashgate, 2006), 10 (quotation). Participation in the confraternity also enabled the women of Confraire de Notre Dame du Rosaire to reconcile themselves to their changed circumstances by participating in the ritual life of their community. For the usefulness of confraternities in strengthening social networks and their role as "a powerful tool for mobilizing solidarity" that served to resolve crises of self-identity, social structure, and social order in early-modern Europe, see Nicholas Terpstra, "De-Institutionalizing Confraternity Studies: Fraternalism and Social Capital in Cross-Cultural Context," in Black and Gravestock, *Early Modern Confraternities,* 264–67.

53. Emily Clark and Virginia Meacham Gould, "The Feminine Face of Afro-Catholicism in New Orleans, 1727–1852," *William and Mary Quarterly,* 3rd ser., 59 (April 2002): 413, 425.

54. Although persons of African descent, many of them enslaved or recently freed (judging by their lack of surnames) often sponsored baptisms of enslaved or indentured Dominguans, the transition from white to black sponsorship may be seen in comparing sacramental records from 1798, when white sponsors, though by no means a majority, appear with some frequency, to records dating from 1802 to 1804, when, out of eleven baptisms, nine sets of sponsors were of African descent. Between 1805 and 1809, of the six recorded baptisms most likely involving black Dominguans, all sponsors were black. "Sacramental Registers at St. Joseph's Church," *RACHS* 17 (1906): 7, 10–12, 15–17, 25; *RACHS* 18 (1907): 223–39, 267–72, 403, 409; *RACHS* 19 (1908): 87, 96–97, 356, 428.

55. "Marriage Registers at St. Joseph's Church," *RACHS* 20 (1909): 132, 137–39, 167, 174, 184.

56. "Sacramental Registers at St. Joseph's Church, Philadelphia," *RACHS* 17 (1906): 335.

57. Laura V. Monti, comp., *A Calendar of Rochambeau Papers at the University of Florida Libraries* (Gainesville: University of Florida Libraries, 1972), 137; Ministère de la guerre, *Annuaire de l'Etat Militaire de France pour l'Annee 1820* (Strasbourg: F. G. Levrault, 1820), 563, 566. Little is known about Margaret Charlotte D'aquin. The sacramental register lists her place of origin simply as "San Domingo."

58. Further discussion of the development of black Dominguan communities in the nineteenth century may be found in Nash, "Reverberations of Haiti," 59–60; Branson and Patrick, "Etrangers dans un Pays Etrange," 202–5; and Davies, "Saint-Dominguan Refugees."

◆
6

"A SLAVE THAT WILL STEAL FROM A SLAVE, IS CALLED *MEAN* AS *MASTER*"

Thefts and Violence inside Southern Slave Quarters

JEFF FORRET

They are proverbially *thieves*," groused Charles Colcock Jones in reference to the South's slave population. Bondpeople, the Georgia slave owner complained, pilfered constantly and indiscriminately, "from each other; from their masters[;] from any body." The grievance was widely shared among southern slaveholders. In slave scholarship, theft has been portrayed as a mild form of day-to-day resistance to slaveholder authority. The act of pilfering from the owner proved not only materially beneficial but also psychologically gratifying. Containing elements of risk and sport, successful burglaries gave slaves a satisfying, momentary triumph over the master or other white victim. Although many enslaved parents, including Henry "Box" Brown's mother, instructed their children "not to steal," historian Eugene D. Genovese pointed out that the ethic of the quarters excused thefts from owners as mere "taking" rather than "stealing." If masters owned as property both slaves and the commodities they filched, any of the goods bondpeople appropriated without permission to eat or use for themselves ultimately remained in the master's possession, so masters suffered no net loss. Indeed, Alex Lichtenstein framed bondpeople's thefts from their owners as a vital part of an ongoing negotiation between master and slave over the moral economy of the plantation. Although certainly frustrated, most slaveholders resigned themselves to some loss of property through bondpeople's thievery. They generally expressed greater alarm only when slaves sold or bartered stolen goods in the marketplace or through underground economic networks that included blacks as well as poor whites—exchanges that posed a somewhat more direct challenge to the slave system.[1]

But slaves, as Charles Colcock Jones indicated, did not always restrict thefts to white victims. When they targeted the goods or cash belonging to others of their own color, they altered the fundamental dynamics of the act. Slaves took quick umbrage with peers who would violate their trust and readily resorted to violence to remedy the egregious violation of the quarters' unwritten law that forbade stealing from one another. Conflicts over property marked an important fissure within the slave community.[2]

Southern demographics usually assured that the blacks whom enslaved thieves preyed upon were similarly enslaved, but slaves sometimes stole from free blacks as well. One Virginia bondman accosted the free black Isaac Brown "on the public road & robbed him of bacon, coffee & sugar" in 1819. Incidents between slaves and free blacks were more likely in Upper South states such as Virginia, which alone contained 28 percent of all free people of color living in the South in 1820. Eight of every ten southern free blacks lived in Delaware, Maryland, Virginia, and North Carolina, so slave thefts from free blacks were most probable in those states. Even in the Upper South, however, slaves who stole from other blacks typically deprived of their property not free persons of color but fellow bondpeople. In 1820 the slave population of the South was more than 11.5 times greater than its free black population; slaves outnumbered free people of color by almost 1.4 million. No wonder, then, that when the light-fingered slave Bob of Frederick County, Virginia, stole "sundry . . . articles," the goods belonged to three different slaves.[3]

Certainly in their cramped slave cabins, most bondpeople lacked any truly safe repository for their possessions. They might conceal goods under a loose floorboard or other favorite hiding spot, but the quarters' dearth of privacy often made these presumptively secret locations virtually common knowledge among the slaves. Some slaves accumulated and saved cash or secured valuable possessions by depositing them with the master for safe keeping, but this required surrendering control of their goods and placing inordinate trust in the hands of their oppressors, who might easily and without fear of legal repercussions swindle bondpeople out of their belongings. Banks, rare in the Old South, were practically never an option; with only a few, isolated exceptions among industrial slaves, southern blacks did not gain experience with such institutions until the creation of the Freedman's Savings Bank at the end of the Civil War.[4]

Bondpeople who earned money, acquired consumer goods, or stole commodities that other slaves envied therefore needed to exercise caution and vigilance. Employing creativity in secreting their possessions did not hurt. In Mississippi, an enslaved husband and wife buried stolen money in a tin box in a hen house, while other slaves stashed their loot in a trunk belonging to a lower-class white man whom they trusted. Similarly, one prolific enslaved thief in Southampton County, Virginia, knew he could not safely stow his bonanza in or near his dwelling; rather, he secreted his bounty "in a stump," in "a Hollow Tree," in "another Tree," and under a log. With no better alternative available, a different Virginia slave hid in the woods the small treasures he had robbed from a bondwoman.[5]

However isolated or remote, these sylvan locations were hardly secure. Slaves' cash and commodities were therefore at risk of plundering by fellow bondpeople. In up-country South Carolina's Pickens District in 1853, mistress Sarah Burgess's bondman Wiley, "a man of coler, Did steele some Tobacco and half a dollar in mony . . . on the sabeth from Jesse a man of color the Property of Elizabeth Fields." As John Campbell has explained, slaveholders' efforts to rein in bondpeople's independent economic activities were making cash increasingly scarce among up-country South Carolina slaves in the 1840s and 1850s. As a result, there would likely have been a concomitant escalation of temptation when slaves spied untended or irresponsibly guarded money.[6]

Some bondpeople went so far as to purchase locks to help secure valuables from the depredations of fellow slaves. "They have locks on their doors," observed traveler William Thomson, "which are necessary, for they steal like rats." Ubiquitous locks reinforced whites' perception that dishonesty plagued the quarters. "Locks, bolts, and bars secure articles desirable to them," wrote Charles Colcock Jones. Prudence dictated that "the *keys*, must always be carried." Travelers to the South frequently commented upon slaves' use of security devices and the motives behind their use. Touring the slave huts of low-country South Carolina, one contemporary "observed that many of the doors were fastened by a padlock and chain outside." Upon inquiring into the matter, he learned that "honesty is not a virtue they have towards each other. They would find their things stolen if they did not lock their doors." On a plantation in the Georgia low country, Charles Lyell noticed "a large wooden padlock" that slaves used "to guard their valuables from their neighbors when they are at work in the field, for there is much pilfering among them." Since "the slave quarters were generally deserted through the entire day," cautious slaves "closed and locked" the "Negro cabins" of Mississippi, too. According to Frederick Law Olmsted, along the James River in Virginia, some quarters boasted "lock-up closets" to secure slaves' belongings. In Charlotte County, the enslaved woman Matilda "had two chests that she kept her nice clothes in, and always kept them locked." "Mother always kept her clothes locked up," Matilda's son remembered. "She was very particular with her clothes." She "wouldn't trust [even] her husband to go to them."[7]

The prevalence of locks in the quarters meant that it would not have been unusual for slaves to keep keys on their person. Matilda routinely "carried her bunch of keys in her pocket." When she was found murdered, the keys to her trunks were missing. Whereas when slaves carried their own keys, they demonstrated their mistrust of other residents of the quarters, when masters deemed slaves sufficiently trustworthy to bestow upon them a set of keys, they implicitly testified to the confidence they placed in those bondpersons. Keys, thus laden with symbolic, relational value, inspired passionate emotions. An enslaved blacksmith in Dougherty County, Georgia, mortally wounded another slave with an axe helve for "stealing shop keys and stable keys" that belonged to the master but which he guarded as though they were his own.[8]

Theft from fellow slaves met with widespread disapproval and rebuke in the quarters. Slave culture was firmly grounded in a highly localized sense of place. Those slaves who were not forcibly relocated with their masters or made victims of the domestic slave trade often never ventured far from the home plantation over the course of their lifetime. Passes or tickets dispensed by the master were required for slaves to travel even short distances unmolested by patrollers or other whites they encountered along the road, any of whom might accost and interrogate an enslaved sojourner. Compared to enslaved women, enslaved men enjoyed somewhat greater freedom of movement, taking advantage of opportunities to leave the plantation either on business for the master, to court a sweetheart on a nearby holding, or to visit an abroad spouse living nearby. Yet even for enslaved men, the ability to travel was limited. A few trips to the mill notwithstanding, Virginia bondmen Henry "Box" Brown and his brother "would have known nothing whatever of what was going on anywhere in the world, excepting on our master's plantation."[9]

In slaves' circumscribed world, relationships with fellow bondpeople mattered greatly. For reasons of family, distance, and—considering the unreliable sources of food and water and the prospect of encountering patrols or hostile whites—the sheer odds against success, most slaves could not realistically risk an attempted flight to freedom. Like it or not, they lived and worked with a given cohort, some larger than others, of fellow bondpeople on the home plantation and in the immediate vicinity. To be sure, membership in these enslaved peer groups was fluid, given the buying and selling of the internal slave trade and the compulsory migrations prompted by masters' often incessant search for more profitable lands, but in no case did a sense of camaraderie or belonging among a group of bondpeople come automatically. Slaves needed to create ties of trust to forge the bonds of neighborhood and community.[10]

When they stole from one another, they undermined that trust by violating the ethic that bound them together. "I am sure that, as a rule, any one of us who would have thought nothing of stealing a hog, or a sack of corn, from our master," declared successful fugitive John Brown, "would have allowed himself to be cut to pieces rather than betray the confidence of his fellow-slave." Thefts from masters could be justified; thefts from other slaves could not. Bondpeople denounced and condemned those among them whose demeanor and actions marked them as "mean." "A slave that will steal from a slave, is called *mean* as *master*," explained former bondman Lewis Clarke. "This is the lowest comparison slaves know how to use: 'just as mean as white folks.'" Masters were the ultimate thieves, stealing slaves' time, the products of their labor, their parents, their spouses, their children, and their lives. Nevertheless, Clarke insisted, the "nigger dat . . . steal from nigger, he meaner nor all." Such individuals unraveled the social fabric of the quarters.[11]

Some enslaved thieves caught in their crimes committed violence upon the bondpeople who caught them in the act, to prevent them from revealing their treachery to the master or to other slaves. Traveling in the vicinity of Athens, Georgia, England's James Silk Buckingham heard stories of slaves "in which poisonings and secret murders had been committed by them on their own relatives, to prevent disclosures" of thefts. Dishonest bondpeople surely did want to conceal their crimes to avoid the master's discipline as well as the opprobrium of their fellow residents of the quarters. Slaves' widely held contempt for the thieves among them may have proven the most effective deterrent to misdeeds. In Kathleen Hillard's analysis of 234 cases of property crimes committed in the up-country South Carolina districts of Anderson and Spartanburg, only fourteen, or 6 percent, of the indictments "involved accusations of intra-plantation theft by slaves from slaves."[12]

A reputation for honesty inside the quarters was so highly valued that enslaved women and men took offense even when merely accused of theft. The bondwoman Milly in DeSoto County, Mississippi, acknowledged that she had a "quarrel with Laura . . . because Laura accused her of Stealing Some of her things." Near Montgomery, Alabama, a slave ferryman confronted a "d—d nigger" for stealing his gourd. The second slave resented the allegation and threatened to "smash your wool skull in if you call me tief." The ferryman replied with a violent threat of his own. Some slaves went beyond verbal attacks by committing physically violent assaults to avenge a charge of stealing.[13]

In fact, most property-related violence between slaves revolved around theft. Two cases from up-country South Carolina illustrate how allegations of theft might trigger a violent response from the accused bondman. After the slave Dick of Anderson District declared that Toney "had stolen more leather than his back could pay for," Toney confronted Dick and assaulted him, "severely hurting him verry much." Toney also fought the slave Sy for what "Sy had said about him in regard to some stolen leather." When Spartanburg District slave Sam accused George of stealing his hammer, George took offense and fatally smote Sam on the head with an axe and a pole. Neither Toney nor George wanted to be diminished in the eyes of their fellow bondpeople, so they relied on violence to defend their reputations. It is also quite possible that they feared their accusers might inform the master on them, inviting punishment.[14]

Slaves occasionally employed violence to prevent theft of their valuable possessions. Solomon Northup, a northern free black kidnapped and sold into slavery in Louisiana, was walking a road late one night, "carrying a dressed pig in a bag swung over my shoulder." A pair of fugitive slaves attempted to waylay and rob him. Northup dodged them as they "snatched at the bag," grabbed a "pine knot," and hurled it at the head of one of his assailants, knocking him "apparently senseless to the ground." Thus, Northup staved off the attack and preserved possession of the pig. Similarly violent episodes unfolded when bondpeople caught other slaves in the act of thievery, whether on the public roads, in the woods, or in a slave cabin.[15]

Despite the social opprobrium bondpeople attached to theft within the quarters, stealing among slaves remained a persistent problem over time and, on certain plantations, reached epidemic proportions.[16] Most frequently, the object of such thefts was food. Of all categories of nourishment, slaves most commonly stole meat from one another, perhaps a chicken, a whole pig, or a slab of bacon. Less commonly, they pilfered any number of commodities not included in standard plantation fare: eggs, butter, sugar, coffee, or liquor. Although masters typically allotted their slaves rations of meal and molasses, some were compelled to augment their supply by filching from other bondpeople. That food was the most frequent target of enslaved thefts of other bondpeople's property suggests that they were driven to steal by necessity. Hungry slaves were desperate slaves, willing to violate social norms against thievery in the quarters and risk their reputations.

Currency, including both cash and coin, marked the second most common item slaves stole from one another. Money was so insecure in the quarters that many slaves elected to spend whatever amounts came into their possession almost immediately at a local store or crossroads grogshop rather than risk losing it to another bondperson. That money was so frequently stolen suggests its pervasiveness as a medium of exchange among enslaved consumers. Most slaves lacked the opportunity to accumulate and save substantial sums, however, so the quantities stolen were generally small.

Slaves scored more impressive sums when they robbed whites or white-owned stores and shops. Enslaved thieves in Virginia divested white victims of "a quantity of Silver and Copper Money of the value of Fifty dollars" and "certain Bank notes of the value of fifty five dollars and certain silver coin current money of this Commonwealth to the amount of $12.65 cents." The efforts of another yielded a more modest "six half dollars," "forty six dimes," and "two half dimes current coins of the United States," along with "four silver coins of the Kingdom of Spain, of the value of twelve and a half cents each." Successful thefts from whites probably injected a good share of the cash that circulated within the slave economy. After food and money, the commodities slaves most commonly stole from other slaves were tobacco and other articles they could claim as theirs and either use or sell at market. Practical items such as clothing also ranked high in desirability.[17]

Slaves typically stole from one another furtively, when their victims' backs were turned, but they also occasionally committed violent robberies. In Spanish Louisiana, the enslaved overseer Pierre returned from market laden with cash "because he sold some pigs in the city and had not spent all the money." Unlike the numbers of enslaved men, in particular, who promptly deposited the money that came to them with purveyors of alcohol, "Pierre did not drink." Those who knew the teetotaling Pierre would have had some idea of the sums in his possession despite the urban temptations presented him. Pierre's brother Clement was a notorious thief, and Pierre, in his capacity as overseer, "had told him that the first time he stole again he would be killed with the beating he would receive." Brotherly bonds strained, Clement reportedly "feared Pierre more than he did his master." When Pierre went missing on his way home, suspicion naturally fell to Clement. When Pierre's blood-stained purse was found in Clement's sheaf of rice, Clement revealed the location of the gun he used to commit the robbery and fratricide and, under threat of punishment, led whites to his brother's body. Decades later, a "very stout" bondman named Austin was "found dead . . . on the road" in Hinds County, Mississippi, the rope that strangled him still wrapped around his neck. Theft was a likely motive for the murder, for "the dead negro's pocket had been rifled after death." In a similar case, Scott, enslaved in Lunenburg County, Virginia, viciously beat and robbed the bondman Bob one Sunday evening in March 1823. Bob had just purchased "a bottle of Rum & some Sugar" at Thomas A. Filbert's grocery store at Lunenburg Courthouse. Present at the store, Scott followed Bob home and waylaid him with a stick. Bob survived the attack long enough to share what had transpired, fingering Scott as his assailant. Scott had taken the rum, the sugar, and the "three quarters of a dollar in silver" that Bob had in his pocket when he left Filbert's store. At trial, Filbert identified the unique bottle that he had filled with rum for Bob, which was found where Scott lived, spattered with blood. Scott had gone home the evening of the murder, "groggy" or "very drunk" from quaffing a tumbler or bottle of spirits that he invited the slaves Sarah and Solomon to share with him. He also had "some sugar in his hands" and either one or two of the stolen silver quarters. Altogether, there was ample evidence to guarantee that Scott would hang for the murder.[18]

When slaves committed thefts inside the quarters, the victim might pursue different avenues for recourse. Some appealed to the master or overseer. Like many slaveholders, Virginia's Richard Eppes, who commanded his slaves not to steal from anyone, including "your . . . fellow servants," implored his bondpeople to alert the overseer "immediately" upon realizing any goods were missing so that he might root out "the rogue" and administer the proper punishment. Some slaves elected to follow this sort of direction. During the Civil War, Dougherty County, Georgia, slave Henry accused the bondman Gilbert of "eating his chicken," while Gilbert claimed "that Henry had taken two dollars from him." Seeking resolution, they started off together "to see Mas John about it." A pair of slaves in Isle of Wight County, Virginia, simultaneously protected their foodstuffs and performed loyal service to the master by trapping an enslaved thief they discovered sneaking about the plantation. A bondman named Nat "was going to see his wife" when he noticed the smokehouse door ajar. Upon hearing a noise inside, he went to the kitchen and informed "the old negro woman" Silvy. Together they crept up to investigate and spied an enslaved thief named Jordan lingering suspiciously among the cured meats. While Nat and a third slave detained the intruder inside the smokehouse, Silvy hastened to inform the master. Slaves on one Mississippi plantation persuaded their owner to sell a particularly aggravating, kleptomaniacal slave woman who chronically stole from them. Cognizant of thefts among his slaves, one planter in Georgia established a rule that, any time "one negro steals from another," the driver was required to seize the equivalent value "of the marauder's goods and chattels" to make restitution. If the enslaved thief proved unable to compensate the victim within a reasonable time frame, punishment ensued. Most commonly, masters employed the whip in their futile efforts to cleanse the quarters of thievery.[19]

Reporting thefts to the master might backfire against the enslaved victim, however, by fueling the resentment of the bondperson who suffered "correction." On the Amherst County, Virginia, holding of Charles Taliaferro, a dispute erupted between slaves Isaac and Robin in November 1819. Isaac accused Robin of stealing his clothes, prompting Addison Taliaferro to administer Robin a severe whipping. One bondman heard Robin blame Isaac for the lashing he received and threaten to kill him. Robin gained his vengeance by bludgeoning Isaac with a pestle, fracturing the slave's skull. When slaves such as Isaac sought the master's intervention, some bondpeople saw betrayal. Ultimate loyalty must reside with one's fellow slaves; consulting the master qualified as tattling, ratting out, or snitching, and enslaved snitches made themselves vulnerable to retribution in the quarters. When the Copiah County, Mississippi, bondman Simon murdered Norvall in a "misunderstanding about mollasses," the victim was not a suspected thief but rather a hapless witness to thievery: "Simon said he killed Norvall because Norvall had seen him stealing molasses & had told his master about it or . . . would tell him & . . . Simon was afraid his master would whip him."[20]

Because slaves did not legally own the property they possessed, they were unable to air their grievances in courts of law, with but rare exception. When enslaved thief and enslaved victim belonged to different masters, litigious slaveholders might guide a case of theft through the court system. In Chesterfield County, Virginia, Thomas Traylor's slave Peyton was charged with highway robbery, stealing "a bundle of clothes and [a]bout 5$ in cash" from Mrs. Cheatham's bondwoman Sarah. Sarah was returning home from market shortly after Christmas 1817 when she overtook and passed Peyton on the public road. Peyton then approached her from behind, "struck her with a stick and demanded her money, which he took, together with a bundle of clothes which she had in a basket."[21]

The imprudent use or display of purloined goods was often the undoing of slaves who stole from their peers. The slave Isham confirmed the identity of Sarah's assailant after spying Peyton "with one of his shirts on, of which Sarah had been robbed." Isham's testimony exposes one of the great difficulties inherent in thefts from other slaves. Bondpeople knew precisely what goods they owned, and they proved astute observers of the commodities others possessed as well. To evade detection and blame, the enslaved thief was best served by either consuming stolen property immediately or pawning it off to another individual, black or white, and taking other goods or cash in exchange. Attempting to wear, use, or display stolen merchandise was fraught with danger. In 1856, for example, the South Carolina bondman Dan gazed longingly at the shoes of fellow slave George. So covetous was Dan of the shoes that he offered to purchase them. George refused. The next morning, George awoke to find his window open and his shoes missing. He instantly thought of Dan, and the next week at church, Dan was wearing the filched footwear. Suspicion confirmed.[22]

The biracial evangelical churches of the slaveholding South occasionally intervened in the property disputes of enslaved congregants. Church disciplinary committees frequently investigated charges of theft lodged against their members. Sometimes white churchgoers levied accusations of theft against other white members as an alternative to court action. Very rarely, a white man might even be accused of stealing from a black. At Bethabara Baptist Church in Laurens District, South Carolina, "brother Samuel Jones" was excluded from fellowship in 1837 on charges of "drunkenness, and other gross offences," such as "taking some money from a colord man at a muster ground in the neighbourhood." Churches were vastly more interested in the depredations committed by enslaved members upon property owned by whites. They commonly charged slaves with theft and the concomitant charge of lying to mask the deed. In the gang-labor regimes of the tobacco-producing Virginia Piedmont and cotton-growing Middle Georgia, churches most frequently accused slaves of stealing meat—the pork and poultry that filled slaves' bellies as a supplement to paltry rations. The congregation of Beaverdam Baptist Church in Wilkes County, Georgia, came to understand that some masters even encouraged their slaves' thievery. As John M. Strozier purportedly instructed his slave Willis, "if you did not get enough to eate to steal it." In South Carolina, where variations of the task system were more widely employed, a greater proportion of slaves were granted permission to raise stock or to grow their own fruits and vegetables in garden plots allotted by the master. In consequence, South Carolina churches were more apt to charge slaves with the theft of cotton, tobacco, or wheat that they might sell at market, rather than consume as food. Churches also cited enslaved members as accessories to theft. Bethel Baptist Church of Hancock County, Georgia, charged the bondwoman Celia with "consealing stolen property for her children and telling lies" about it. In Wilkes County, Fishing Creek Baptist Church likewise condemned the enslaved woman Sarah as an "accomplice" in "the pilfering act of her Daughter." Their respective congregations excluded such protective slave mothers from fellowship.[23]

Although enslaved members of southern evangelical churches were subject to intense scrutiny and possible disciplinary action, they could also use those same religious institutions to mediate conflicts among black churchgoers over thefts in the quarters and other issues. In 1822 Philips Mill Baptist Church in Wilkes County, Georgia, received "some unfavorable reports" about the bondman Daniel for having stolen unspecified goods and gotten into "an affray with Major Terrels servants" as a result. Daniel gave satisfaction and remained within the fold. Another Wilkes County church forgave an enslaved man who confessed in May 1850 "that he took two dozen eggs of a woman of Color the property of Neal Meadows." In acknowledging "he had [done] rong," he expressed sufficient sorrow to retain fellowship. As these examples suggest, churches more willingly excused slave thefts when the victim was also enslaved rather than white. But forgiveness was not automatic in such cases. In July 1838, Horeb Baptist Church in Georgia's Hancock County heard a complaint against "brother Deedham, a man of colour, the property of brother Tucker," for "taking Bacon and Butter, from . . . [a] negro woman and disposing of the same to his own benefit." Church testimony confirmed that "he had received both Bacon and Butter, at different times, which had been stolen." For his misdeeds, "he was excluded from the fellowship of the church."[24]

Rather than summoning the assistance of the master or invoking the disciplinary authority of the church, however, slaves usually handled cases of theft in the quarters on their own, without external interference. Ex-slave Jacob Stroyer explained in elaborate detail the supernatural techniques (sometimes fused with Christian elements) through which bondpeople in his South Carolina neighborhood in the 1850s detected thieves among them. Sometimes they read the movement of either a Bible or a sieve suspended from a string. Another method, imported from West Africa and purportedly more reliable, employed graveyard dust. Slaves took dust from the grave of the most recently deceased slave, placed it in a bottle, and poured in water to dissolve the dust. If a suspected thief drank the mixture and was innocent, nothing happened. If guilty, it was said, the thief would die, go to hell, and burn in fire and brimstone. Because so many slaves believed in magic and conjuration, this ritual often elicited confessions. If none of these techniques rooted out the thief, the slaves chalked up the theft to strangers from outside the neighborhood.[25]

Slaves who ferreted out the thieves among them devised their own solutions to the crisis of community signified by theft. Some slaves mediated disputes or acted as agents on behalf of others. When the Dougherty County, Georgia, bondman Gilbert complained to his enslaved friend John that Henry had taken Gilbert's two dollars, John labored with Henry—unsuccessfully—"to get the money for Gilbert." Social ostracism served as one potent weapon wielded by bondpeople to punish light-fingered slaves. To be made an outcast shunned by fellow bondpeople not only deterred some thefts from taking place but also spurred enslaved thieves to make amends. For restoration into a community of slaves, the robber must perform the appropriate penance. According to Jacob Stroyer, when slaves identified the individual who stole a chicken, "if he had any chickens he had to give four for one, and if he had none he made it good by promising that he would do so no more." Slaves without compensatory poultry thus escaped any retributive punishment; an apology and pledge to do better sufficed. The leniency slaves showed such persons may indicate their recognition that the guilty bondperson probably stole out of dire need. At the other end of the enslaved socioeconomic spectrum, a relatively prosperous slave who already owned ample fowl but nonetheless stole a chicken paid for the crime fourfold. In many other cases, slaves accepted recompense at the ratio of one to one. If the stolen property could not be returned or an identical commodity supplied to its enslaved owner, substitute goods were permitted at the discretion of the victim of theft. In Muscogee County, Georgia, the bond-man Neil charged Phil in 1853 with stealing his money and using it to buy alcohol. Neil was willing to take the jug of liquor as his just compensation.[26]

Cunning slaves might also reestablish social harmony by framing an enslaved thief. Although this was probably not done frequently, it was theoretically possible for them to steal goods themselves, plant them about the premises or on the person of the enslaved offender, and lead the master or other white authority to the evidence. According to British traveler James Silk Buckingham, slaves "revenged themselves" for a host of "offences committed by brothers and sisters, by stealing articles, and placing them secretly in the pockets of those they wished to injure, then accusing them, and becoming witnesses to convict them of the crime." Isaac, a slave with a reputation as "a quarrelsome, drunken vicious negro," devised such a strategy as a means to secure "recompense" from Emanuel, a fellow bondman with whom he worked at a Richmond, Virginia, tobacco factory. Laboring under the false impression that Emanuel had informed their common employer that Isaac had stolen tobacco, Isaac vowed to "have his 'recompense' out of Emanuel, that night, if not before." According to one eyewitness to their quarrel, "Isaac . . . swore that if he could not be revenged in any other way, he would steal something and put it in Emanuel's house, and then inform the police of it and bring them to the place." Slaves who cleverly planted evidence to effect the punishment of an enslaved adversary, Buckingham related, "often subsequently [confessed] their wickedness, and [boasted] in the success of their plots."[27]

Many slaves directly confronted those bondwomen and bondmen who violated their claims to property. Because most bondpeople owned very little, they placed a premium on what they did possess and rallied in defense of their goods against the incursion of thieves among them. A pair of cases from Anderson District, South Carolina, illustrates the ways in which slaves broached the subject of theft. In 1844 Louisa, Austin, and Yancy "had Lost some meat." Suspicion fell on the slaves of J. W. Norris, so they plotted to "Lay out J.W. Norris['s] Negroes on Sunday to make them confess about stealing the Bacon." Florilla, the property of Norris, was on her way to church when the aggrieved bondpeople accosted her and threatened to "kick her Durned Brains" out to elicit a confession. The trio of slaves "did assault beat & in a Riotous manner abuse Florilla." In another case, when one witness saw the slave John "leaving Mrs. Guitans premises just before day break with a bout ½ B[ushel] of corn in a Bage" in November 1855, he assumed it was "stolen property." Margaret Guitan's bondman Dan also spotted John, approached the thief, and "put his hand on the corn," informing John, "you are two [too] fat this morning." John instructed Dan to "say nothing A bout it," as "it did not come from here." Dan was apparently not appeased by the claim, for a fight broke out. John and an enslaved friend attacked Dan with a stick. Outnumbered, Dan still managed to inflict some "wounds with an Ax" or stick, sending John away "with his head brused and Blody."[28]

In both of these instances, slaves relied on violence as a means of self-preservation. They had a vested interest in the crime that took place. The theft of bacon or corn meant less food in their own bellies. Therefore, slaves willingly fought to safeguard their provisions. Trespassers likely understood what was at stake; otherwise, John would not have emphasized that his bag of stolen corn "did not come from *here*." He implicitly assumed that if the theft did not reduce Dan's rations, Dan would permit John to slip off with the pilfered food-stuff. But John was wrong. Slaves protected the master's property even when it had no immediate value to them. In 1854, for example, William Duckworth's Ned, another Anderson District slave, crept "in to the Black Smith Shop" of Tom N. Smith, "pilfering and as tho he wished to Steal some of his Iron until his negros run him out of the shop." Five of Smith's slaves and one bondman of Mrs. Guitan ran Ned off, but not before Ned struck the slave "Bill 2 Blows with his fist," sparking a melee. The slaves who entered the fray likely did not do so out of simple allegiance to the master, though. Had they not prevented the theft, they may have taken the blame for the missing iron and suffered unwarranted punishment.[29]

Thefts in the quarters often provoked violent reactions among enslaved men eager to punish thieves and send a clear message to deter other, would-be criminals. When Pickens District, South Carolina, slave Jesse, peaceably playing marbles one Sunday with fellow bondman Wiley, suddenly whirled and identified Wiley as "the Negro that stole his tobac[c]o," the two slaves quarreled. Jesse informed Wiley that "he came there after his tobacco and if he could not get it he could whip him." True to his word, Jesse "struck the first lick." After the Muscogee County, Georgia, slave Phil failed to repay the money he had allegedly stolen from Neil or to surrender the jug of liquor he purportedly bought with it, the two bondmen faced off, one wielding a plough handle, the other a wooden club. A third slave intervened and placed a momentary stop to their skirmish, but afterward their battle resumed. Neil then fatally stabbed Phil with a bowie knife.[30]

Slaves who pursued violent retribution upon other bondmen they accused of theft sometimes failed to exact the vengeance they sought. They might instead become the victims of the encounters they had initiated. During the Civil War, Mat, an enslaved Georgian, lost some money. Rummaging through the pocketbook of the bondman Elbert, Mat discovered a three-cent piece he claimed as his. The pair argued a while before dispersing, but two nights later, still obsessed with his missing money, Mat seized a pickaxe to attack Elbert. On this occasion, violence afforded no satisfaction to the aggrieved slave. Mat's plan to harm Elbert physically backfired when his intended victim preemptively struck Mat on the head with an axe, killing him. The story was much the same in Charlotte County, Virginia, where the slave Dick complained that "his wife had stolen 7 dollars" from him. Dick reserved the greater share of his venom, however, for the bondman Julius, whom he described as a "D-d Rascal" who protected "his . . . wife, in a wrong." Dick proclaimed his intention "to cut [Julius's] G_d d_d guts out of him" and "to see him in hell before day." Dick got the worse of their encounter, but as he lay dying, he still believed he had taken the proper course of action. "You all think I am a fool," he said as he breathed his last, "but thank God I am not a fool yet." Many enslaved men no doubt concurred with Dick that violence had its proper place inside the slave community.[31]

In a moral ethic uniquely forged in the crucible of bondage, slaves countenanced thefts from whites but not from each other. Nevertheless, temptation occasionally overwhelmed bondpeople and compelled them to violate their mutually understood code. It could hardly have been any other way. The dense web of economic relationships in which slaves participated permitted some to acquire money and goods to materially improve their lives and those of their loved ones. Yet bondpeople's experiences in the market produced a profound ambivalence. The inequitable distribution of material wealth among slaves generated social distinctions and status differentiation despite their shared bondage. The very success that might elicit the respect and admiration of fellow bondpeople might just as easily inspire jealousy, rivalry, and the compulsion to steal. The infiltration of cash and commodities into bondpeople's lives thus eroded the communal ethic of southern slave quarters.

NOTES

1. Charles C. Jones, *The Religious Instruction of the Negroes: In the United States* (Savannah: Thomas Purse, 1842), 135; John Ernest, ed., *Narrative of the Life of Henry Box Brown, Written by Himself* (Chapel Hill: University of North Carolina Press, 2008), 52; Eugene D. Genovese, *Roll, Jordan, Roll: The World the Slaves Made* (1974; New York; Vintage Books, 1976), 606; Alex Lichtenstein, "'That Disposition to Theft, with Which They Have Been Branded': Moral Economy, Slave Management, and the Law," *Journal of Social History* 21 (Spring 1988): 415; Jeff Forret, *Race Relations at the Margins: Slaves and Poor Whites in the Antebellum Southern Countryside* (Baton Rouge: Louisiana State University Press, 2006), ch. 2. Material for this chapter may also be found in Jeff Forret, *Slave against Slave: Plantation Violence in the Old South* (Baton Rouge: Louisiana State University Press, 2015), ch. 5.

2. Compared to thefts from the master, thefts among slaves have received very little scholarly attention, although they are mentioned in Genovese, *Roll, Jordan, Roll*, 606–7, 631; and Dylan C. Penningroth, "My People, My People: The Dynamics of Community in Southern Slavery," in *New Studies in the History of American Slavery*, ed. Edward E. Baptist and Stephanie M. H. Camp (Athens: University of Georgia Press, 2006), 171–72. Less understood still are thefts from slaves by whites. In 1853, for example, a white man in Mississippi robbed a slave of a fifteen-dollar gold watch and some money. See *State v. Daniel G. Smith* (1854), case 21846, group 1850, box 16, file 21, Adams County Courthouse Collection, Historic Natchez Foundation, Natchez, Mississippi. On theft within the slave quarters in the colonial era, see Philip D. Morgan, *Slave Counterpoint: Black Culture in the Eighteenth-Century Chesapeake and Lowcountry* (Chapel Hill: University of North Carolina Press, 1998), 469–70.

3. Auditor of Public Accounts, Condemned Blacks Executed or Transported Records—Condemned Slaves, Court Orders, and Valuations, 1810–1822, Misc. Reel 2551, frame 922, LVA; Historical Census Browser, University of Virginia, Geospatial and Statistical Data Center (2004), http://fisher.lib.virginia.edu/collections/stats/histcensus/index.html (accessed March 17, 2012); Auditor of Public Accounts, Condemned Blacks Executed or Transported, Records—Condemned Slaves, Court Orders, and Valuations, 1781–1793, Misc. Reel 2549, frame 439, LVA.

4. Dylan C. Penningroth, *The Claims of Kinfolk: African American Property and Community in the Nineteenth-Century South* (Chapel Hill: University of North Carolina Press, 2003), 97; Charles B. Dew, "Disciplining Slave Ironworkers in the Antebellum South: Coercion, Conciliation, and Accommodation," *American Historical Review* 79 (April 1974): 411, 412.

5. Michael Wayne, *Death of an Overseer: Reopening a Murder Investigation from the Plantation South* (New York: Oxford University Press, 2001), 12–13; Auditor of Public Accounts, Condemned Blacks Executed or Transported Records—Condemned Slaves, Court Orders, and Valuations, 1810–1822, Misc. Reel 2551, frame 998, LVA (quotations); Executive Papers, James Patton Preston, February–May 1818, box 4, folder 1, LVA.

6. Pickens District, Court of Magistrates and Freeholders, Trial Papers, 1829–1862, folder 11, SCDAH; John Campbell, "As 'A Kind of Freeman'? Slaves' Market-Related Activities in the South Carolina Upcountry, 1800–1860," in *The Slaves' Economy: Independent Production by Slaves in the Americas*, ed. Ira Berlin and Philip D. Morgan (London: Frank Cass, 1991), 147–48, 153. On slaves' ability to save money, including for such long-term purposes as purchasing freedom, see Kathleen Mary Hilliard, "Spending in Black and White: Race, Slavery, and Consumer Values in the Antebellum South" (PhD diss., University of South Carolina, 2006), 90–93 and ch. 6.

7. Lawrence T. McDonnell, "Money Knows No Master: Market Relations and the American Slave Community," in *Developing Dixie: Modernization in a Traditional Society*, ed. Winfred B. Moore Jr., Joseph F. Tripp, and Lyon G. Tyler Jr. (Westport, CT: Greenwood Press, 1988), 37; Genovese, *Roll, Jordan, Roll*, 607; William Thomson, *A Tradesman's Travels in the United States and Canada, in the Years 1840, 41, and 42* (Edinburgh: Oliver & Boyd, 1842), 189; Jones, *Religious Instruction of the Negroes*, 135; William Howard Russell, *My Diary North and South*, ed. Fletcher Pratt (New York: Harper, 1954), 77, 78; Charles Lyell, *A Second Visit to the United States of North America* (New York: Harper, 1849), 1:264; Charles Sackett Sydnor, *Slavery in Mississippi* (New York: D. Appleton-Century, 1933), 41; Frederick Law Olmsted, *A Journey in the Seaboard Slave States, with Remarks on Their Economy* (New York: Dix & Edwards, 1856), 111–12; Executive Papers, William Smith, Misc. Reel 5022, box 4, folder 4, frames 59–69, LVA.

8. Executive Papers, William Smith, Misc. Reel 5022, box 4, folder 4, frames 59–69, LVA (first quotation); Executive Papers, Henry A. Wise, Misc. Reel 4202, box 8, folder 4, frame 690, LVA; *Henry, a Slave v. the State* (1863), Supreme Court of Georgia, 33 Ga. 441, 1863 Ga. LEXIS 6 (second quotation).

9. Morgan, *Slave Counterpoint*, 469; Sally E. Hadden, *Slave Patrols: Law and Violence in Virginia and the Carolinas* (Cambridge, MA: Harvard University Press, 2001); Stephanie M. H. Camp, *Closer to Freedom: Enslaved Women and Everyday Resistance in the Plantation South* (Chapel Hill: University of North Carolina Press, 2004), ch. 1; Ernest, *Life of Henry Box Brown*, 55.

10. Anthony E. Kaye, *Joining Places: Slave Neighborhoods in the Old South* (Chapel Hill: University of North Carolina Press, 2007).

11. L. A. Chamerovzow, ed., *Slave Life in Georgia: A Narrative of the Life, Sufferings, and Escape of John Brown, a Fugitive Slave, Now in England* (London, 1855), 83; *Narratives of the Sufferings of Lewis and Milton Clarke, Sons of a Soldier of the Revolution, during a Captivity of More than Twenty Years among the Slaveholders of Kentucky, One of the So Called Christian States of North America: Dictated by Themselves* (Boston: Bela Marsh, 1846), 119–20.

12. J. S. Buckingham, *The Slave States of America* (1842; reprint, New York: Negro Universities Press, 1968), 2:87 (first quotation); Hilliard, "Spending in Black and White," 161, 166 (second quotation).

13. *Laura, a Slave v. the State of Mississippi* (1852), box 5830, case 6763, MDAH (first quotation); Penningroth, *Claims of Kinfolk*, 99 (second and third quotations).

14. Anderson District, Court of Magistrates and Freeholders, Trial Papers, reel C2775, case 400, SCDAH; Spartanburg District, Court of Magistrates and Freeholders, Trial Papers, reel C2922, case 296, SCDAH. George was found guilty of manslaughter, jailed for two months, and given three hundred total lashes distributed in weekly increments of fifty. See also McDonnell, "Money Knows No Master," 37, 38.

15. Sue Eakin, *Solomon Northup's Twelve Years a Slave and Plantation Life in the Antebellum South* (Lafayette: Center for Louisiana Studies, University of Louisiana at Lafayette, 2007), 241–42.

16. Genovese, *Roll, Jordan, Roll,* 607.

17. Auditor of Public Accounts, Condemned Blacks Executed or Transported, Records—Condemned Slaves, Court Orders, and Valuations, 1794–1809, Misc. Reel 2550, frame 252, LVA (first and second quotations); Auditor of Public Accounts, Condemned Blacks Executed or Transported, Records—Condemned Slaves, Court Orders, and Valuations, 1833–1845, Misc. Reel 2553, frames 166, 814, LVA (third through sixth quotations).

18. *Re Clement and Jacobo* (1777), 12 La. Hist. Q. 682, in *Judicial Cases concerning American Slavery and the Negro,* ed. Helen Tunnicliff Catterall (Washington, DC: Carnegie Institution of Washington, 1932), 3:437–38; *John (a Slave) v. State* (1852), Supreme Court of Mississippi, 24 Miss. 569, 1852 Miss. LEXIS 103; Lunenburg County, Order Book 24, 1821–1823, reel 34, LVA.

19. Quoted in Hilliard, "Spending in Black and White," 140 (first quotation), 141 (second and third quotations); *Henry, a Slave v. the State* (1863), Supreme Court of Georgia, 33 Ga. 441, 1863 Ga. LEXIS 6 (fourth through sixth quotations); Auditor of Public Accounts, Condemned Blacks Executed or Transported Records—Condemned Slaves, Court Orders, and Valuations, 1810–1822, Misc. Reel 2551, frame 919, LVA (seventh and eighth quotations); Genovese, *Roll, Jordan, Roll,* 607; James O. Breeden, ed., *Advice among Masters: The Ideal in Slave Management in the Old South* (Westport, CT: Greenwood Press, 1980), 51 (ninth and tenth quotations).

20. Amherst County, Order Book 1815–1820, reel 30, LVA; *Simon, a Slave v. the State of Mississippi* (1859), box 5849, case 8900, MDAH.

21. Executive Papers, James Patton Preston, February–May 1818, box 4, folder 1, LVA.

22. Ibid. (quotation); Hilliard, "Spending in Black and White," 178.

23. Penningroth, *Claims of Kinfolk,* 100–101; Bethabara Baptist Church (Laurens District, SC), Records, 1801–1881, September 1837, SCL; Beaverdam Baptist Church (Wilkes County, GA), Minutes, 1836–1855, August 1849, drawer 9, reel 22, GArch; Bethel Baptist Church (Hancock County, GA), Minutes, 1828–1887, December 1839, drawer 77, reel 26, GArch; Fishing Creek Baptist Church (Wilkes County, GA), Minutes, 1821–1873, September 1855, drawer 171, reel 28, GArch.

24. Philips Mill Baptist Church (Wilkes County, GA), Minutes, 1785–1948, June 1822, September 1822, drawer 45, reel 13, GArch; Beaverdam Baptist Church (Wilkes County, GA), Minutes, 1836–1855, May 1850, drawer 9, reel 22, GArch; Horeb Baptist Church (Hancock County, GA), Minutes, 1792–1916, July 1838, drawer 32, reel 77, GArch.

25. Jacob Stroyer, *Sketches of My Life in the South,* part 1 (Salem, MA: Salem Press, 1879), 47–50. See also Herbert G. Gutman, *The Black Family in Slavery and Freedom, 1750–1925* (New York: Pantheon, 1976), 279–82.

26. *Henry, a Slave v. the State* (1863), Supreme Court of Georgia, 33 Ga. 441, 1863 Ga. LEXIS 6; Stroyer, *Sketches of My Life,* 50; *State v. Neil* (1853), Records of the Superior Court of Muscogee County, drawer 80, reel 64, GArch, in Glenn M. McNair, "Justice Bound: Aframericans, Crime, and Criminal Justice in Georgia, 1751–1865" (PhD diss., Emory University, 2001), 120–21.

27. Buckingham, *Slave States of America,* 2:87 (first and second quotations), 88 (seventh quotation); Executive Papers, John M. Gregory, November 1842, box 2, folder 4, LVA (third through sixth quotations).

28. Anderson District, Court of Magistrates and Freeholders, Trial Papers, reel C2917, case 154, SCDAH; Anderson District, Court of Magistrates and Freeholders, Trial Papers, reel C2918, case 289, SCDAH. On Florilla, see also McDonnell, "Money Knows No Master," 37.

29. Anderson District, Court of Magistrates and Freeholders, Trial Papers, reel C2918, case 268, SCDAH.

30. Pickens District, Court of Magistrates and Freeholders, Trial Papers, 1829–1862, folder 11, SCDAH (quotations); *State v. Neil* (1853), Records of the Superior Court of Muscogee County, drawer 80, reel 64, GArch, in McNair, "Justice Bound," 121. See also *Henry, a Slave v. the State* (1863), Supreme Court of Georgia, 33 Ga. 441, 1863 Ga. LEXIS 6. In Pickens District, both slaves ultimately received more than three dozen lashes for "Fighting on the sabeth and gaming."

31. *State v. Elbert* (1863), Records of the Superior Court of Newton County, drawer 11, reel 3, GArch, in McNair, "Justice Bound," 121–22; Executive Papers, Henry A. Wise, Misc. Reel 4195, box 2, folder 5, frames 3–11, April 1856, LVA.

BONDS BURST ASUNDER

*The Transformation of the Internal Economy
in Confederate Richmond*

KATHLEEN M. HILLIARD

"*Unclaimed Stolen Goods*," announced the April 12, 1864, edition of the Richmond *Daily Dispatch:*

> One canister of allspice, a water-cooler filled with black tea, twelve pounds
> black pepper, one fluting and case, two dozen lead pencils, one piece of cotton edging, a lot of spool cotton, a quantity of writing paper, envelopes and
> music, five pairs of ladies' shoes, a lot of silk dress buttons, one piece of gold
> lace, one revolving pistol, a white silk bonnet, a quantity of drafting paper,
> five pairs of ladies' flannel drawers, two gingham handkerchiefs, two gold
> pencils, and one valuable gold watch.[1]

In months past, "large quantities of stationery of every description" had disappeared from the "various departments of Government." Prompted by the loss
of some "thousand dollars' worth of steel pens" and a tip from a local resident, Treasury Department watchman Valentine Brown directed officials to a
book and stationery store known as the "Central News Agency" just behind
St. Paul's Episcopal Church. In addition to the cache of goods listed above,
officers discovered a large portion of the missing pens, a bag containing more
than one thousand dollars' worth of letter, note, and bill paper, a "large pile
of the Bibles obtained abroad by the Rev Moses D Hoge," and a mass of
other goods. That "valuable gold watch"? Worth an estimated five thousand
dollars, it was, by far, the most expensive item found. Authorities confiscated
the "magnificent" timepiece from the pocket of the shop's "ostensible propri-

etor" Grandison, one of the besieged city's many trading, trafficking, street-wise slaves.[2]

By spring 1864, few war-worn Richmonders would have been surprised by the crime, though the scale of operations and those involved in it must have caused consternation. "A set of well kept single entry books" revealed that Grandison and "two other negroes," one slave and one free, were doing quite the "lucrative business" and that Grandison himself "was the Treasurer of a thriving secret Benevolent Society." Worse, the man who had hired Grandison was in on the game, having invested "$500 into the business when it was first started," claiming "a dollar or two now and then" from the store's profits. The source of the store's stock was more worrisome still. Interviews with Grandison and his fellows revealed that the thousand dollars worth of stolen paper products had been brought in only a day before by a "negro who traded in the army."[3] Ultimately, though, this polymorphous enterprise, both white and black, slave and free, written-down and underground, went a step too far.

Illegal interracial trade, theft, dwindling Confederate stores, slaves grasping weapons, cash, and the finest of goods: interwoven within Grandison's tale was a striking narrative of Richmond's precipitous fall.[4] As the Union blockade tightened and the Army of the Potomac threatened, Richmond's shops and hucksters' stalls grew increasingly bare. Historians have told of Richmond's women rising in riot to protest the price of bread in April 1863, but these worrisome scenes were just the most visible sign of economic, social, and political relations breaking apart.[5] As shortages of goods and currency inflation brought hardship to city residents, day-to-day economic transactions came to resemble the shaded world of illicit economic exchange long exploited by enslaved people—and their masters—throughout the South.[6] But where once trade had offered slaves opportunities as individuals to differentiate themselves from fellow bondpeople and more nearly—if still only slightly—approach the level of free white society, now war propelled whites as a class sharply downward, engendering fears, sharp and sudden, that soon their material standing and perhaps political power, too, might fall below that of rising slaves. In the convergence of black and white economic fortunes, we see political and social mastery lost, the inadequacies of the new southern nation dangerously exposed.[7]

This catastrophic breakdown was the last moment of a decades-long metastasizing of contradictions within the system of slavery broadly and in slaves' economic relations specifically. Throughout the antebellum period, in small towns and big cities, yeoman farms and grand plantations, enslaved men and women like Grandison had entered into market relations in a thriving "informal" or "internal" economy. Earning and spending prospects limited by custom or law, slaves moved exchange to realms outside white surveillance. There, enslaved people bought and sold goods and services with each other, certainly, but also in and among the broader population of poor white farmers and laborers, free people of color, and slaveholders. In Richmond, where so many enslaved men and women were "hired out," economic activity was particularly vigorous and exceedingly porous. Sanctioned and prohibited exchange went hand-in-hand, with fenced goods and those legally procured flowing in and out of slaves' hands promiscuously.[8]

No doubt the master class fretted over lines crossed but understood, too, that such exchange, problematic though it was, invested slaves in the very system that oppressed them. And so, while slaves bought and sold, stole and fenced, slaveholders gritted their teeth and reconfigured strategies to accommodate the conscious and unconscious challenges slaves as economic actors hurled against their regime. But as the thrill of secession and early Confederate victories waned, exigencies of war made a mockery of the world slaveholders had so carefully crafted. White residents found themselves scheming, strategizing, and scratching out subsistence for themselves in a local economy straitened by Union strangling and Confederate financial blunders. Long accustomed to working the informal economy's underground channels, slaves navigated this netherworld alongside them. In this moment of economic leveling, white Richmonders saw disaster looming.

There was no shortage of complaints about the state of Richmond's local economy as the war progressed. As early as the fall of 1861, shortages and currency inflation wracked the city. Historian Emory Thomas summed its causes succinctly: "The blockade, lack of sufficient transportation facilities, wartime disruption of farming, and the presence of an ever-consuming army" triggered rising prices.[9] Added to these problems were the influx of refugees, clerks, and bureaucrats attached to the capital, as well as entrepreneurs looking to make their fortunes in the bustling hub of industry and government; Richmond's infrastructure and resources were thus stretched beyond capacity from the earliest days of the conflict. The city's white population—from old elites and new, struggling immigrants to commercial traders—felt the pain. While Rebel high society saw social lives lowered—once gallant balls turned to "starvation parties," balls of knitting yarn in every woman's hand—the city's middle and working-class white population felt scarcity even more acutely.[10]

White Richmond tightened belts in tough times, adapting life and labor to meet the demands of "the pressure and the burden of the war." German immigrant John Lange closed his dramshop and turned to cobbling and producing "battery bags" for sale. By the summer of 1864, "without occupation or income," he could "hardly make ends meet," and "got busy in [his] garden," explaining that "it sure was necessary since everything was so scarce." Scraping together what cash he could and working connections down in Shockoe Slip, he purchased odds and ends in bulk—matches, small lots of fragrant soaps, boxes of cigars, and shoe laces—and had his sons "peddle them in the streets and markets."[11] Noting the city's growing familiarity with "economy" in December 1862, Confederate War Department clerk John B. Jones sighed that such living was "something new in the South." His government salary unequal to rising inflation, he eventually moved his family to a house with a "smart vegetable garden" that he, like Lange, "cultivate[d] with careful assiduity in hopes of saving some dollars in the items of potatoes, tomatoes, beets, etc."[12] Emma Mordecai claimed that the blockade had made southern women "ingenious and independent," as she and her neighbors plaited straw for hats, learned to crush sorghum, darned and sold socks, and feasted on blackberry dumplings made by "confederate receipt"—flour, blackberries, and hot water. Still others took special care with worn clothes, mending where needed and using homespun for new, made do without sugar, and replaced coffee with chicory or rye.[13] But even strategies like those employed by Lange, Jones, and Mordecai failed to sate in a city where goods were so scarce. Unsurprisingly, burglaries plagued Richmond, the mayor passing judgment daily on dozens of men and women charged with property crimes from theft to the trade and possession of stolen goods. In short, war drove white Richmonders to learn the tricks of the trade that slaves had long practiced in the underground economy.[14]

To enslaved people who had long worked the margins of Richmond's economy—scrapping and saving, marketing independently produced wares and truck, fencing goods and trading up—the straitened scheming of their city masters must have both bemused and worried them. Slaves, too, suffered as war took its toll, but the work white folks endured to make ends meet was far from unfamiliar. Historian Midori Takagi has argued that wartime deprivation and restrictions struck enslaved Richmonders particularly hard, temporarily strengthening slavery's bonds. The "independent slave community" that developed through the antebellum period, she contends, became less so under increased surveillance, new restrictions, and renewed determination to enforce oft-ignored laws on movement and economic activity. Most distressing, bond-people found opportunities for employment dwindling rapidly. Impressed into government or military service, many slaves lost the ability to negotiate terms of hire, forfeited overtime bonuses, and saw earnings cut. Fewer private opportunities presented themselves as increasing numbers of manufactories and tobacco warehouses closed their doors and strapped white families hired less domestic help.[15]

Takagi's tale of increasing oppression rightly emphasizes the ways white fear, legal statute, and wartime exigency came together to inhibit slave livelihoods. But because Takagi mostly focuses on white-sanctioned opportunities and transactions, she misses the ways more marginal and subterranean networks of exchange turned local economy and the master-slave relation itself inside out.[16] Pulsing just below the surface of law and propriety was a far more complex, confounding set of market relations, guided as almost nowhere else in American history by Adam Smith's famous "invisible hand," unfettered by government regulation, racial norms, or class prescriptions. Everywhere in Richmond, in these years, men and women, black and white, slave and free, lived out the truth of that central law of the marketplace, *caveat emptor:* let the buyer beware.

That irony grated mightily on white Richmonders long before the crash came. In the spring of 1861, budding Confederates had hailed the creation of the southern nation for the economic freedoms secession promised. Bursting the bonds of national union would be the first step toward forging new ties with Europe—and the Yankees, too—on better and more profitable terms. Gaining political self-mastery would begin a steady climb toward full coffers and a booming economy. The source of all this triumph would be the South's superior labor system, paternalist masters deftly guiding grateful slaves.

But war quickly exploded all those hopes. It was not grand battlefield reverses alone that seemed to capsize their fortunes; in picayune skirmishes on the home front, in the marketplace, and especially in illicit transactions between whites and blacks, signs of their doom were made manifest.[17] In better times, masters might have been able to dismiss the more worrisome aspects of the internal economy, imposing moralizing judgment on slave spending and citing nettlesome thefts and underground marketing to justify their rule. War's straitening circumstances, however, transformed the internal economy's meaning. War not only flattened white Richmonders materially; it leveled their gaze as well. The more white folks struggled, the more difficult it became to ignore troubling economic behavior on the part of slaves. This new angle of vision—from within the internal economy instead of above it—revealed the crumbling foundations of the slaveholders' world.[18]

Contra Takagi, scarcity secured masters to slaves in new and disquieting ways. As Richmond slipped into decline, city slaveholders found themselves increasingly and distressingly dependent on their bondpeople. Servicing the households of the city's most wealthy and influential, slaves scoured the streets and shopped the markets for provisions to stock family larders. But how, with goods so scarce, could enslaved men and women find those items city papers claimed had all but vanished from storekeepers' and hucksters' stalls? Faced with household shortages, some slaveholders simply chose not to ask. Confederate mistress Mary Chesnut lamented the plight of the starving city as well as the toll it took on her social life. Fed up with her complaints, her husband's valet Laurence spat, "You give me the money, I'll find everything you want." Goods were there for those with the guile to get them, he knew. So, too, perhaps, did Chesnut, who never questioned the provenance of provender readily provided, noting only that his schemes were "simple ideas but effective." And so she passed over cash, and Laurence disappeared into the streets each day, coming home with turkey, ice, and sundries enough to keep the family "plentifully supplied" in the toughest of times.[19]

What Chesnut might have seen, had she had not turned a blind eye to Laurence's wandering, was a growing network of exchange largely dependent on theft from private and Confederate stores. To be sure, enslaved people were not solely responsible for the surge of property crimes that gripped the city, but what white Richmonder could deny their role? Both in October of 1862 and October of 1863, the *Daily Dispatch* warned that the city's "usual" season of thieving had begun, as "hundreds of burglaries ... will be attempted in the fall and winter." Whereas in 1863, the paper mourned "desperadoes" generally, the year before, editors had classified depredators more precisely. On the outskirts of the city, "desperate riff-raff"—treacherous whites—committed violent highway robberies. Within the city proper, editors argued that it was the "colored population" who perpetrated crimes in Richmond's private residences. The uptick in activity by these *"chevaliers de industrie"* was a sure sign that the "morals of the city are not in the most healthy condition."[20] That was doubly bad news, indeed.

White southerners had long lamented slaves' "stealing," and so it was not surprising that they would condemn thieving generally. But behind such criticism lay profound unease over the fraying fabric of southern society. Mastery's warp and weft unraveled as a class enslaved to do city whites' bidding found ways to exploit age-old relations to material advantage. By autumn 1863, Richmond mistress Sallie Brock Putnam lamented, "Domestic troubles . . . arose to vex and annoy us." Thefts and robberies of "the most provoking character were everywhere perpetrated," she recalled, placing blame squarely on household servants.[21] Others in white Richmond told similar stories. In January 1865, Theodore Law woke with a start to "the strong smell of smoke which pervaded his house." Running to the rear room, he found his bureau smoldering. Upon further investigation, he discovered that the drawer had been broken open and a good bit of money and jewelry purloined. With no sign of forced entry, he turned to slave Celia. With the help of a local watchman, he searched the girl, "pulling out the money from different parts of her clothing," $3,280 in Confederate cash hidden in her stockings and, "in her bosom . . . a roll of bank notes." Dismissing her "cock-and-bull story" of a pistol-wielding intruder, Law brought her before the Hustings Court.[22] Robert Leckay's suspicions were similarly raised when groceries began disappearing from his Richmond shop. Seeing no sign of forced entry, he turned his gaze to the bondwoman Cynthia, whom he had "long suspected . . . of robbing him." The mystery was solved in late 1864, when he caught her slipping into the store by means of a duplicate key.[23] These two examples must stand for thousands more, all confronting Richmond whites with the same terrifying truth: It was not the loss of money or things that so focused their fears; it was the sudden ebb of mastery itself. Not even Jefferson Davis was spared that fall. In February 1864, the president's slave Cornelius was charged with "stealing money from his master," part of a larger plan of escape to enemy lines. After he was caught with "snack" enough for a "long journey" and the pilfered cash, authorities brought him to the station house, where he escaped once again from his captors. Whether this second jailbreak was ultimately successful remains unknown, but Cornelius, like hundreds of other enslaved men and women in the surrounded city, had made his political point perfectly plain.[24]

Indeed, depredations became so common that even Mary Chesnut—who benefited from shadowy economic dealings—began to worry. In 1864 she reported that her neighbor had been robbed of a barrel of sugar. "A calamity," Chesnut recorded, not just because sundries were so scarce. She could not help but think of her housemaid Molly's warning: "Always, the stealing is from the inside of the house, your own black people." Knowledge of thefts stirred anxieties in the Chestnut household. Laurence, the fellow who could "find everything" for the family, had long caused consternation. Since moving to Richmond, he had "done all of [the Chesnuts'] shopping" and had within reach much of the family's money. "Watch, clothes, [and] two or three hundred gold pieces" all lay in an open trunk: What kept him from pocketing the goods and "pack[ing] off to Yankees"? Mary's husband cavalierly dismissed her concerns. But as "ticklish times" advanced and with "gold ... at such a premium," she took stricter control, sewing specie and diamonds into a belt "tied under [her] hoops." Laurence never commented on her "latest fancy," she noted, always wearing "the same bronze mask" as he went about his daily affairs. But he asked for "twice as much money now when he goes to buy things—at least twice as much as he used to take when it was lying about in the tray."[25] Were Laurence's requests simply a symptom of currency inflation and economic upheaval? Might Molly's admonition come to pass in Mary's own home?

Questions like these were on the lips of many in Richmond as war progressed. But more than relations with individual masters came under strain. Slaves, free people of color, and white men had long served as haulers and drivers, moving goods and people throughout the city. As conscription tapped the pool of white labor, slaves continued to ply city streets, a growing number of carts, wagons, and drays at their disposal. What they did with those conveyances, Richmonders complained, brought disorder to the community.[26] In January 1865, the *Dispatch* noted that in "ninety-nine cases out of every hundred," city slaves were responsible for brazen thefts, enslaved wagon drivers and other bondpeople "going at large" pegged as the major culprits.[27] Visitors and residents alike told of the hubbub engulfing the city's central railroad depot, the perfect spot for slaves to pinch goods from the milling crowd.[28] Among the most lucrative schemes was an ancestor of the modern taxi scam: shouting bondpeople beckoning strangers to waiting hacks, omnibuses, and wagons; hauling them to desired destinations; and then departing posthaste with a bag or satchel as light-fingered tribute. Even resident Richmonder Elizabeth

Hubbard, familiar with the depot scene, fell victim in 1864. Enslaved haulers John and Stephen promised good service upon her alighting from a train but took her hatbox and other goods as supplementary payment. Parmelia Wilson suffered the same fate at the hands of Thomas Johnston's slave Marshall. Promising "to deliver [her baggage] to her lodging-place in a safe and prompt manner," the drayman showed up three hours later, one of the trunks broken open and three hundred dollars worth of beef and bacon missing. Such crimes, however minor, were far from petty. The theft of bags and goods by black thieves could be made right; it was the rifling of paternalist power and social relations that was the true and irreparable crime in the eyes of white Richmonders.[29]

But even more than bonds with slaves, masters worried, were coming apart. The vexing problem of black theft that mushroomed across the years of war and siege engulfed the white community, too, both wittingly and unwittingly. Richmond whites acted as black criminals' confederates, intermediaries, and consumers of purloined property. Indeed, by 1865, it became virtually impossible for loyal Rebels to go shopping in the capital without worrying whether their own acts of consumption contributed to subverting social order and national existence. Virginia law prohibited whites from buying goods, "however trivial," the *Dispatch* reminded Richmonders in 1863, from slaves without their masters' consent: That long-standing statute was in need of "rigid" enforcement, "especially . . . now."[30] Property thefts soared as the economy tightened. "Nine out of every ten" robbers were family servants, the paper despaired, but these miscreants "readily find purchasers for what they steal" among even more culpable whites "and are thus encouraged in their robberies."[31]

How to sort out this trouble? Bondpeople and free blacks bought pilfered goods, certainly, but hardly deserved the harshest blame. White ignorance, too, contributed to the problem. As the *Dispatch* complained, "many strangers in this city . . . seem to know nothing of the laws of Virginia relative to negroes, and . . . traffic with them at all times." Still worse, white Richmonders did not bother to discriminate, readily buying items from enslaved and free alike. Consequently, "the owners of slaves are deeply wronged, and the morals of their servants ruined." Sallie Putnam blamed the "low and depraved in questionable quarters of the city" for black market purchases, yet all could name one or more Mary Chesnuts who bought and winked and paraded their patriotism proudly.[32]

Innumerable tales from the Mayor's Court give public witness of the link between light-fingered slaves and grasping whites, without supplying anything like a workable remedy. Consider the perplexing plight of shopkeeper George Bluford in the winter of 1863, when he cornered his slave ascending the cellar steps with a bundle on his shoulder. The slave confessed that he had been "stealing for some time," supplying one of the merchants in the city. However dumbfounding that news must have been, Bluford could hardly have known that months later he would still be wandering Richmond streets searching stores and shops all over town for his goods. After days of hunting, the frustrated man thought he saw a missing roll of leather in the shop of Gideon Garber. But Garber demurred: That item had been consigned to him by another fellow named Morris Kauffman. Regardless of how the chain of culpability snaked, Bluford demanded justice. Yet if the merchant felt flummoxed by his inability to regulate a thieving slave, how bewildered he must have been to hear the judgments rendered upon instigating and collaborating whites in the Mayor's and Hustings courts. Were fines of ten or fifteen dollars at all likely to curb the trading tendencies of white villains at a time when Confederate currency values were plummeting? And if the actions of courts and newspapers aimed at shaming fellows like L. Dwyer, who traded money and honor for a bag of onions, was justice for Richmond's Blufords or correction for their adversaries any more than a cruel joke? In years past, a man like Allen Nunnally, long suspected of "trading with negroes," would have been hauled to court for vending illicit wares—most commonly liquor. But times had changed: now Nunnally faced prosecution as consumer, not seller, accused of buying apple brandy from a slave. That little revolution must have made worried whites wonder how low their neighbors would finally sink.[33]

Writ large, such individual failings bespoke deep danger. "A Traitor," cried the *Examiner*. John Bosher had fallen for a Confederate sting, trading information on the posting of Rebel pickets for Yankee payment. His treachery surprised no one, though, as he had once been suspected of "trading with negroes, but was sharp enough always to avoid detection." A rope might remedy this betrayal, but how to stem the tide of greed or deprivation that drove free white buyers to more minor treasons was a mystery none could unravel.[34]

Where whites saw trouble, slaves saw opportunity. Bondpeople exploited prewar links with masters and hirers, expectations of menial and manual service on city streets, and underground dealings with free whites and blacks to

advantage as the war progressed.[35] As disturbing were signs of entrepreneurship on the part of slave traders. Cultivating ties across the city and putting
to work commercial skills honed in more secure times, bondpeople built sophisticated underground economic networks. At first glance, the arrest of Jane,
an enslaved woman accused in November 1861 of stealing a hog, looked plain
and simple. It soon became alarmingly clear, however, that Jane "was carrying
on an extensive pork-packing business," fueled mostly by purloined swine. In
1864 five slaves faced charges of even greater larceny. They were "a regularly
organized band of chicken thieves, doing business on a large scale." Investigating the small Marshall Street house in which their enterprise was based,
authorities found "a large number of cocks and hens, with their necks recently
wrung; a lot of burglars tools and implements; several new felt hats, and pieces
of clothing and dry goods," as well as a pistol, a double-barreled shotgun, and
a yard full of "chicken heads, feet, and offal." More worrisome still, that same
year an assortment of white men and slaves were arrested by Petersburg authorities for operation of a regional pork ring involving theft of Confederate
stores in that city. Five slaves had pilfered pork by the barrel and were selling
these rationed goods in Richmond. The division of crooked proceeds, in this
case, mirrored a division of criminal labor—and redoubled white alarm—with
only half the loot going to the slave conspirators themselves. The balance was
doled out to the Rebel *"guard at the store."*[36]

But not all such businesses ran completely underground. Black and white
markets blurred everywhere. White Richmonders complained bitterly of "negro cook shops and hucksters" who were "furnished with meats, poultry, and
other necessaries, stolen by servants of their masters."[37] These shops were run
by slaves whose masters allowed them to hire their own time, ranging free
throughout the city or finding a white person to "stand master for them." They
conspired with household servants, offering their "abodes" and "cook shops" as
"storage for their plunder." With little oversight and a stock of fenced goods
at their disposal, these slaves then "trad[ed] as free men" throughout the city.[38]
Such "repositories of stolen goods" were a nuisance, one paper complained, as
it lauded recent efforts by the City Council to fine masters who allowed slaves
to hire their own time and run rampant through the city.[39] In October 1864,
the council banned slaves from operating a "cook shop, eating house, drinking
saloon, room, or store for the sale of anything, unless the owner or hirer of
said slave resides in the same house." The *Examiner,* decrying these "sink holes

for the dropping of negro plunder" that plagued the city, projected that "five hundred negro shops of one degree of negro enterprise and another" would soon shutter their doors. But expecting to dismantle such pervasive networks of black ambition, complexity, and guile with the stroke of a pen was like whistling Dixie.[40]

The hour of slave subservience was passing fast. Everywhere in Richmond, signs of rising black fortunes—and fading white hopes—were unmistakable. Exploiting connections, honing entrepreneurial skill, and organizing thriving underground trade, enslaved people sent Confederate anxieties soaring. Shadowy networks and midnight dealings might be downplayed. But a watch missing from the master's bureau, plump hens stolen from the coop, goods and money changing hands brazenly on the street betrayed subversive connections too plainly to ignore. City papers, memoirs, and diaries offer hundreds of distressing minor incidents in which slaves turned entrepreneurs turned yet again into consumers, showcasing their purchases proudly. The *Examiner* of June 28, 1864, listed, among the usual tally of property crimes, detectives' efforts to root out a "den of negro thieves" from a Cary Street flat. Bad enough that the slaves possessed "a complete assortment of all sorts and sizes of keys"; more alarming, their room was full of "goods of considerable taste," plain signs of "high life and sumptuous living."[41] At a time when so many whites struggled to put food on the table, that image must have cut to the quick.

Increasingly direct comparisons between rising black and falling white economic fortunes—alarming evidence of slaves' purchasing power alongside grumbling about shortages and inflation—piled up ominously as the war progressed. By 1862 "the Franklin street millionaire" stood "for an hour in the market place" fruitlessly trying to "cheapen a fat turkey," while a man of lesser means "steps up, with his breeches pocket plethoric with shinplasters . . . and bears off the luscious fowl." If only "poor people would practice some self-denial," the *Examiner* whined, prices would drop, all might be sated, and social order could be restored. At this point, newspapers did not admonish enslaved Richmonders specifically, but as wartime pressures grew, so too did white Confederate resentment. By October 1863, the *Daily Dispatch* cheered strengthened gaming laws: No longer would "persons seeking a few birds for sick friends" be "elbowed out of the way by sleek negroes with hamper baskets." Or so they hoped. Striving slaves with money to spend still competed with beggared whites in the marketplace, and in the end, money talked.[42]

Cutting and caustic, comparisons mounted. "It is a well known fact that, at this time, when the white population of Richmond are compelled to strain every nerve to procure food to eat, and but few of them are able to purchase the necessary items of clothing, the negroes dress better have more money than was ever known before," the *Dispatch* scowled. Typical was the arrest of a "negro fellow, named Van Amburg," slave of Robert Davis, who had in his possession a lot of pantaloons, vests, frock coats, military coats, a gold button, a bowie knife, and fifteen linen collars. Asked where he got the clothes, he explained that he bought them from a local tailor with "money . . . made 'between times' by putting away coal, going on errands, &c."[43] So pernicious was slave spending—and, in some cases, hoarding—that Richmond editors even laid failed Confederate monetary policy at their feet. Concerned with the "exorbitant price of gold," the *Dispatch* blamed faithless white freemen who dumped property before fleeing the city and, strikingly, "the negroes, who have been hoarding Confederate currency" and then "disposing of it, preparatory to running off."[44]

Such laments rang out from Richmonders reeling under increasing economic pressure. White residents told sad tales of fortunes fractured and goods pawned. Confederate officer and journalist Thomas DeLeon noted that by 1863 the "pinch began to be felt by many who had never known it before." With income and salaries unable to match rampant inflation, "almost every one, who had any surplus portables, was willing to turn them into money." Thomas Bayne, too, remembered selling or bartering "anything we had for provisions." His wife parted with a bonnet for six hundred dollars, "taking payment in five turkeys." After selling off "all that [he] could sell, including a diamond ring," he begged friends for help.[45] In Richmond's hock shops, "bonnets rested on the sturdy legs of cavalry boots; rolls of ribbon were festooned along the crossed barrel of a rifle and the dingy cotton umbrella; while cartridges, loaves of bread, packages of groceries, gloves, letter paper, packs of cards, prayer-books and canteens, jostled each other in admirable confusion."[46] To avoid pawning possessions publicly, other Richmonders turned to their slaves. "It was no unusual thing," Sallie Putnam recalled, "to have presented at our doors a basket in the hands of a negro servant who sold on commission articles disposed of by the necessitous to obtain food." She described jewelry stores full of "diamonds and pearls, watches and valuable plate," all sold "to procure necessary articles of food and raiment." Mistresses might make these arrangements on the sly, but heightened anxiety about slaves' economic activity could very well expose shameful shedding of now superfluous luxuries.[47] In October 1863, authorities arrested two enslaved women bearing "ten baskets of clothing, a variety of jewelry, several pairs of boots, and divers[e] other articles" on suspicion of theft. The overburdened women's excuse? They had been sent out by their mistresses to "make the sales." Noting that many "were forced to part with portions of their wardrobes in order to get the necessaries of life," the mayor called for continued investigation of the matter. Though the enslaved hawkers may have escaped punishment, their owners did not. Not only did the *Examiner* publish the families' names; it chastised them for failing to give these pawners-by-proxy a note explaining their actions. In one way or another, it seemed, failing family fortunes would be exposed.[48]

Hundreds more turned to auction houses seeking to stave off ruin. "Auctions became the means of brokerage," DeLeon noted, "and their number increased to such an extent that half a dozen red flags at last dotted every block on Main street." In 1862 Confederate clerk John B. Jones offered up a "silver (lever) watch," for which he had paid twenty-five dollars. The price it brought "sufficed for fuel for a month, and a Christmas dinner," he noted gladly. His daughter surrendered a pair of earrings a year later.[49] Jones was not alone. Auction ads in city papers reveal libraries dissolved and parlors dismantled, the red flag of the auction house a common sight throughout the business district. Early on, that flash of crimson meant that blockade runners' goods had reached the city, and auction houses became places where Richmonders, especially the hated agents of "speculation" and "extortion," might find larger lots of goods like sugar, flour, and cloth for purchase.[50] As the war progressed, however, auctioneers' offerings shifted. By early 1864, "the red flag [was] displayed less frequently on Main street," speculating merchants "who were wont to gather under its scarlet folds . . . well nigh dispersed." As Wilmington, North Carolina—the Confederacy's main port of entry for blockade runners' goods—came under federal pressure, the flow of "Yankee gew-gaws" slowed. But though the "dulcet and dove-like tones of the crying auctioneer" faded, they did not disappear entirely.[51] Newspapers still listed auctions daily, though the red flag less often announced blockade runners' successes than neighbors' failures. "BEDSTEADS, MATTRESSES, TABLES, CHAIRS, CROCKERY and GLASSWARE, PARLOR and COOKING-STOVES, READY-MADE CLOTHING, BLANKETS, SHOES, HATS, DRY GOODS, GROCERIES &c., GOLD and SILVER WATCHES, JEWELERY,

&c.," cried Main Street auctioneer G. W. Willis in a January 1865 ad. Over on Fourth Street, E. B. Cook dropped the hammer on "the residence of Mrs. S. Clinely," sending a wealth of treasures—"A handsome bookcase," "Cups and Saucers, Plates and Dishes," "A choice Library of Books, embracing Histories, Works on Literature, Science, &c."—out the door. Furniture and housewares, clothing and carpets, all of Richmond seemed up for sale in 1864 and 1865.[52]

For those with extra cash, auctions meant getting goods on the cheap at neighbors' expense. Even John B. Jones, whose silver watch found its way to the auction block, occasionally bought items when the market was right. We can imagine the bustling scene—merchants lurking, workmen with notes stuffed in their pockets straining to make their voices heard, socialites quietly surveying goods under the gavel. And, strikingly, one more group: "This is another innovation that the times have brought upon us; another symptom of the breaking down of the barriers that, until this war, kept the negro in his proper sphere," the *Examiner* warned. During the Confederacy's last worrisome winter, the "gathering of negroes at the auctions" had become too much to bear. Using "grossly improper language" in the "presence of, and even to, white women," slaves seemed a social nuisance and a political threat. How they rollicked at these spectacles of dismantled wealth remains lost to history. Glad carousing and rough talk, perhaps? Subtle digs at masters' failing fortunes? White Richmonders heard far worse, city papers told: full-throated assertions of slaves' economic power. "Now ladies and gentlemen at auctions are forced to bid in competition with swathy negroes, who monopolize the most eligible positions and claim the nod of the auctioneer," the *Examiner* lamented. "Not an auction is held but the negro element is largely developed and some darky 'Mrs. Toodles' is always around enjoying the first pick and putting her label on the goods of her choice." This "promiscuous selling to slaves without permission of their owners," the paper reminded readers for the hundredth time, was a violation of city ordinances. But truly that was the least of their troubles.[53]

Richmond's slaves had long feared the gavel's fall, auctions dispersing family and friends south and west at masters' whims. Now city masters were stricken. Livelihoods buffeted by fickle crops and shaky markets, white southerners had experienced loss before. This time was different. For "those who had anything to sell," pawnshops and auction houses allowed city residents "to live."[54] But at what cost? White misfortune and black opportunity converged at the point of sale. Even for those free men and women who avoided the auctioneer's mocking patter, the sight of slaves carting off Confederates' treasures must have been deeply troubling.

Dallas Tucker, a young boy during the war, understood this convergence well. Years after Appomattox, he recalled Richmond's fall. As Yankee soldiers moved in, he and his fellows roamed Richmond's streets, an "inconsiderable sum of $500" of inflated Rebel currency in his pocket to procure food for his family's table. Black-eyed peas at $25 per quart, a square of mutton given by a "kindly" butcher for $250, the little Rebel handed over his bills and dropped the goods back home. With the remaining bit of cash in hand, he "sallied forth" once again, facing a wall of fire as the city began to burn. Equally imposing was "the gathered crowd of hungry, despairing people" he met, swarming "pell-mell" into the city's warehouses. Joining the mob, Tucker raced from building to building, scrambling to street level when the blaze came too near. "We had all filled our hands, our pockets, and our arms with such things as we could find," he remembered, and then gathered in an alley to sort out the booty. But there would be no reward that day. All scattered as the cry rang out: "The Yankees are coming." Tucker "took to [his] heels," the only item salvaged from the pile a "pair of rough, tanned, brogan shoes, such as corn-field hands might wear."[55]

Hours later, Tucker made his way to the capitol and there, hidden behind a tree, watched the Union's banner rise "on the flag-pole above, where the Stars and Bars had floated for years." In that moment, he realized, he was witnessing the "Alpha and Omega—the beginning and the end—of the Southern Confederacy in old Virginia." He thought back to family and fortune lost and his "heart . . . filled with bitter hate," his lips "pour[ing] maledictions on our triumphant foes." With nothing but a pocketful of worthless currency and a pair of shoes once bound for a poor slave's feet, the defeated boy headed home, steeling himself for tough times ahead.[56]

Ruined whites, rampaging Yankees, rejoicing blacks, slaves no more: In the weeks and months after Richmond's fall, defeated Confederates found all their worst fears realized, a rough, strange, humiliating shoe placed finally on the other foot. Worn by war, the economic, social, and political bonds of the internal economy so carefully tended in mastery's heyday had finally burst asunder. However flawed and unfinished the revolution of Reconstruction would turn out, there was no going back from here.

NOTES

1. *Richmond Daily Dispatch,* April 12, 1864.
2. Ibid., April 6, 1864. See also *Daily Richmond Enquirer,* April 6, 1864.
3. *Richmond Daily Dispatch,* April 6, 1864. See also *Daily Richmond Enquirer,* April 6, 1864; *Daily Richmond Examiner,* April 14, 1864. In the end, Grandison suffered twenty-five lashes at the hands of the Mayor's Court and was released at large. Six months later, though, Grandison found himself before the mayor once again, charged not with possessing stolen goods but with "standing in the store of a white person [in this case, his owner's confectionary shop], selling to slaves and bartering with negroes generally." No whipping this time, the mayor decreed, with the owner's promise that the entrepreneurial slave would be sent to the batteries to do his part to bolster the Confederacy's flagging defenses. *Daily Richmond Examiner,* October 7, 1864. See also *Richmond Daily Dispatch,* October 7, 1864.
4. The most comprehensive treatment of Richmond during the Civil War is Emory M. Thomas, *The Confederate State of Richmond: A Biography of the Capital* (Austin: University of Texas Press, 1971). For other narratives, see Ernest B. Furgurson, *Ashes of Glory: Richmond at War* (New York: Vintage, 1996); Nelson Lankford, *Richmond Burning: The Last Days of the Confederate Capital* (New York: Penguin, 2002); Gregg D. Kimball, *American City, Southern Place: A Cultural History of Antebellum Richmond* (Athens: University of Georgia Press, 2000), 217–52.
5. Though many historians have analyzed the famed Richmond Bread Riots, the most thoughtful is Michael B. Chesson, "Harlots or Heroines: A New Look at the Richmond Bread Riot," *Virginia Magazine of History and Biography* 92 (April 1984): 131–75. For more recent coverage, see Stephanie McCurry, *Confederate Reckoning: Power and Politics in the Civil War South* (Cambridge, MA: Harvard University Press, 2010), 178–217.
6. Scholarship on the internal economy of the slave South is extensive and complex. For a summary, with an explication of my own views, see Kathleen M. Hilliard, *Masters, Slaves, and Exchange: Power's Purchase in the Old South* (New York: Cambridge University Press, 2014).
7. Lawrence T. McDonnell has argued that bondpeople's economic activities in the antebellum period could bring the lives of poor whites and the enslaved into convergence, that the market was a liminal space in which money was master and the alienating nature of commodity exchange might have eroded social hierarchies. This chapter argues that market exchange—and the deteriorating Confederate economy, in particular—made that sort of leveling a reality. Lawrence T. McDonnell, "Work, Culture, and Society in the Slave South, 1790–1861," in *Black and White Cultural Interaction in the Antebellum South,* ed. Ted Ownby (Jackson: University Press of Mississippi, 1993), 125–47.
8. For a particularly illuminating study of this intersection of licit and illicit trade, see Sudhir Alladi Venkatesh, *Off the Books: The Underground Economy of the Urban Poor* (Cambridge, MA: Harvard University Press, 2006).
9. Thomas, *Confederate State of Richmond,* 73–74.
10. Edward M. Alfriend, "Social Life in Richmond during the War," *Cosmopolitan* 11 (1891): 229–32; Sallie Brock Putnam, *Richmond during the War: Four Years of Personal Observation* (New York: G. W. Carleton, 1867), 250–57, 270; C. Vann Woodward, ed., *Mary Chesnut's Civil War* (New

Haven, CT: Yale University Press, 1981), 167. Though boosters bragged that few Richmonders descended to beggary, calls for poor relief increasingly animated city discourse. For an extended discussion on poverty and poor relief in Confederate Richmond, see Elna C. Green, *This Business of Relief: Confronting Poverty in a Southern City, 1740–1940* (Athens: University of Georgia Press, 2003), 68–84.

11. John Gottfried Lange, "The Changed Name, or the Shoemaker of the Old and New World, Thirty Years in Europe and Thirty Years in America," ca. 1870–1880, typescript, trans. Ida S. Windmeuller, VHS, 143, 171 (first quotation), 147 (second quotation), 178 (third, fifth, and sixth quotations), 181 (fourth quotation), 183 (seventh quotation). The translator includes a question mark after "battery," apparently unsure of the translation. Whatever he produced, the entrepreneurial Lange clearly sought out ways to make cash and feed his family in tough times.

12. John B. Jones, *A Rebel War Clerk's Diary at the Confederate States Capital* (Philadelphia: J. B. Lippincott, 1866), 1:217 (first and second quotations), 266 (third quotation), 340 (fourth quotation).

13. Emma Mordecai Diary, 1864–1865, typescript, folder 104, Mordecai Family Papers, SHC, 62 (first quotation), 60 (second quotation), 71, 78, 80, 85. For a more detailed discussion of deprivation on the Confederate home front, see Mary Elizabeth Massey, *Ersatz in the Confederacy: Shortages and Substitutes on the Southern Homefront* (Columbia: University of South Carolina Press, 1952).

14. Thomas, *Confederate State of Richmond,* 69, 168. Richmond's main newspapers—the *Daily Dispatch,* the *Enquirer,* the *Examiner,* and the *Whig*—covered the daily proceedings of the Mayor's Court, where most minor property crimes were tried. Aside from these newspaper reports, no records from the Mayor's Court remain. The mayor often referred more serious crimes to the city's Hustings Court. Though the Library of Virginia possesses these records, they are of little value for detailed information about alleged crimes, because they list little more than identifying information and verdict for each case. Thomas, *Confederate State of Richmond,* 133, 199.

15. Midori Takagi, *"Rearing Wolves to Our Own Destruction": Slavery in Richmond, Virginia, 1782–1865* (Charlottesville: University Press of Virginia, 1999), 124–44. The phrase "independent slave community" derives from the title of Takagi's fifth chapter, "The Formation of an Independent Slave Community," 96–123.

16. Ibid., 139.

17. By this I mean to differentiate my views from those of Stephanie McCurry, whose analysis of these sources of Confederate defeat in *Confederate Reckoning* places less stress on the narrowly military fortunes of the South.

18. In this sense, the convergence of gaze between falling whites and rising blacks made the "moment of truth" described by scholars like James L. Roark and Willie Lee Rose more palpable and vexing. See Roark, *Masters without Slaves: Southern Planters in the Civil War and Reconstruction* (New York: Norton, 1978); and Rose, *Slavery and Freedom* (New York: Oxford, 1982), esp. 73–89.

19. Woodward, *Mary Chesnut's Civil War,* 432 (first and second quotations), 434 (third quotation).

20. *Richmond Daily Dispatch,* October 4, 1862 (first and fourth through seventh quotations);

and October 6, 1863 (second and third quotations). For editorial comment on Richmond's transformation into "a noisy, reckless and bloated metropolis of vice," see *Daily Richmond Examiner,* January 25, 1862. For further discussion of "crime and robbery" run rampant in Richmond, see Murdoch John McSween, *Confederate Incognito: The Civil War Reports of "Long Grabs," a.k.a. Murdoch John McSween, 26th and 35th North Carolina Infantry,* ed. E. B. Munson (Jefferson, NC: McFarland, 2013), 65, 76–77.

21. Putnam, *Richmond during the War,* 264.

22. *Richmond Daily Dispatch,* January 13, 1865 (first through third quotations); *Daily Richmond Examiner,* January 13, 1865 (fourth quotation).

23. *Richmond Daily Dispatch,* December 3, 1864.

24. Ibid., February 16, 1864 (first quotation); Jones, *Rebel War Clerk's Diary,* 2:150 (second and third quotations).

25. Woodward, *Mary Chesnut's Civil War,* 544 (first and second quotations), 432 (third quotation), 132, (fourth and seventh through twelfth quotations), 101 (fifth and sixth quotations).

26. By 1863 civic institutions were warning of this growing threat. In October 1863, Mayor Joseph Mayo cautioned that enslaved hack drivers were perpetrating or aiding burglaries throughout the city. *Richmond Daily Dispatch,* October 23, 1863. In November 1863, the City Council acted, strengthening "the Ordinance Concerning Wagons, Drays, Carts, &c.," toughening licensing requirements, and placing limits on slave and free black use of such conveyances. Richmond City Council, Minutes, November 30, 1863, in Louis H. Manarin, ed., *Richmond at War: The Minutes of the City Council, 1861–1865* (Chapel Hill: University of North Carolina Press, 1966), 396.

27. *Richmond Daily Dispatch,* January 31, 1865.

28. For a description of activity around the railroad depot, see W. C. Corsan, *Two Months in the Confederate States: An Englishman's Travels through the South,* ed. Benjamin H. Trask (Baton Rouge: Louisiana State University Press, 1996), 74.

29. *Daily Richmond Examiner,* October 28, 1864; *Richmond Daily Dispatch,* March 28, 1865 (quotation). For other examples of such schemes, see *Richmond Daily Dispatch,* February 18, 27, 1862; April 16, 1864; and January 24, 1865.

30. *Richmond Daily Dispatch,* August 7, 1863.

31. Ibid., December 15, 1863.

32. Ibid.; Putnam, *Richmond during the War,* 264.

33. *Richmond Daily Dispatch,* October 13, 1864 (first quotation); April 23, 1864; *Daily Richmond Examiner,* August 31, 1863; *Richmond Daily Dispatch,* June 6, 1863; *Daily Richmond Examiner,* October 26, 1863 (second quotation).

34. *Daily Richmond Examiner,* May 22, 1862.

35. In *Confederate Reckoning,* Stephanie McCurry aptly argues for a "politics of subsistence" on the home front, but only attributes such maneuvering to interactions involving soldiers' wives. Such analysis better suits Richmond slaves' efforts during the war than the interpretation of unconflicted slave agency she offers. Where McCurry sees a groundswell of resistance, I argue that Richmond slaves aimed to exploit old economic and political connections within the city rather than break them immediately. McCurry, *Confederate Reckoning,* 133–77, 218–357.

36. *Richmond Daily Dispatch,* November 30, 1861 (first quotation); April 19, 1864 (second and fourth quotations); *Daily Richmond Examiner,* April 18, 1864 (third quotation); *Richmond Daily Dispatch,* February 1, 1864 (fifth quotation).

37. *Richmond Daily Dispatch,* December 19, 1863.

38. Ibid., December 23, 1863.

39. Ibid., December 30, 1863.

40. Richmond City Council, Minutes, October 10, 1864, in Manarin, *Richmond at War,* 519; *Richmond Daily Examiner,* October 19, 1864. See also ibid., October 11, 1864.

41. *Daily Richmond Examiner,* June 28, 1864.

42. Ibid., March 10, 1862; *Richmond Daily Dispatch,* October 20, 1863.

43. *Richmond Daily Dispatch,* June 11, 1864 (quotations); June 13, 1864; *Daily Richmond Enquirer,* June 11, 1864.

44. *Richmond Daily Dispatch,* January 18, 1865.

45. Thomas C. DeLeon, *Four Years in Rebel Capitals: An Inside View of Life in the Southern Confederacy, from Birth to Death; from Original Notes, Collated in the Years 1861 to 1865* (Mobile, AL: Gossip, 1892), 236; Thomas Livingston Bayne, "Life in Richmond, 1863–1865," *Confederate Veteran* 30 (1922): 100.

46. DeLeon, *Four Years in Rebel Capitals,* 237.

47. Putnam, *Richmond during the War,* 253.

48. *Daily Richmond Enquirer,* October 21, 1863 (first quotation); *Richmond Daily Dispatch,* October 21, 1863 (second and third quotations).

49. DeLeon, *Four Years in Rebel Capitals,* 236 (first and second quotations); Jones, *Rebel War Clerk's Diary,* 1:224–25 (third and fourth quotations), 274.

50. *Daily Richmond Examiner,* March 30, 1864.

51. Ibid., January 5, 1864.

52. These descriptions of auction advertisements come from the *Richmond Daily Dispatch,* January 19, 1865, but dozens of advertisement appeared weekly in the city's papers in 1864 and 1865.

53. *Daily Richmond Examiner,* December 2, 1864 (first and fifth through seventh quotations); *Richmond Whig and Public Advertiser,* January 3, 1865 (second through fourth quotations).

54. DeLeon, *Four Years in Rebel Capitals,* 236.

55. Dallas Tucker, "The Fall of Richmond: Graphic Descriptions of Events of Evacuation-Day," *Southern Historical Society Papers* 29 (1901): 157–58.

56. Ibid., 159.

THE PROBLEM OF AUTONOMY

Toward a Postliberal History

ANTHONY E. KAYE

For the past forty years, historians of the United States have strained to think beyond the framework of liberalism. Practitioners of the new social history were determined to break up a consensus history that insisted liberal thought was the only political thought the United States had ever had.[1] Yet new social histories have had a way of doubling back unwittingly toward liberalism. Historians of republicanism, for example, attributed this ideology to so many different groups in so many variations that critics ultimately questioned whether it differed from liberalism at all.[2] Recently, some scholars have scrutinized how liberalism is inscribed in social historians' own analytical categories, namely race and agency. Slavery has figured prominently in these inquiries. Race, Barbara J. Fields argues, originated in the early republic as an ideological solution to the contradiction between a nation founded on the practice of slavery and the principle that all men are created equal. Race is an ideology, not an analytical category that scholars can invoke to explain history; it holds no answers for historians, only questions.[3] Agency, writes Walter Johnson, is an abstraction that elides the conditions of enslavement, the internal politics of the enslaved, and any collective action that failed to conform to the model of "the self-determining liberal individual."[4] The pages to come focus on a particular concept of agency: autonomy. They contribute to the groundwork of a postliberal historiography by interrogating the many meanings and constitutive character of autonomy in both liberal theory and revisionist literature on slavery.

Historians of slavery in the United States began writing about autonomy in reply to the Elkins thesis. Stanley M. Elkins famously argued that slavery was a total institution, analogous to Nazi concentration camps, that stripped the slaves of every remnant of African culture and attachments to any significant other but the master.[5] During the 1970s, revisionist historians refuted Elkins point by point, documenting in rich, empirical studies the ties of kinship that constituted the extended slave family, a vital African American culture redolent with African motifs, and innumerable acts of slave resistance. For John W. Blassingame, George P. Rawick, Sterling Stuckey, Lawrence W. Levine, and Deborah Gray White, among many other revisionists, autonomy was a useful heuristic device for synthesizing these disparate social practices into "the slave community" that stood between slaves and masters' supposedly absolute power.[6]

Revisionist historians engaged in a spirited debate about the degree of slaves' autonomy. Peter Kolchin offered one of the most creative and concrete critiques of autonomy in his comparison of Russian serfdom and southern slavery. "In short," he concluded, "communal independence rested on economic autonomy." From that standpoint, the peasant commune—the *obshchina*—provided a stronger foundation than the informal recognition of slave families and of their title to garden plots. The commune exercised powerful collective authority over the property rights of both serfs and noble lords. It distributed inheritances among serf families, determined the rents they owed their lords, and laid the basis for a common-law recognition of serfs' family property, including their title to land. The lords, in contrast to southern slaveholders, who had untrammeled rights over their human property, could not sell serfs apart from their land.[7] Revisionist historians have proved beyond cavil that slaves formed enduring families; struggled with slaveholders across a spectrum of resistance from absconding to insurrection; engaged in extensive independent production and brisk trade; and created a brilliant oral culture of jokes, stories, songs, and sermons. Autonomy has outlived its usefulness not because the empirical claims of revisionist historiography are wrong but because they are proved.

The Elkins thesis has few defenders today, yet the edifice of autonomy erected by the revisionists still stands. In a recent comparative history of North American slavery, David Brion Davis's synthesis of the literature on antebellum slave society is true to the state of the field, where scholars are coming alive to the inadequacies of autonomy but cannot let it go. Although he notes, "Some writers have exaggerated the autonomy" of slave culture, the concept seeps into his account through metaphors of enclosure. "African American culture could flourish in a largely black world," preserve "crucial areas of life and thought from white control or domination," and create "a sanctuary of human dignity."[8] Recent work continues to stake new claims for the autonomy of slaves in new subfields and new locales: in the North, on rivers from the Atlantic coast to the Mississippi, and among the Seminoles and, by some accounts, the Cherokee. Historians of slavery elsewhere in the Americas did not have much truck with autonomy until recently, yet as historians trained in the United States venture into the Atlantic world, the concept is entering the literature on the Caribbean as well. This old conceptual framework is embedded in important and otherwise innovative approaches, such as the diasporic interpretation of slave culture. Arguments that Africans in the Americas recreated practices and systems of belief from their homelands are predicated on the notion that slaves could build a culture of their own making on a foundation of autonomy. "The pursuit of African history into the diaspora," writes Paul E. Lovejoy in a seminal essay, "demonstrates how slaves could create a world that was largely autonomous from white, European society."[9]

This chapter challenges writers of American history to move beyond the liberal framework of autonomy. Several scholars have explicitly challenged its usefulness for the study of slave society in trenchant criticisms of other analytical categories.[10] One limitation of "the resistance paradigm," Dylan C. Penningroth writes, is that "it implicitly presumes that autonomy is what oppressed people want, but as observers of both continents have indicated, autonomy is not a universal goal."[11] Yet the concept of autonomy persists in no small measure because it has not received sustained scrutiny from either its champions or its critics. This chapter elaborates some of the varied meanings of autonomy by comparing how it is used in the historiography of antebellum slavery and in liberal theory, then points toward a postliberal historiography of slavery by sketching some of the insights historians have gleaned from theories that break down the dichotomy of agency and structure.

One would never know from the historiography of slavery that autonomy is a defining concept of liberalism. Liberal thinkers from the Enlightenment to the present day have posited autonomy as a prerequisite for the exercise of reason; for self-legislating individuals who can think freely, make moral choices, keep promises, and pursue their own course of self-development; for a public sphere where citizens justly adjudicate claims on society. Amid many disagreements among different strands of liberalism, liberal thinkers agree that autonomy is a necessary condition for the rational individual, justice, even liberal society itself. A survey of autonomy in the work of several liberal theorists brings to light fundamental assumptions and characteristic moves in the historiography of antebellum slavery.[12] These thinkers remind us, too, how deeply the concept of autonomy is embedded in liberal thought and, in turn, how deeply liberalism is inscribed in revisionist writing on slavery. Liberal theory suggests, in sum, that the concept of autonomy is anachronistic to slavery and thus underscores the need for historians to fashion new frameworks for the interpretation of slavery.

The new social history shared a formative impulse with the original formulation of autonomy in embracing the moral capacities of ordinary people. In *Grounding for the Metaphysics of Morals*, Immanuel Kant derives the concept of autonomy from maxims of popular morality, reformulated in terms of increasingly refined modes of thought—practical reason, pure practical reason. Kant's method, like the new social historians', works "from the bottom up." In substance, however, Kant reveals an arresting contradiction in the revisionist historiography of slavery: Autonomy is, from its first elaboration in liberal theory, a conception of *freedom*. This is the crux of Kant's theory of morality, announced in the heading of the concluding section: "*The Concept of Freedom is the Key for an Explanation of the Autonomy of the Will.*"[13] This is the foundation of the common man's capacity to act rationally and morally.

If a conception of freedom is a problematic framework for the interpretation of slavery, this quality of autonomy nevertheless creeps into writing about slavery. Slaves belonging to a conscientious evangelical planter in the Sea Islands enjoyed "a freedom of spirit that was not crushed by the confines of slavery; they had within their little island world a cultural freedom." William Wells Brown, who later became a leading abolitionist, was typical of slaves on the move, "freed from the personal domination" of masters in "moments of autonomy." Such claims offer little help in understanding slaves' struggles. For if slaves gained freedom in slavery, we can hardly make sense of enslaved people who ran away to the North, such as Brown, planned revolts, or left owners en masse during the Civil War.

In the literature on slave resistance, Kant's formulation of autonomy has other disturbing implications when scholars conceptualize slaves in terms of agency and structure. In this duality, historians, indeed scholars in all the human sciences, imagine social action in a field where an agent encounters society as a series of constraints. Theorists, especially sociologists, have long debated what counts as structure, whether it includes not only institutions of the state but also such intangible features of society as ideology, morals, and manners. Much scholarship in the humanities and social sciences amounts to an account of how agents confront, withdraw from, or maneuver around such social structures. In the historiography of slavery, slaves confront slaveholders, slaveholders' discipline, their paternalism, their Christianity, their expectations of mastery. Historians array slaves' actions—from revolt and other forms of violence to running away and other forms of everyday resistance, such as backtalk, complaint, and other forms of more-or-less willing obedience—along a spectrum of resistance and accommodation. The achievement of the revisionist literature on resistance was to replace static interpretations of slave personality, the Sambo thesis of Elkins, with a dynamic understanding that any slave was capable of acts of rebellion and obedience and everything in between.

If the dichotomy of agency and structure tends to array resistance along a spectrum from rebellion to obedience, however, Kantian autonomy makes actions along the spectrum tending toward obedience increasingly problematic. For the freedom held out to all agents by Kant's notion of autonomy as freedom of the will is choice. Even an agent acting under severe constraint—an official compelled to carry out the policy of his government in Kant's famous example—can act autonomously if he chooses to do what he is told for his own reason. Revisionist historians similarly posit a slave who, despite all the exactions of bondage, could at any moment choose to rebel. Yet if slaves had autonomy in the Kantian sense of free will, it also follows that when slaves obeyed their masters, they chose accommodation, which is to say, slaves chose to accommodate slavery. This comes uncomfortably close to saying slaves chose slavery, but of course, revisionist historians believed no such thing, which is why they wrote a good deal more about rebellion than accommodation. Autonomy equipped the revisionists well to write about revolts but left them no vocabulary to make sense of slaves' methods of struggle that fell short of rebellion. The increasingly conventional usage of *enslaved people* pushes back against the counterintuitive implications of autonomy by underscoring that they were neither born nor chose to be slaves but were made slaves. Historians who have written about everyday slavery have had to go further and eschew both the concept of autonomy and the dichotomy of agency and structure.

John Stuart Mill elaborated the most capacious conception of autonomy in classical liberal thought. Unlike Kant, Mill defines morality in terms of consequences rather than intent and elaborates rigorous conditions for the exercise of autonomy in both the private and public spheres. Mill reformulated British utilitarianism by recalibrating Jeremy Bentham's ethics of the pleasure principle. Instead of seeking justice in actions promoting the least pain and the most pleasure, Mill values actions for the quality as well as the quantity of pleasure they afford. His revisionist utilitarianism reformulates autonomy in terms of "individuality" and "development" or "the free development of individuality." Moreover, he outlines interlocking preconditions for autonomy in "security" and "liberty." And he defines security broadly with a correspondingly broad claim on society for protection. Security means "making safe for us the very groundwork of our existence," and it must be provided "uninterruptedly": liberty, "without hindrance, either physical or moral from . . . fellow-men." Liberty of self-development, encompassing liberty of thought, expression, association, is the sine qua non of autonomy. "The only freedom which deserves the name," he writes, "is that of pursuing our own good in our own way."[14]

Slaves, of course, enjoyed none of Mill's prerequisites for autonomy. He insists on slaves' lack of security in numerous works. In *Principles of Political Economy*, slavery is a stark exception to the common interests of capital and labor. Where slaves could be bought cheaply in numbers, "self-interest [would] recommend working the slaves to death, and replacing them by importation in preference to the slow and expensive process of breeding them."[15] His absolutist notion of security dispelled any illusions that American planters were better than their West Indian peers. In two essays urging Britons to support the North during the Civil War, Mill argued that one need not determine whether the norm in the South was better represented by "the Legrees or the St. Clairs" (Harriet Beecher Stowe's representative figures of the worst and best of the master class, respectively) to know that American slaveholders were guilty of the worst atrocities imaginable. Slavery was not just "the name of one social evil among many others" but rather "the summing-up and concentration of them all." When people are held under the worst "oppression," he wrote, "they are compared to slaves," and "the despots" to "slave-masters, or slave-drivers."[16] Throughout *The Subjection of Women*, Mill stigmatized modern relations of gender with indignant comparisons to slavery.[17] Indeed, slavery served admirably as a metaphor for all manner of oppressions in Mill's writings—in addition to political despotism and gender inequality, the impressment of British sailors, deference to customary authority, repression of individual thought— because slavery distilled oppression itself.[18] Mill's preconditions for autonomy are expansive precisely because he understood that the influence of society is so invasive. They also make his theory anachronistic to a slave society, where his preconditions for autonomy were so sorely lacking.

Mill's expansive conception of autonomy, with its correspondingly exacting preconditions and his frank statements about the despotism of slavery, suggest why revisionist historians prefer not to write much about slaveholders. A robust concept of autonomy would not bear up well to a straightforward reckoning with the slaveholders' onslaught. Although historians of the slave community have been accused of romanticizing slave society, they are no more inclined than Mill to regard slavery as a school for self-development. No one would argue that antebellum slavery afforded slaves the security that Mill insisted autonomy requires, much less met the standards of his expansive understanding of liberty. Rather than confront owners' many encroachments on slaves head-on, most historians secure the preconditions of autonomy by removing slaveholders from the analysis at the outset. The title of Rawick's landmark volume *From Sundown to Sunup* all but announces this sleight of hand. After all, slaves worked under owners and their agents from sunup to sundown. The convention of writing about slaves in the absence of slaveholders has become so common that historians seldom bother to justify the procedure.

Charles Taylor offers further clues to why the concept of autonomy became an unexamined and unchallenged axiom in revisionist historiography. In *The Ethics of Authenticity,* he objects to what he calls the "liberalism of neutrality," like that of Kant, which is neutral on the ends of a good society and consigns all our ends to a private realm beyond the judgment of others. Because liberalism casts autonomy as a neutral good, we tend not to acknowledge autonomy as a subjective ideal at all, nor do we feel entitled to judge, let alone criticize, those who hold, express, or act on this ideal. For historians, as for all thinkers, in Taylor's view, the silence surrounding autonomy is reinforced by the discourse of social science, which eschews moral ideals.[19] For historians of slavery, then, the discourse of social science obscures that the concept of autonomy is neither a social scientific concept nor an analytical category but a moral ideal, and a highly subjective one at that.

Democratic theorist Robert Dahl sheds light on a tendency in revisionist historiography to institutionalize slave society. For Dahl, the problem of political autonomy is at the crux of the *Dilemmas of Pluralist Democracy*. He defines autonomy in terms of one actor's independence from another's control. People are under the control of another when their actions conform to "the preferences, desires, or intentions of one or more actors." Autonomous organizations, he observes, are necessary to democratic processes and an intrinsic result of the rise of democratic nation-states. The fundamental problem for such states is to at once control these organizations and afford them autonomy. Hence Dahl's subtitle, *Autonomy vs. Control*. Slavery and autonomy are not, to his way of thinking, mutually exclusive. He briefly cites slaves and owners as examples of classes who might theoretically have autonomy from the other's control. Yet for Dahl, autonomous actors are necessarily institutional actors: unions, corporations, political parties, local government, branches of government (the executive, the legislature, the judiciary), and the like. The institutional nature of autonomous actors is critical because Dahl believes autonomy requires them to have sovereignty over their respective domains. That requires the state to recognize the autonomy of such institutions. After all, nation-states can only exercise sovereignty over all spheres if the sovereign power of autonomous institutions is conferred by the state itself. So the most pressing dilemmas of pluralist democracy, in Dahl's judgment, are resolved by grants of the state, such as regional autonomy, national independence, or constitutional reform.[20]

Slaves in the United States were in no position to exercise the political autonomy contemplated by Dahl. Elkins had defined slavery as a problem in American institutional and intellectual life, as he put it in the subtitle of his book. In reply, revisionist historians have been keen to suggest the institutional character of the slave's autonomy. This is the claim implicitly staked in phrases that objectify slave society in monolithic terms, such as *The Slave Community*, *The Black Family*, or *Slave Religion: The "Invisible Institution."*[21] Although Dahl counts families among institutions that can exercise "relative autonomy," slave families would not qualify from his standpoint because they crucially lacked recognition by the state. During the 1660s, Virginia and Maryland adopted laws that children born of unions between free people and slaves acquired the status of the mother—free if she was so, slave if she was enslaved. The rule of maternal descent protected slaveholding men's undisputed right to their bondwomen's children and their sexual access to slave women. To recognize slave marriage by law would have given away what slaveholders had appropriated by this legal definition of slavery. Legal recognition of slave marriages would necessarily have conferred exclusive conjugal rights to spouses and constrained slaveholders' right to sell families apart. So it was that marriage between slaves was unrecognized in southern statutes and explicitly denied by southern jurists.[22] From Dahl's perspective, slave law resolved the tension between slaves' control over their families and slaveholders' control over their human property not by granting autonomy to slaves but by preserving slaveholders' control. Political autonomy requires a recognition by the state that the democracy of the Old South, such as it was, steadfastly denied to slaves.

Eugene D. Genovese's contradictory stances on autonomy point to the difficulties of writing a postliberal history of slavery. Over the years, he variously scored liberal historians of slavery, Marxist social historians, new social historians, black nationalists, and white new leftists, all for conceding too much to liberalism. In a broad critique of social history, Genovese and Elizabeth Fox-Genovese castigated historians of slave culture for eliding the master class in the "emphasis on black achievement and autonomy" and dismissed "this liberal view" along with all of its "reactionary moral and political implications."[23] Genovese's objection to autonomy followed logically from his arguments for paternalism. John Rawls, the leading modern exponent of contractarian liberalism, articulated a consensus in liberal theory that paternalism and autonomy are irreconcilable, "for slaves are not counted as capable of having duties or obligations. Laws that prohibit the abuse and maltreatment of slaves are not founded on claims made by slaves in their own behalf, but on claims originating either from slaveholders or from the general interests of society (which do not include the interests of slaves)."[24] Contrary to Rawls, in *Roll, Jordan, Roll* Genovese portrayed paternalism as a set of reciprocal rights and duties accepted but differently interpreted by master and slave. Yet Genovese was perfectly consistent with Rawls to the extent that the master class formulated the rules of paternalism based on masters' estimate of what was best for their slaves, not on what slaves thought was best for themselves.

A close reading of Genovese illustrates his own crooked path to autonomy. Since the refutation of the Elkins thesis by revisionist historians, autonomy has retained some of its currency in opposition to Genovese's formulation of paternalism. Yet Genovese, too, conceptualized the master-slave relation squarely within the revisionist framework of autonomy. "At the crux of the master-slave relation," Genovese wrote, were the master's determination to reduce slaves to an extension of his own will and the slaves' struggle "to assert themselves as autonomous human beings."[25] His work reminds us that appropriating theoretical frameworks from radical critiques of liberalism can also lead historians back to autonomy, in Genovese's case by way of G. W. F. Hegel and Antonio Gramsci.

The conceptual overture in part 1 of *Roll, Jordan, Roll* begins and ends with glosses on Hegel's account of lordship and bondage.[26] Hegel distills this relationship in a struggle to the death between a master and the slave who has displeased him. The master raises his hand in a fury; the slave fearfully submits; the master returns to his senses, the slave to his labor. Yet the conflict transforms both lord and bondman in how they think of themselves, their relationship, and freedom. The lord lets the bondman escape with his life, recognizes that his own consciousness is independent from the slave's, and thus achieves autonomy. The slave, for his part, also derives the notion of autonomy from the struggle, recognizes its value, but understands that autonomy is not for him. He emerges with a new self-consciousness of his dependence on his master, a new self-consciousness that he is a slave. According to Hegel, the slaves' struggle for autonomy fails, only to generate a new conception of freedom that transcends the master's after emancipation.[27]

In Genovese's version of the master-slave dialectic, the slave's struggle for autonomy is partly successful within slavery. Neither the masters nor the slaves achieved autonomy, though the slaves came closer than Hegel suggested. Paternalism intertwines them in an enmeshed relationship from which neither can escape: "Neither could express the simplest human feeling without reference to the other," Genovese wrote in the opening paragraph to his tome. During the Civil War—"The Moment of Truth," he called it—masters learned they had never known their slaves at all, especially in their desire for freedom.[28] In the slaves' appropriation of Christianity, they reaped a broad, albeit qualified, autonomy, "an autonomous spiritual life," which slaveholders regarded with contempt because it signified "that the slaves had achieved a degree of cultural and psychological autonomy." Genovese registered the slaves' partial success in their struggle for autonomy with qualifiers such as a "measure of autonomy" or, most commonly, a "degree of autonomy."[29] Genovese's assertions that slaves achieved a qualified autonomy, of course, were echoed by countless other revisionist historians.

Whereas Genovese used Hegel to conceptualize the partial success of the slaves' struggle for autonomy, he defined its political failure in Gramscian terms of hegemony: "In Gramsci's terms, they had to wage a prolonged, embittered struggle with themselves as well as with their oppressors to 'feel their strength' and to 'become conscious of their responsibility and their value.' It was not that slaves did not act like men. Rather, it was that they could not grasp their collective strength as a people and act like political men."[30] Five years earlier, in 1967, Genovese had also quoted these phrases on struggle and self-consciousness, not in reference to the slaves but in an essay arguing that Gramsci's ideas had the potential to revitalize Western Marxism and socialist parties in Europe and the United States and to lend direction and discipline to the New Left.[31]

Gramsci led Genovese back to autonomy because, though Gramsci did not theorize about autonomy per se, he used it during the 1920s as a conceptual tool in theorizing about the necessary tasks for the working class to take power in Italy. "Are intellectuals an autonomous and independent social class?" he asked in one of his most important entries on "The Formation of Intellectuals" in his prison notebooks. No, Gramsci explained, they were appended to other social classes, drawing his now familiar distinction between traditional intellectuals and organic intellectuals. Intellectuals were important lieutenants to the ruling class and played an important role in its hegemony over society, helping to secure "the 'spontaneous' consent given by the great masses of the population" and, as judicial officers of the state, to ensure "the discipline of those groups which do not 'consent.'"[32] Gramsci cast revolutionary workers' movements as "proletarians . . . struggling for industrial autonomy" and argued that, in Italy, factory committees were the most promising institution for "autonomous revolutionary action by the working class."[33] Autonomy also figured prominently in Gramsci's considerations on "the Southern Question"—Italy's own divide between an industrial North and an agrarian South. The working class needed to establish under its own leadership an alliance with southern peasants, and this would require wresting them from "the southern bloc," their domination by organic intellectuals attached to the petty and middle bourgeoisie, large-scale landowners and traditional intellectuals. This, too, was a project of autonomy in Gramsci's view: "The proletariat will destroy the southern agrarian *bloc* to the extent to which, through its Party, it succeeds in organizing ever larger masses of peasants in autonomous and independent formations."[34]

Genovese's interpretation of slaveholders' hegemony over slaves rested on Gramsci's model of an autonomous socialist party. "The autonomy of the party" was one of Gramsci's "life-long themes," Genovese wrote. "In Gramscian terms a political party is an agent of education and civilization" that schools its "followers in the principles of moral conduct, the duties, and the obligations appropriate to that order," in sum, "a system of class rule." A socialist party fulfilled this political role by fostering, first, "a rank-and-file . . . characterized by discipline and faith"; second, a leadership to give it "cohesion"; and third, "cadres, which mediate morally, physically, and intellectually between the other two."[35] Southern slaves had no autonomous political party, of course, and Genovese portrayed them in *Roll, Jordan, Roll* as specifically lacking in discipline and cohesion. Slaves, he wrote, were prone to theft, which buttressed slaveholders' confidence in their own rule and undermined the slaves' solidarity, "their self-respect and their ability to forge a collective discipline appropriate to the long-term demands of their national liberation."[36] Genovese took the drivers' measure by the yardstick of the mediating role of Gramscian party cadres. The drivers were "men between" who "strove to mediate between the Big House and the quarters" and used their "power to get more and better work for the master," yet "also . . . to raise the standard of civility, cleanliness, and morality among the people."[37] Black preachers, in Genovese's view, came closest to assuming the task of political leadership but instead took on the more practical, modest role of assuaging the slaves' self-respect: "The slaves relied on their black preachers for solace and moral guidance, but the preachers could not transform that support into political action." Taking stock of the political resources that the preachers and drivers brought to emancipation, Genovese reckoned, "An incipient autonomous black leadership had died a-borning."[38]

Genovese's crooked path to autonomy is unusual in the revisionist literature only in the length of its train of implicit analogies: between the master-slave relation in the Old South and the struggle for self-consciousness in Hegel's account of lordship and bondage; between the Old South and an underdeveloped Italy; between the slaves and Gramsci's account of a self-conscious working class; between, on the one hand, the relationship among field laborers, drivers, and preachers, and, on the other hand, workers and the leadership of a vital socialist party. And yet for all that, Genovese arrived at the same conclusion that many other revisionist historians reached by the comparatively simple implicit analogy between the slave and the liberal individual, or the slave community and liberal society: The slaves had achieved a measure or degree of autonomy.

Among all the formulations of autonomy by historians of slavery, this qualified formulation of autonomy finds the most warrant in liberal theory.[39] Feminist theorists, most notably Diana T. Meyers, have elaborated a concept of "relational autonomy" to resolve several tensions in feminism and liberalism, especially between autonomy, authenticity, and "the traditional woman." Feminists long regarded women who embraced traditional roles of wives and mothers as products of a gendered inequality in which society cultivated a psychology of dependency and self-sacrifice in women and presented these social norms as natural characteristics of femininity. During the 1980s, however, difference feminists valorized the traditional woman and reformulated her gendered roles as a set of capacities—intimacy, caring, resolving differences—that were, compared to men's capacities, different yet equal. Relational autonomy offers an account of how a woman's choice of traditional roles, though partly the product of socially reinforced beliefs, could also be autonomous, or partly so.[40]

This conception of autonomy is relational in at least three respects. It argues that social relations contribute to autonomy, or the lack of it; compares the autonomy of women and men in comparable situations; and treats autonomy as a condition that can be attained by degrees. Relational autonomy posits that one need not be entirely rational, possess perfect self-knowledge, or exercise unconstrained control over her actions to be autonomous. Rather, autonomy can be episodic, limited to a particular range of activities, and based on partial understandings of the influences that constrain one's desires, plans, and identity. One can act autonomously in certain situations, embark on certain programs autonomously, glimpse "partial insights into one's authentic self," and "gain a measure of autonomy."[41]

Relational autonomy is perhaps the most promising formulation for historians of slavery. The insistence on considering autonomy within a social framework is congenial to social historians' insistence on situating agency in the context of social relations. Theorists of relational autonomy are also interested in categories that have defined American social history—people subordinated, for instance, at the intersections of race, class, and gender.[42] Most important, relational autonomy breaks with the absolutism and universalism of liberal theory that is inimical to historicism. In liberal theory, autonomy is typically, like love, death, or tenure, an absolute state. Either you have it or feel it, or you don't; either you are, or you aren't. Relational autonomy says, on the contrary, autonomy is a process, necessarily incomplete for many people, a repertoire of skills acquired by degrees.

Revisionists inclined to press on with the concept of autonomy would do well to consider liberal feminists' suggestions that some people possess the requisite skills for autonomy, while others do not; people gain a degree of autonomy in some spheres of life, but not in others, and in relation to some people, but not to others. These implications and qualifications have eluded revisionist historians, who write as if slaves took their measure of autonomy with them wherever they went. Taking relational autonomy seriously would invite historians to specify which kinds of slaves (field laborers, house servants, bondmen, bondwomen, for instance) gained autonomy and which did not; in which arenas (work, family, religion, sociability) they gained autonomy; and in relation to whom (owners, overseers, drivers, spouses, other family members). Exploring the skills slaves needed to gain autonomy to different degrees, in different relationships, in different arenas could add welcome nuance to the revisionist account of slaves' autonomy.

Still, if relational autonomy has provocative implications for revisionists, the theory also carries assumptions that historians will find difficult to integrate with slavery. Relational autonomy, designed to fit the dilemmas of the modern homemaker, is anachronistic to slavery, too. According to Meyers, autonomy rests in part on the power to decide a range of questions about how one wants to live, including "'What line of work do I want to get into?'" Obviously, slaves were not free to answer such questions as they willed. This is why Marina A. L. Oshana is not sanguine about even the relative autonomy of slaves. For the slave has lost power over social relations that bend his will and shape his life, she argues. He always acts in full knowledge of his owner's expectation of obedience and the possibility of punishment should he act otherwise. The slave is not "self-governing because his external environment renders him incapable of functioning in a self-governing way."[43]

The comparison of autonomy in liberal theory and the historiography of slavery suggests, at a minimum, that historians who persist in employing this concept have some explaining to do. It is reasonable to expect, to begin with, that they specify which of autonomy's many meanings they have in mind and which sort of autonomy they believe slaves achieved: a narrow Kantian one in which bondpeople were able to think for themselves and do their duty for their own reasons; Mill's expansive notion of self-development; political autonomy; or liberal feminists' relational autonomy. The latter is the most promising, if only because it could help historians think concretely about who gained autonomy, in what arenas, on what terms, and to what degree. They must elaborate, moreover, how slaves gained the preconditions for autonomy spelled out by liberal theorists or how slaves achieved autonomy in the absence of its preconditions. Whatever formulation historians may adopt, it is incumbent upon them, finally, to demonstrate what they have long assumed, namely that autonomy was the slaves' primary objective.

But perhaps the time has come for historians of slavery to put an end to the eternal recurrence of autonomy. It has locked the analysis of slave society into a single conception of agency that finds little warrant among liberal theorists who have thought carefully about it. Few philosophers regard enslaved people as autonomous. Nor could they. Autonomy is, from its first formulation by Kant to its most recent iterations, a conception of freedom. Any concept devised to explain how citizens of liberal nation-states navigate the impositions of government, traditional culture, and modern civil society to live in freedom is a blunt instrument for sorting out the conditions of slaves.[44] After all, the government denied that slaves were citizens, society questioned their humanity, and the law left them not to their own devices but to their owners' devices. As a political ideal, specifically a liberal political ideal, autonomy is an ideological concept, not an analytical tool.

The clearest path to a postliberal historiography lies with approaches that break through the agency-structure opposition. No simple appropriation of any one theorist will lead the historiography of slavery beyond autonomy. Yet several historians have taken this approach from a variety of directions, such as comparative history, poststructuralist feminism, and human geography.

Studies of slaves' struggles over places are grounded in a growing field of human geography. Over the past thirty years, geographers have explored how social spaces are made, drawing eclectically on Marxism, feminism, and reflexive sociology.[45] Common to the field, though, is an insistence on moving beyond agency and structure by unhinging this dichotomy and the constant opposition it posits between actors and society. Actors do not simply take society as a given series of obstacles, Anthony Giddens has argued, but simultaneously create and recreate the conventions and institutions they confront, using them to facilitate their own ends. This "duality of structure," as Giddens calls it, is inscribed in human geography in the dynamic relationship between people and places in the making of social spaces.[46] In the human geography of slavery, slaves made and remade ties in both conflict and collaboration with slaveholders and other slaves. They made places in transit across plantation lines, between town and country, and along rivers; in the interstices between plantations, in neighborhoods, and via networks. Situating social ties in the places where slaves made them—cross-plantation marriages, neighborhood conspiracies, secret parties in hollows, woods, and other liminal spaces— reveals alliances that were contingent, conditional, and cross-cutting.[47]

Judith Butler's theory of performed identities points to another avenue beyond the liberal framework of autonomy. In *Gender Trouble,* Butler deconstructs the duality of sex and gender in feminist discourse. She dispatches autonomy in the opening paragraph as an artifact of this duality: "The radical dependency of the masculine subject on the female 'Other' suddenly exposes his autonomy as illusory." Butler disposes of the duality of agency and structure with the gendered body. The feminist conception of gender distinguished between culturally prescribed norms of femininity and masculinity as opposed to the physical nature of male and female sex. Sex is thereby essentialized as a biological fact, and gender is cast as a subjective ideology. But the category of sex, Butler argues, is subjective as well, and the duality of masculine and feminine is not inherent to bodies but imposed on them. Sex was not a material fact discovered by the human sciences but a category produced by languages, practices, and institutions in the regulation of sexuality. If there is no masculine or feminine body prior to the discourse of gender, the agent and the structure are both gendered and entirely imbricated. Sex is as much a performance as gender, the presentation of bodies engendered to make sense as male and female.[48]

Historians have used Butler's theory of performed identity to probe the instability of racism and how enslaved people contested it.[49] Although analogies between race and gender are hardly new to historical analysis, they make a good deal more sense from Butler's perspective than from that of liberal feminism. Race was not, strictly speaking, analogous to gender if the latter was, as feminists claimed, an ideological interpretation of objective physical differences. After all, scholars in the human sciences proved some time ago that physical differences alleged to distinguish people of African and European descent varied more widely within those groups than between them.[50] If the physical difference between the sexes is a discursive effect, though, as Butler argues, then the analogy between race and gender becomes revealing. The discourses of race and gender both create the facts of nature they purport to discover. In the South, hundreds of court cases turned on determinations of race, including proceedings to enforce criminal laws restricting the rights of free black people, civil cases pertaining to inheritance and other property disputes, slander suits, and freedom suits.[51]

Ariela J. Gross has shown how vexed race could become when an enslaved woman, Alexina Morrison, sued her owner for freedom on the grounds she was white, had been kidnapped and enslaved in Arkansas, and then was sold to a slaveholder in Jefferson Parish, Louisiana. Such cases often came down to judging between rival accounts of how she had performed her race, as if it were an essential, natural quality that must manifest itself, if not in her color, then in her speech and deportment. A plaintiff and her supporting witnesses told stories of her modesty, intelligence, discretion, and other qualities of white womanhood. Slaveholders and their witnesses, for their part, gave accounts of how she had performed her blackness in acts of promiscuity or indiscretion. Morrison's jailer, after she ran away in 1857, testified at trial that he was sufficiently persuaded she was white to take her into his home, to invite her to balls with his family, and to introduce her to white society.[52] Other witnesses of Morrison's told the court they had found nothing amiss in her presence at balls and had put her up for the night in their daughters' beds. As one witness testified, "she conducted herself as a white girl. She is so in her conduct and actions."[53]

Performing whiteness was a powerful mode of struggle that cannot be understood in terms of autonomy. In the three trials in Morrison's case, one jury found in her favor and two ended in hung juries, including the last to try her case. Yet the other eleven women claiming to be white whom Gross uncovered in suits against their owners all gained their freedom. Legally, none framed their arguments in the language of autonomy but instead claimed their freedom in the common terms of the contemporary discourse of race. Their manner and appearance embodied conventional standards "of white womanhood as beauty, purity, and physical and moral goodness," Gross writes, "requiring protection by honorable gentlemen."[54]

Histories that approach race as performed identity break through the dichotomy of agency and structure by taking a bead on the inextricable relationship between the performer and her audience. To gain gentlemen's protection, Walter Johnson points out, Morrison underwent the indignities of the slave market, disrobing to the waist in court and at a local hotel for jurors and local white people to gaze over her half-naked body. Dependencies between slaves and slaveholders ran both ways in the performance of whiteness. A light-skinned bondwoman sold for a premium in the slave market. For her owners to realize her value, planters had to be willing to pay dearly for the distinction of owning a woman with the virtues of white womanhood, and the slave had to perform her imagined whiteness to good effect. The value of light-skinned enslaved women, Johnson concludes, was based on "the *synergetic* whiteness of slave and slaveholder."[55]

Legal historians are also bringing to light slaves' previously unseen role as lawmakers. In cases of racial determination, Gross argues, customary understandings did not so much triumph over law as law itself was "created by a variety of lawmakers."[56] Customary standards of law often did trump statute law in the Carolinas, where county courts were less attentive to state law than to local reputation. Laura F. Edwards has shown how one customary principle, the people's peace, opened a space where people denied standing by statute influenced local legal proceedings. Slaves, as well as free black people and white women of every social rank, cut a figure in neighborhood networks of gossip, kinship, everyday social relations, and honed their local reputations. Slaves with reputations as honest and peaceable were acquitted in court on charges of theft and violence or had cases resolved favorably without trial.[57] Theories of structuration and performed identities are not the only tools available to excavate this legal history of slaves. Edwards draws her conclusions partly from recent work on slavery grounded in these theories, partly from her own eclectic reading in feminist and critical race theory, but mostly from extensive archival research.

A long-overdue comparative history of slavery in the U.S. South and West Africa offers another path beyond autonomy. Dylan Penningroth's work on family and property during the mid-nineteenth century among Akan slaves on the southern Gold Coast and slaves in the U.S. South recasts slave resistance as struggles for incorporation. Since the mid-1970s, many Africanists have interpreted slavery in West Africa as "an Institution of Marginality." Enslaved outsiders were appropriated by the Akan and many other West African societies as kinless people. Slaveholders wielded a power over slaves that was unique in societies where everyone's status depended on hierarchies of kinship. Over time, typically generations, slaves and their descendants entered into different relations with owners and were incorporated into their households, lineages, and polities as concubines or spouses, sisters or daughters, agents of their owners or owners' kin in trade or government. The rules of incorporation varied among different societies, and historians debate its extent. Recent work emphasizes the limits of incorporation and the struggles that ensued when slaves and slaveholders contested claims of belonging.[58]

As slavery expanded in southern Gold Coast and the U.S. South during the nineteenth century, kinship became increasingly prominent in the ideology of slavery. After British abolition of the slave trade in 1807, slaves formerly sold to the Americas sharply increased slaveholdings in West Africa, growing to about one-half the Akan population by 1850. Masters in southern Gold Coast distinguished among slaves in terms that emphasized the foreignness of some and belonging for others. They spoke of "bought slaves" or "northern" slaves versus "domestics" or slaves "born in the house." Slaveholders described slaves in idioms of both kinship and kinlessness, depending on their purposes: as orphans when expanding claims over their people's bodies, their labor, their belongings, and their children; as members of their own lineage to deflect claims over slaves by their wives' matrilineage.[59]

Akan slaveholders' tendency to manipulate the boundary between slavery and kinship gave slaves and their descendants a purchase on ownership of property and membership in families. Some slaveholders, rather than see their property inherited by a distant relative, bestowed titles as heads of households or lineages on a former slave. In 1844 one slave who became head of his owner's household duly settled some of its debts by selling members of his late owner's family. "Slaves established social ties all the time, including biological ties with their own masters," Penningroth writes, "and so it was *through* community and kinship, not in its absence, that slaves and masters fought their battles." Akan struggles over incorporation set in bold relief American slaves' strategies of incorporation to advance claims to family and property.[60]

Penningroth, like Edwards, is interested in how slaves made claims stick in the interstices between customary practice and written law, which recognized neither slaves' property nor their families. In theory and by statute, slaves *were* property, and people who belonged to their owner could not belong to spouses, parents, or other kin; their belongings were their owners' property, too. Among slaves, Penningroth writes, "what turned possessions into property was a complex interchange of display and acknowledgment, guided by people's shifting notions of what was customary in their neighborhood." Slaves claimed ownership over their belongings by counting their chickens when other slaves were in the quarters at evening times, wearing their "finery" to church, by talking about the state of their gardens, their horses, and other livestock.[61]

Enslaved people's relations of family and property were mutually constitutive. Many southern slaves got a start accumulating property with an inheritance from their parents. Slaves, by the same token, used property to sure up bonds of kinship. "By bequeathing property," Penningroth writes, "slaves over and over again defined not only *what* belonged to them but also *who*." Families adopted other slaves unrelated by descent who helped them make property. As the domestic slave trade systematically removed people from the Upper South to the Deep South, making and distributing property became means for strangers to incorporate themselves into an unfamiliar neighborhood. Charles Ball, separated from his wife and children in Maryland, negotiated his adoption by the family whose cabin he shared in Georgia, offering his labor and earnings in return for kinship and "a portion of the proceeds of their patch or garden." Property and kinship constituted relations of power among slaves, too. Enslaved people invoked hierarchies of kinship to command other slaves' labor, such as parents who collected pay for their children's overwork picking cotton.[62]

Historians of African slavery among American Indians in the Deep South have explored the struggle for incorporation between slaves and slaveholders.[63] As the Five Tribes—the Cherokee, the Creek, the Choctaw, the Chickasaw, and the Seminole—adopted southern ways during the nineteenth century, they also increasingly resembled West African societies with plantations and African slavery in addition to traditional systems of matrilineal descent. Barbara Krauthamer demonstrates that, for the Choctaw and the Chickasaw in eastern Mississippi, slavery transformed understandings of gender, property, and power. For slaveholding men, accumulating property in people bolstered lines of paternal descent and established individual wealth as a new basis of political power.[64] In southern Gold Coast, masters took a slave as a junior wife for similar purposes, because they could readily control her and her children. A freeborn wife, by contrast, could mobilize members of her own lineage, who could assert their own claims to her children.[65] The Choctaw and the Chickasaw drew sharp boundaries on incorporation, too, along racial lines. They increasingly defined people of African descent as black, redefining Indianness in opposition to both whiteness and blackness.[66] Choctaw and Chickasaw slaves were still contending for emancipation in 1866. The Thirteenth Amendment did not apply to Indian Territory, so the Chickasaw and the Choctaw abolished slavery by treaty with the United States. Freedmen contemplated citizenship in the United States in the summer of 1869 but instead petitioned for Choctaw and Chickasaw citizenship in September. "We consider ourselves full citizens of those nations," a convention in Skullyville resolved, "and fully entitled to all the rights, privileges, and benefits as such, the same as citizens of Indian extraction."[67]

Comparative history, poststructuralist feminism, reflexive sociology, and human geography can help historians see more in slaves than appealing likenesses of our liberal selves. These approaches, to be sure, can backtrack to autonomy. One way to pull down the edifice of autonomy, though, is to take down its scaffolding in the opposition between agency and structure. As other disciplines in the human sciences break away from this dichotomy, and historians increasingly find their interdisciplinary moorings, the avenues beyond autonomy become more accessible and multiply. Comparisons are emerging between southern, West African, and American Indian slaveries, and provocative similarities loom large. New terrains of struggle and relations of power are coming into view among slaves as well as with slaveholders: struggles for incorporation; contentions over family, property, and law in courts; everyday social networks; and neighborhoods. Slavery and the South are starting to look different.

NOTES

This chapter has benefited from suggestions by John P. Christman, Brian Fay, and participants in the 2007 annual meeting of BrANCH at Madingley Hall, Cambridge University.

1. For an influential synthesis of the consensus view of American history, see Louis Hartz, *The Liberal Tradition in America: An Interpretation of American Political Thought since the Revolution* (New York: Harcourt, Brace & World, 1955). Tellingly, Hartz found proslavery thinkers in the antebellum South the most difficult to subsume in his liberal consensus (chs. 6–7).

2. Isaac Kramnick, *Republicanism and Bourgeois Radicalism: Political Ideology in Late Eighteenth-Century England and America* (Ithaca, NY: Cornell University Press, 1990); Daniel T. Rodgers, "Republicanism: The Career of a Concept," *Journal of American History* 79 (June 1992): 11–38.

3. Barbara J. Fields, "Slavery, Race, and Ideology in the United States of America," in *Race-craft: The Soul of Inequality in American Life*, by Karen E. Fields and Barbara J. Fields (London: Verso, 2012), 111–48. See also 1–74, 261–90; and Barbara J. Fields, "Whiteness, Racism, and Identity," *International Labor and Working-Class History* 60 (Fall 2001): 48–56.

4. Walter Johnson, "Slavery, Reparations, and the Mythic March of Freedom," *Raritan* 27 (Fall 2007): 44, 50–54 (quotation 50). See also Walter Johnson, "On Agency," *Journal of Social History* 37 (Fall 2003): 113–24, esp. 115; Walter Johnson, "Agency: A Ghost Story," in *Slavery's Ghost: The Problem of Freedom in the Age of Emancipation,* by Richard Follett, Eric Foner, and Walter Johnson (Baltimore: Johns Hopkins University Press, 2011), 8–30.

5. Stanley M. Elkins, *Slavery: A Problem in American Institutional and Intellectual Life,* 3rd ed. (Chicago: University of Chicago Press, 1976).

6. John W. Blassingame, *The Slave Community: Plantation Life in the Antebellum South,* rev. ed. (New York: Oxford University Press, 1979), 90–91, 105–6, 130–31, 145–48, 249–50, 287–90; George P. Rawick, *From Sundown to Sunup: The Making of the Black Community* (Westport, CT: Greenwood, 1972), 8–12; Lawrence W. Levine, *Black Culture and Black Consciousness: Afro-American Folk Thought from Slavery to Freedom* (New York: Oxford University Press, 1977), xi, 29–30, 33–37, 70, 96–97; Deborah Gray White, *Ar'n't I a Woman? Female Slaves in the Plantation South* (New York: Norton, 1985), 153–58; Sterling Stuckey, *Slave Culture: Nationalist Theory and the Foundations of Black America* (New York: Oxford University Press, 1987), vi–ix, 8, 30, 34–35, 79, 93. For useful introductions to revisionist historiography of antebellum slavery, see Peter Kolchin, "American Historians and Antebellum Southern Slavery, 1959–1984," in *A Master's Due: Essays in Honor of David Herbert Donald,* ed. William J. Cooper Jr., Michael F. Holt, and John McCardle (Baton Rouge: Louisiana State University Press, 1985), 87–111; Peter Kolchin, *American Slavery, 1619–1877,* rev. ed. (New York: Hill and Wang, 2003).

7. Peter Kolchin, *Unfree Labor: American Slavery and Russian Serfdom* (Cambridge, MA: Belknap Press of Harvard University Press, 1987), part 2, esp. 217, 233–36 (quotation 236).

8. David Brion Davis, *Inhuman Bondage: The Rise and Fall of Slavery in the New World* (New York: Oxford University Press, 2006), 199–204, 378n18 (quotations 200, 203, 204).

9. Paul E. Lovejoy, "The African Diaspora: Revisionist Interpretations of Ethnicity, Culture and Religion under Slavery," *Studies in the World History of Slavery, Abolition and Emancipation* 2, no. 1 (1997): n.p., www.yorku.ca/nhp/publications/Lovejoy_Studies%20in%20the%20World%20History%20of%20Slavery.pdf.

10. Saidiya V. Hartman, *Scenes of Subjection: Terror, Slavery, and Self-Making in Nineteenth-Century America* (New York: Oxford University Press, 1997); Anthony E. Kaye, "Neighbourhoods and Solidarity in the Natchez District of Mississippi: Rethinking the Antebellum Slave Community," *Slavery and Abolition* 23 (April 2002): 1–24; Kaye, *Joining Places: Slave Neighborhoods in the Old South* (Chapel Hill: University of North Carolina Press, 2007), esp. 9–11; Sharla M. Fett, *Working Cures: Healing, Health, and Power on Southern Slave Plantations* (Chapel Hill: University of North Carolina Press, 2002), 6–7; Dylan C. Penningroth, *The Claims of Kinfolk: African American Property and Community in the Nineteenth-Century South* (Chapel Hill: University of North Carolina Press, 2003), 1, 43, 81, 161; Stephanie M. H. Camp, *Closer to Freedom: Enslaved Women and Everyday Resistance in the Plantation South* (Chapel Hill: University of North Carolina Press,

2004), 7; Thavolia Glymph, *Out of the House of Bondage: The Transformation of the Plantation Household* (New York: Cambridge University Press, 2008), 9.

11. Dylan C. Penningroth, "The Claims of Slaves and Ex-Slaves to Family and Property: A Transatlantic Comparison," *American Historical Review* 112 (October 2007): 1044–45n16.

12. This paragraph is adapted from Kaye, *Joining Places,* 9–10. This chapter is not a comprehensive survey of liberal thought or the critical debates about the particular conceptions of autonomy discussed below. For introductions, see John P. Christman, *The Politics of Persons: Individual Autonomy and Socio-historical Selves* (Cambridge: Cambridge University Press, 2009); Christman, "Autonomy in Moral and Political Philosophy," *The Stanford Encyclopedia of Philosophy* (2002), http://plato.stanford.edu; Joseph Raz, *The Morality of Freedom* (Oxford: Clarendon Press, 1986); Gerald Dworkin, *The Theory and Practice of Autonomy* (New York: Cambridge University Press, 1988).

13. Immanuel Kant, *Groundwork for the Metaphysics of Morals,* trans. James W. Ellington, 3rd ed. (Indianapolis: Hackett, 1993), 49 (quotation, emphasis original); J. B. Schneewind, *The Invention of Autonomy: A History of Modern Philosophy* (Cambridge: Cambridge University Press, 1998), esp. 3–6, 483–92, 507.

14. John Stuart Mill, *Utilitarianism* and *On Liberty,* both in *The Collected Works of John Stuart Mill,* ed. J. M. Robson (Toronto: University of Toronto Press, 1963–91), 10:203–59 (fourth, sixth, and seventh quotations on 10:251); 18:213–310 (first, third, and eighth quotations on 18:260–61; second quotation on 18:267; fifth, ninth, and tenth quotations on 18:225–27); Wendy Donner, *The Liberal Self: John Stuart Mill's Moral and Political Philosophy* (Ithaca, NY: Cornell University Press, 1991), esp. 10–26, 37–41, 57–65.

15. Mill, *Collected Works,* 2:245.

16. Mill, "The Contest in America" and "The Slave Power," *Collected Works,* 21:125–64, esp. 136, 158 (quotations).

17. Mill, *Collected Works,* 21:264–65, 267, 269, 273, 276, 281, 284–87, 294, 296, 301, 320–21, 323.

18. Ibid., 1:615; 6:178–81; 18:243.

19. Charles Taylor, *The Ethics of Authenticity* (Cambridge, MA: Harvard University Press, 1991), 17–21.

20. Robert Dahl, *Dilemmas of Pluralist Democracy* (New Haven, CT: Yale University Press, 1982), 1–8, 16–28, 89–95.

21. Albert J. Raboteau, *Slave Religion: The "Invisible Institution" in the Antebellum South* (New York: Oxford University Press, 1978); Herbert G. Gutman, *The Black Family in Slavery and Freedom, 1750–1925* (New York: Pantheon, 1976); Blassingame, *Slave Community.*

22. Margaret A. Burnham, "An Impossible Marriage: Slave Law and Family Law," *Law and Inequality* 5 (July 1987): 187–225. For comparative perspectives on the legal descent of slave status in Virginia slave law, see Robert J. Cottrol, *The Long Lingering Shadow: Slavery, Race, and Law in the American Hemisphere* (Athens: University of Georgia Press, 2013), 85–90; Jennifer L. Morgan, *Laboring Women: Reproduction and Gender in New World Slavery* (Philadelphia: University of Pennsylvania Press, 2004), 71–76, 167–73.

23. Elizabeth Fox-Genovese and Eugene D. Genovese, "The Political Crisis of Social History: Class Struggle as Subject and Object," in *Fruits of Merchant Capital: Slavery and Bourgeois*

Property in the Rise and Expansion of Capitalism, by Fox-Genovese and Genovese (Oxford: Oxford University Press, 1983), 179–212 (quotation 197); Eugene D. Genovese, *In Red and Black: Marxian Explorations in Southern and Afro-American History* (Knoxville: University of Tennessee Press, 1984), 66–67, 105, 316–18, 332, 360–61.

24. John Rawls, *Justice as Fairness: A Restatement*, ed. Erin Kelly (Cambridge, MA: Harvard University Press, 2001), 22–23. On the incompatibility of paternalism and autonomy, see also Marina A. L. Oshana, "Personal Autonomy and Society," *Journal of Social Philosophy* 29 (Spring 1998): 82.

25. Eugene D. Genovese, *Roll, Jordan, Roll: The World the Slaves Made* (New York: Vintage, 1976), 91. For an early statement of this formulation, see Genovese, *Red and Black*, 102–28, esp. 103.

26. For Genovese's glosses on Hegel, see *Roll, Jordan, Roll*, 3–7, 97–98. Genovese referred more explicitly to Hegel's account of lordship and bondage in earlier works. See Eugene D. Genovese, *The Political Economy of Slavery: Studies in the Economy and Society of the Slave South* (1965; reprint, New York: Vintage Books, 1967), 32–34, 71; Genovese, *Red and Black*, 52n63, 284–85; Eugene D. Genovese, *The World the Slaveholders Made: Two Essays in Interpretation* (1969; reprint, Middletown, CT: Wesleyan University Press, 1988), 7–8.

27. G. W. F. Hegel, *Phenomenology of Spirit*, trans. A. V. Miller (Oxford: Oxford University Press, 1977), 111–19. For an influential commentary on Hegel and a still-useful explication of his account of lordship and bondage, see Alexandre Kojéve, *Introduction to the Reading of Hegel*, comp. Raymond Queneau, ed. Allan Bloom, trans. James H. Nichols Jr. (New York: Basic, 1969), 3–70. Cf. David Brion Davis, *The Problem of Slavery in the Age of Revolution, 1770–1823* (Ithaca, NY: Cornell University Press, 1975), epilogue.

28. Genovese, *Roll, Jordan, Roll*, 3, 97–112 (quotation 97).

29. Ibid., 148, 181, 221, 232, 236, 238, 656. When Genovese glossed Hegel in his description of docile slaves turned rebellious and kind masters turned wild beast, he quoted Gramsci. See ibid., 148. See the passage quoted in the next paragraph of the text.

30. Ibid., 148–49.

31. Genovese, "On Antonio Gramsci," in Genovese, *Red and Black*, 391–422.

32. Antonio Gramsci, *The Modern Prince, and Other Writings* (New York: International, 1968), 118–25 (quotations 118, 124).

33. Ibid., 22–27 (quotations 23, 25).

34. Ibid., 28–51, esp. 42–46 (quotations 44, 51). Gramsci's reflections on breaking up the southern bloc led him to subsidiary formulations on the autonomy of southern cities and historical reflections on the lack of autonomy of the Action Party, radical democrats led by Giuseppe Mazzini, and the loss of autonomy by the Catholic Church during the Risorgimento. Antonio Gramsci, *Prison Notebooks*, ed. Joseph A. Buttigieg, trans. Buttigieg and Antonio Callari (New York: Columbia University Press, 1992), 1:133–35, 412n7, 138–39, 223–35.

35. Genovese, "On Antonio Gramsci," 403–4, 406.

36. Genovese, *Roll, Jordan, Roll*, 599–609 (quotation 609).

37. Ibid., 365–88 (quotations 378–79, 384).

38. Ibid., 255–79, 388 (quotations 273, 388).

39. On relational autonomy, see Catriona Mackenzie and Natalie Stoljar, introduction to

Relational Autonomy: Feminist Perspectives on Autonomy, Agency, and the Social Self, ed. Mackenzie and Stoljar (New York: Oxford University Press, 2000), 3–31; Diana T. Meyers, "Interactional Identity and the Authentic Self?" in Mackenzie and Stoljar, *Relational Autonomy,* 151–80; Meyers, *Self, Society, and Personal Choice* (New York: Columbia University Press, 1989); Jennifer Nedelsky, "Reconceiving Autonomy: Sources, Thoughts, and Possibilities," *Yale Journal of Philosophy* 84 (November 1987): 7–19, 33–36. For a sympathetic critique, see John P. Christman, "Relational Autonomy, Liberal Individualism, and the Social Constitution of Selves," *Philosophical Studies* 117 (January 2004): 143–64.

40. Diana T. Meyers, "Personal Autonomy and the Paradox of Feminine Socialization," *Journal of Philosophy* 84 (November 1987): 619–26.

41. Ibid. (quotations 624, 625).

42. On recent scholarship probing the intersections of gender, race, class, and sex, see Leslie M. Alexander, "The Challenge of Race: Rethinking the Position of Black Women in the Field of Women's History," *Journal of Women's History* 16 (Winter 2004): 50–60; Cornelia H. Dayton and Lisa Levenstein, "The Big Tent of U.S. Women's and Gender History: A State of the Field," *Journal of American History* 99 (December 2012): 797–802; Crystal N. Feimster, "The Impact of Racial and Sexual Politics on Women's History," *Journal of American History* 99 (December 2012): 822–26.

43. Meyers, "Personal Autonomy," 624; Oshana, "Personal Autonomy and Society," 82, 86–89, 97 (quotation).

44. Christman, "Relational Autonomy," 147, 156–57.

45. For points of entry to the literature of human geography, see David Harvey, *The Limits to Capital,* new ed. (1982; London: Verso, 1999); Henri Lefebvre, *The Production of Space,* trans. Donald Nicholson-Smith (Oxford: Blackwell, 1991); Allan Pred, "Place as Historically Contingent Process: Structuration and the Time-Geography of Becoming Places," *Annals of the Association of American Geographers* 74 (June 1984): 279–97; Doreen B. Massey, *Space, Place, and Gender* (Minneapolis: University of Minnesota Press, 1994); Linda McDowell, *Gender, Identity and Place: Understanding Feminist Geographies* (Minneapolis: University of Minnesota Press, 1999); Yi-fu Tuan, *Space and Place: The Perspective of Experience* (Minneapolis: University of Minnesota Press, 1977); Edward W. Soja, *Postmodern Geographies: The Reassertion of Space in Critical Theory* (London: Verso, 1989); Michel de Certeau, *The Practice of Everyday Life* (Berkeley: University of California Press, 1984), 91–130.

46. Anthony Giddens, *The Constitution of Society: Outline of the Theory of Structuration* (Berkeley: University of California Press, 1984). Pierre Bourdieu explores similar themes with the concept of the "habitus," through a different problematic and lexicon. See Bourdieu, *Outline of a Theory of Practice* (Cambridge: Cambridge University Press, 1977). For a discussion of Giddens and Bourdieu, with a pointed emphasis on their differences, see Loïc J. D. Wacquant, "Toward a Social Praxeology: The Structure and Logic of Bourdieu's Sociology," in *An Invitation to Reflexive Sociology,* by Bourdieu and Wacquant (Chicago: University of Chicago Press, 1992), 33–39, 48–49.

47. Kaye, *Joining Places;* Camp, *Closer to Freedom.* For an interesting discussion of slaves' networks, see Calvin J. Schermerhorn, *Money over Mastery, Family over Freedom: Slavery in the Antebellum Upper South* (Baltimore: Johns Hopkins University Press, 2011).

48. Judith P. Butler, *Gender Trouble: Feminism and the Subversion of Identity* (New York: Routledge, 1990), ix (quotation), 16–18, 23. See also Judith P. Butler, *Bodies That Matter: On the Discursive Limits of "Sex"* (New York: Routledge, 1993).

49. Ariela Gross, "Reflections on Law, Culture, and Slavery," in *Slavery and the American South,* ed. Winthrop D. Jordan (Jackson: University of Mississippi Press, 2003), 66–67, 188n35; Ariela J. Gross, "Litigating Whiteness: Trials of Racial Determination in the Nineteenth Century South," *Yale Journal* 108 (October 1998): 111–13n6, 156–77.

50. Fields and Fields, *Racecraft,* 4–11, 50–52, 112–13.

51. Ariela J. Gross, *What Blood Won't Tell: A History of Race on Trial in America* (Cambridge, MA: Harvard University Press, 2008), 8–11, 42–43, 53–65, 70–71.

52. Ibid., 58, 1.

53. Walter Johnson, "The Slave Trader, the White Slave, and the Politics of Racial Determination in the 1850s," *Journal of American History* 87 (June 2000): 24.

54. Gross, *What Blood Won't Tell,* 3, 58; Gross, "Litigating Whiteness," 176 (quotations).

55. Johnson, "Slave Trader," 18–20 (quotation 20, emphasis added).

56. Gross, "Litigating Whiteness," 181.

57. Laura F. Edwards, *The People and Their Peace: Legal Culture and the Transformation of Inequality in the Post-Revolutionary South* (Chapel Hill: University of North Carolina Press, 2009).

58. Penningroth, "Claims of Slaves," 1041–46, 1049n28; Igor Kopytoff and Suzanne Miers, "African 'Slavery' as an Institution of Marginality," in *Slavery in Africa: Historical and Anthropological Perspectives,* ed. Miers and Kopytoff (Madison: University of Wisconsin Press, 1977), 3–81; Trevor R. Getz, *Slavery and Reform in West Africa: Toward Emancipation in Nineteenth Century Senegal* (Athens: Ohio University Press, 2004).

59. Penningroth, "Claims of Slaves," 1040, 1046n21, 1048–50 (quotations 1050). For other comparisons of African and U.S. slavery, see works cited in 1041n10.

60. Ibid., 1052–53.

61. Ibid., 1053–55 (quotations 1055); Penningroth, *Claims of Kinfolk,* 95–107, 235n192.

62. Penningroth, "Claims of Slaves," 80, 83–91 (quotations 89, 91), 105–7.

63. Celia E. Naylor, *African Cherokees in Indian Territory: From Chattels to Citizens* (Chapel Hill: University of North Carolina Press, 2008), esp. 7–8, 85–87. For a pathbreaking reinterpretation of American Indian slaveholding in the Southwest influenced by the lineage interpretation of African slavery, see James F. Brooks, *Captives and Cousins: Slavery, Kinship, and Community in the Southwest Borderlands* (Chapel Hill: University of North Carolina Press, 2002), esp. 34–35n54.

64. Barbara Krauthamer, *Black Slaves, Indian Masters: Slavery, Emancipation, and Citizenship in the Native American South* (Chapel Hill: University of North Carolina Press, 2013), 31–32.

65. Penningroth, "Claims of Slaves," 1052.

66. Krauthamer, *Black Slaves, Indian Masters,* 17–18, 30–34, 45, 71.

67. Ibid., 113–23 (quotation 123).

III

COMPARATIVE SLAVERY

SLAVE WOMEN AND URBAN LABOR
IN THE EIGHTEENTH-CENTURY ATLANTIC WORLD

MARIANA DANTAS

Recent scholarship on the topic of slave women in plantation societies of the Americas has helped to replace a male-centered portrayal of western slavery with one in which slave women's labor and agency is acknowledged as equally relevant to the economic and social development of the New World.[1] Yet, within the field of urban slavery in the Americas, less attention has been paid to the presence and importance of slave women in and to the development of urban centers.[2] To be sure, different works have addressed slave women's participation in domestic labor and petty commerce, as well as their visibility in various New World towns and cities.[3] Still, urban female slaves' influence on a range of economic and financial exchanges that helped to shape Atlantic urban economies remains underexplored.[4] Through a comparative analysis of the presence and economic activities of slave women in Baltimore, Maryland, and Sabará, Minas Gerais, Brazil, this chapter discusses the relevance of female slave labor to the development of urban environments in eighteenth-century New World societies. While often employed in what could be considered domestic services, slave women nevertheless helped to diversify local production of goods, promote the circulation of commodities, and increase household earnings, all of which undergirded the urban economies in which they found themselves.

While slave women's labor contributed in similar ways to the development of Baltimore and Sabará, as well as a number of other urban environments in the New World, their ability to benefit from their economic relevance differed significantly. An examination of manumission practices in both towns highlights, for instance, the frequency with which slave women in Sabará transformed their hard work into the means through which they acquired their freedom. These women's ability to access the product of their labor and apply it toward their emancipation was not shared by most slave women in Baltimore. There, factors such as a more diverse urban workforce, the beginnings of industrial production, and the resulting gendered division of labor negatively affected slave women's access to paid jobs or the ability to leverage their work. The example of and explanation for these distinct patterns of female manumission help remind us that the experiences slaves endured in New World societies could be as diverse as the socioeconomic environments in which slavery was practiced. Those experiences, moreover, were often shaped by the extent to which slaves could control the form, and access the output, of their labor.[5]

T he history of enslaved Africans and their descendants in the Americas is most commonly associated with the plantation system that developed in parts of North and South America and served as the main economic unit of production in the Caribbean.[6] Yet bondpeople helped to support a great variety of economic pursuits in the New World and to develop more than one type of social environment. Whether in Mexico City, Lima, Buenos Aires, Salvador, Charleston, New Orleans, Kingston, or other cities and towns of the colonial New World, slaves of African descent, at one point or another, contributed to the construction, sustenance, and diversification of urban economies and urban environments.[7] Baltimore, in the British colony and later American state of Maryland, and Sabará, in the Portuguese colony of Brazil, further illustrate the role enslaved African descendants played as agents of urbanization. Present in these towns already in their formative years, slaves were involved in establishing the main industries that supported their urban economy: shipbuilding in Baltimore and gold mining in Sabará. Slaves also helped to shape the physical space of each town, either as the artisans who produced the materials for and worked on the construction of urban buildings, or as the labor employed in the upkeep and improvement of urban spaces, private and public. Finally, slaves in Baltimore and Sabará carried out many of the activities that made urban life in the early modern period possible, whether by providing a variety of services or by transporting and commercially distributing foodstuffs and petty goods.[8]

Indeed, in both Baltimore and Sabará, the rapid increase of the slave population during periods of marked economic growth and physical expansion indicates a strong relationship between the presence of slaves and urbanization.
Eighteenth-century wills, sales deeds, and tax records reveal, for instance, town
dwellers' commitment to the employment of slave labor. In Sabará, tax records
for the 1720s show a steady growth in the number of slaves, mostly through
the purchase of Africans, and the eventual formation of a slave population
that, by the third quarter of the eighteenth century, represented 53 percent of
all residents in the town and its precincts.[9] In Baltimore, midcentury wills and
deeds of sale and late-eighteenth-century tax records highlight a persistent
investment in slave labor. In the seven years from the tax assessment of 1783 to
the census of 1790, the town's slave population grew an astounding 250 percent.
Perhaps of greater relevance is that, while in 1783 only 12 percent of Baltimore
households included slaves, that figure rose to 22 percent in 1790 and to 43
percent in 1800. Moreover, between 1790 and 1800 Baltimore's slave population
grew at a faster rate than its free population.[10] The slave population in Baltimore never came close to equaling the slave population in Sabará in terms of
size or percentage of the general population, yet both populations experienced
a similar marked growth during each town's formative years and periods of
greatest economic expansion.[11] As I have argued elsewhere, these overlapping
patterns of demographic and economic growth indicate the relevance of slavery to the development of both urban centers.[12]

Another similarity between the slave populations of Baltimore and Sabará
was the marked increase of female slaves during the latter part of the eighteenth
century and the early nineteenth century. While a strong presence of women
among urban slaves is not surprising and has been identified as a characteristic
of urban slavery by some scholars, particularly of the American South, it was
not the reality in Baltimore and Sabará for much of the eighteenth century.[13]
Instead, data relative to the composition of the slave population in Sabará
retrieved from probate records shows a slave population that was 80 percent
male between 1750 and 1775. During the last quarter of the eighteenth century,
however, the proportion of males declined to 71 percent.[14] In Baltimore, data
collected through inventories and tax lists indicate a slave population that was
30 percent adult male and 20 percent adult female between 1750 and 1775, 37
percent adult male and 21 percent adult female in 1783, and 25 percent adult
male and 31 percent adult female in 1804. Although Baltimore records rarely

distinguished the gender of slaves under the age of fourteen or those who were elderly, the data does highlight the dominance of men among the town's adult slave population during its early years of rapid economic expansion.[15] By the turn of the nineteenth century, however, Baltimore's slave population was predominantly female. Sabará, meanwhile, which continued to count on the importation of a male-dominated enslaved African labor force to grow, remained predominantly male while becoming increasingly more gender-balanced.

The predominance of women among urban slaves has been explained as the result of a strong overlap between slave work and domestic work in cities and towns of the Americas. Slave men, in this scenario, were in high demand in the countryside, where they were employed in agricultural or other rural activities. The resulting pull factor left urban slave owners unable to compete for able-bodied male slaves, relying instead on other sources of labor to support their commercial, manufacturing, or service businesses. Urban slaveholders were nevertheless successful in purchasing and hiring female slaves, whom they then employed in domestic work.[16] This narrative, though partially accurate, makes two assumptions that overshadow the reality of urban slavery in Baltimore and Sabará. First, it ignores the fact that both urban environments functioned as the pull factor at different points during the eighteenth century, when economic expansion and high demand for labor allowed urban investors to compete favorably for the available male slaves.[17] Second, it fails to recognize slave women's contribution to the core economic activities of the two towns by overgeneralizing and ignoring the economic significance of their work and domestic roles.[18] In both Baltimore and Sabará, urban investors looked toward existing slave populations and recently imported African slaves to secure the labor force they required to establish and expand their businesses. As revealed in eighteenth-century deeds of sale, probate records, and tax lists, they often sought male slaves to support their pursuits, but at times, perhaps when male slaves were in high demand elsewhere, were declining in numbers, were too expensive, or were not necessarily prioritized, they turned to slave women.[19]

Identifying the occupation or economic activity of slave women can be challenging, because the sources available for Baltimore and Sabará are often silent on the matter. Perhaps the two most common occupations associated with slave women were seamstress and midwife, but even those appear rarely. Unlike male slaves, slave women who were apprenticed, perhaps to learn domestic work, or who through their daily labor may have developed particular skills, were not commonly described by their occupation. The absence of such descriptions, however, should not be read as evidence that these women's labor contribution was limited to domestic work of little or no economic significance. Slave women's involvement in spinning and weaving in Sabará is a case in point. Though often performed as domestic work, these services were on occasion provided to people outside the household, thereby earning slave women or their owners a modest income. The 1785 inventory of looms in Minas Gerais, produced at the Crown's orders to help enforce the royal prohibition on cloth manufacturing, reveals that 40 percent of the households listed in Sabará employed slave women in that activity, and 32 percent of loom owners confessed to making a profit from domestic production.[20] Through their labor, slave women provided diversified and specialized services to their owners and to the population of Sabará at large, increasing the supply of consumer goods in that town at the same time as they helped to increase their owners' household income.

Slave women also helped to support and diversify Sabará's economy and their owner's source of income through their participation in local commerce. The involvement of black women in market activities was a feature of the economy in the region of Sabará practically from the beginning of settlement. The Jesuit priest André João Antonil, in his description of the mining district, published in 1711, noted that slave owners often employed their female property as market women, peddlers, and tavern keepers.[21] Aware of the high demand for various subsistence goods, these early entrepreneurs relied on their bondwomen to access some of the profits that could be generated by supplying local inhabitants with food, *cachaça* (an alcoholic beverage made from distilled sugar cane juice), and other commodities. In the decades following the publication of Antonil's writings, that same demand continued to drive slave women's participation in the regional economy. Tax records, municipal regulations, and commercial licenses issued throughout Minas Gerais, and in the town of Sabará particularly, reveal the rapid increase in the early eighteenth century of the number of *vendas*, small commercial enterprises dedicated to trading foodstuffs and local products.[22] Slave women who worked as *vendeiras* played a prominent role in this sector of the economy. During the second half of the eighteenth century, they appeared frequently among licensed peddlers and market people, representing 10 percent of all commercial licenses issued by the Municipal Council and 80 percent of all licenses issued to slaves.[23] Frequent complaints that slave women engaged in market activities without a license suggest, moreover, that the number of slave *vendeiras* in Sabará and their impact on local commerce was even greater than what is revealed in municipal records.[24] Laboring as traders and peddlers, slave women thus supplied the local population with much-needed goods, promoted economic exchanges between rural producers and urban consumers, and offered material support to mining activities and urban development in the region.[25]

In Baltimore, evidence that slave women's labor had economic relevance that went beyond supplying households with domestic services is more often anecdotal than quantifiable. While female slaves in Baltimore, like their counterparts in Sabará, developed specialized skills and talents that occasionally supported their owner's business, instead of merely their owner's domestic needs, no single document offers a systematic account of the economic impact of their labor. Still, some Baltimore slaveholders may have indeed relied on their female slaves to further or to diversify their economic activities. Adam Lindsay, the owner of a coffeehouse, and at least four other tavern keepers similarly listed in the tax assessment of 1783, owned slave women. While it is possible that their female slaves serviced their homes, it is also likely that they served their customers.[26] Similarly, John Chapple, a shipwright who in 1783 published a runaway ad in an attempt to recover his slave Candance, a "remarkably good spinner," may have relied on the labor of his female slave to furnish his ships.[27] Descriptions of slaves' market activities included in Englishman Richard Parkinson's account of his farming years near Baltimore in the late eighteenth century suggest, moreover, the presence and participation, even if limited, of slave women in local commerce.[28]

Perhaps one of the most systematic ways in which slave women contributed to the economic life of Baltimore, at least based on what eighteenth-century sources reveal, was by working as hirelings. Newspaper ads, account books, manumission records, and other documents contain several examples of slave owners hiring out the labor of their slave women to others, or of slave women hiring out their own labor. Most of these women, it seems, were hired to perform domestic work. In some cases there was mention of an occupation, such as seamstress.[29] Either way, their labor benefited their owners, who gained additional income through the practice.[30] It also occasionally afforded the women themselves the opportunity to participate as consumers in the market economy of Baltimore.[31] Through their labor as hirelings, slave women, even those performing mostly domestic work, helped to increase the income of their owner's household; circulate services, goods, and currency; and support the expansion of economic exchanges in Baltimore.

When the lawyer Miguel da Silva Costa died in 1761 in Sabará, his inventory listed four slaves among other personal property and real estate. One of those slaves was Francisca, a twenty-eight-year-old African woman, who was described as being employed in *todo serviço de rua* (all street services).[32] The description of this slave's occupation or form of employment could equally be applied to a number of female slaves in Sabará and Baltimore. In both towns, slave women provided their owners with diverse "street" as well as domestic services. They also participated in commercial and service activities that helped to support the gold mining and shipbuilding industries, and urban life more generally, through the circulation of foodstuffs, goods and services, and currency.[33] Finally, by increasing the household income through their labor and hired services, they affected the process of economic diversification and development of the two towns. The economies of Baltimore and Sabará were not always conducive to or supportive of economic specialization. A limited demand for certain products or services at times prevented artisans and other professionals from surviving solely on the income generated by their trade or business.[34] Yet, the possibility of counting on the labor of slaves either to complement the household income or simply to avoid financial outlay afforded slave owners a certain level of financial security that allowed them to continue investing in their own specialization.[35]

While there were similarities in the ways slave women participated in and contributed to the urban economies of Sabará and Baltimore, their ability to benefit from the fruits of their own labor could differ significantly. To some extent, both female populations were occasionally afforded the opportunity to use income they generated through their labor to purchase goods that helped improve in modest ways their levels of material comfort. Runaway advertisements, account books, and lists of debts in probate records reveal these women's purchases of clothes, food, oil, and so on.[36] Their ability to apply their earnings to the purchase of their own freedom, however, clearly distinguished the experiences of slave women in Sabará from those of slave women in Baltimore. Studies of the practice of manumission, the legal transaction that secured a slave's release from captivity, point out the greater frequency with which women were able to obtain their freedom in most slave societies of the Americas.[37] Manumission records in Sabará reveal that 60 percent of all manumissions recorded during the second half of the eighteenth century favored women.[38] Because women never represented much more than one-third of the slave population of Sabará, the fact that they were manumitted more frequently than slave men underscores their relative success in securing their freedom.[39] In Baltimore, by contrast, manumission deeds from the same period reveal a greater frequency of male than female manumissions. Because slave men were more numerous than slave women during much of the second half of the eighteenth century, it could be argued that the predominance of male adults among Baltimore's manumitted slaves is not surprising. Still, this tendency persisted throughout the early nineteenth century, when the composition of Baltimore's slave population had changed significantly.[40] Thus, even though by 1804 the number of slave women residing in Baltimore had surpassed that of slave men by a ratio of six to five, slave manumissions recorded between 1800 and 1810 show a gender ratio of three men for every two women.[41] Slave women in Baltimore, therefore, experienced greater difficulty obtaining their freedom—or were freed with greater reluctance—than was the case in much of the rest of the Americas.

The manner in which women obtained their freedom also distinguished the practice of manumission in Baltimore and Sabará. While in Baltimore more than half of the female manumissions were granted conditionally and required slave women to fulfill additional terms of service, in Sabará a majority of the female manumissions were achieved through purchase.[42] Both forms of manumission posed disadvantages to slave women. Those who obtained their manumission conditionally had to surrender additional years of productive labor to their owners in order to secure their freedom; those who obtained their manumission through purchase had to relinquish the product of their labor in exchange for their freedom. Either way, these women entered a life of freedom with few financial resources in exchange for their years of work. Nevertheless, the ability to negotiate the purchase of one's freedom gave slave women greater control over when manumission was achieved and the terms under which they would labor toward their freedom.[43] The higher rate of female manumission by purchase in Sabará suggests, therefore, that slave women in that town enjoyed greater success in negotiating the meaning and output of their labor than did their counterparts in Baltimore.

The predominance of African women among manumitted slaves in Sabará points further to a strong correlation between female manumission and slave women's ability to exercise control over the output of their labor. African women, who represented only 8 percent of the slaves listed in inventories from the second half of the eighteenth century, accounted for 23 percent of all manumitted slaves who appear in manumission records from that same period.[44] Moreover, while some of these women were granted manumission immediately or were required to satisfy labor conditions imposed by their owners, two-thirds of all manumitted African women purchased their freedom.[45] African slave women in Sabará and much of colonial Brazil were known for their involvement in urban commerce and for the relative autonomy they enjoyed to procure paid work. Some historians have suggested a correlation between women's experiences with market activities in Africa and their success with similar economic pursuits in the urban centers of colonial Brazil.[46] The gender division of labor that developed in Sabará during its formative period also explains this scenario. Unlike what has been observed for the plantations of the Caribbean and the American South, where slave women were frequently forced to work in the fields alongside men, mining in Sabará was almost exclusively a male job.[47] African slave women, who were brought into the region alongside their male counterparts, albeit in smaller numbers, were forced by their owners to work instead in what may have seemed the next best option for gainful employment: local trade. Quickly, African slave women secured a dominant role in that business. Their participation in local commerce, like other slave women's participation in textile production and other activities, benefited Sabará's economy by promoting the circulation of goods and services while also improving their owners' social and economic standing by increasing their household earnings. More importantly, the frequency with which slave women appear in manumission records purchasing their freedom reveals their success in translating labor into a commodity that was, above all, economically and socially meaningful to them.

Another characteristic of colonial Sabará and colonial Brazil more generally that benefited slave women and affected their ability to leverage their labor more effectively toward the goal of manumission was the structure of local manufacturing. While colonial sources reveal a local production of textiles, ironware, and tools, and of processed goods such as oil, flour, soap, and *cachaça*, the development of manufacturing in large scale was hindered by metropolitan efforts to suppress such activities in the colonies.[48] In the case of Minas Gerais in particular, the Portuguese Crown, interested in encouraging the continuous expansion and growth of the gold-mining industry, objected to local efforts to diversify the economy and repeatedly prohibited local manufacturing. During the reign of José I, for instance, Secretary of State Sebastião José de Carvalho e Melo, the marquis of Pombal, declared the production and commercial distribution of salt, soap, and textiles a metropolitan monopoly. These economic policies aimed to increase metropolitan revenues by enforcing a more effective exploitation of colonial resources and securing a consumer market for Portuguese goods. Ultimately, they increased prices, threatened supplies in the colonies, and encouraged the emergence of certain cottage industries, many of which operated illegally.[49] The informal and clandestine conditions under which regulated commodities were produced meant that the workers employed in these activities were often the female household or domestic slaves of local entrepreneurs who were not (and were not expected to be) employed in gold mining. In addition to the local production of textiles, slave women in Sabará were also involved in the production of soap and castor oil to replace the more expensive soap and olive oil that was imported from Portugal. Moreover, they were often the ones selling the products in the streets and local markets.[50] Thus, colonists' inability to invest in manufacturing on a larger scale and to commit their male slave workforce to those activities helped to preserve an economic niche for slave women in places like Sabará.

The way labor, race, and gender expectations became interconnected in colonial Brazilian society also contributed to securing certain sectors of the labor market in Sabará for slave women, enabling them potentially to leverage the demand for their labor when negotiating manumission. The argument that took place in 1778 between the judge of the orphans' court and the guardian of the three underage daughters of José de Freitas Costa, a poor white man who lived in a rural precinct of Sabará, sheds some light on colonial attitudes toward female labor. Five years after Costa's death, his daughters' guardian requested permission to use part of their inheritance to buy fabric and clothes with which to adequately dress them. The judge responded that, in order to preserve the value of the inheritance until they came of age, the girls should be placed to work in reputable houses and support themselves through their labor. To this recommendation their guardian replied, "with all due respect," that though this practice may have been acceptable in Portugal, where there were numerous houses that employed domestic servants who only worked indoors, it was unheard of "in these Americas," where few households would maintain servants for indoor jobs only and where outdoor labor put women's honor at risk. He explained that because the girls under his care were white and had an inheritance—that is, property—they should not be forced to serve others and thus risk being exposed to the streets, "which would facilitate the loss of their honor, the most precious jewel of the female sex."[51] The opinions expressed in this case reveal a social environment in which certain types of female occupations were associated with loose morals and a lack of honor and viewed as inappropriate for white or propertied women. Women in Sabará, aware of and complicit in the propagation of these gender expectations, invested whenever they could in the purchase of slave women to carry out activities in the streets from which they themselves wished to remain removed.[52] Freed black women, for instance, often owned female slaves even when they did not own much else.[53] Thus, for much of the eighteenth century, slave women prevailed among street vendors in Sabará, many succeeding in earning the price of their freedom.

In Baltimore, slave women were less successful in transforming their labor into freedom. Whereas female slave labor helped to support the local economy and generate income for slave owners, it did not afford bondwomen the economic means or leverage to pursue manumission in the same way or as frequently as it did in Sabará. Patterns of demographic growth and their impact on the labor market in Baltimore help to explain this distinction. As census records from 1790 and 1810 reveal, the white population in Baltimore increasingly outnumbered the slave population: While in 1790 there were 11,925 free white inhabitants and 1,255 slaves, by 1810 those numbers had increased to 36,212 and 4,672, respectively. The slave population in Baltimore grew at a faster rate than the white population during that period, and its percentage of the total population in the city increased, but in terms of sheer numbers, by 1810 Baltimore and its workforce likely seemed whiter to the city's employers.[54] Indeed, during the turn of the nineteenth century, the city of Baltimore became a port of destination for a growing number of European immigrants who arrived in the United States in search of new economic opportunities. Yet, unlike the white indentured servants, who were quickly absorbed into the town and the county's labor force in the years following the American Revolution, this new wave of migrants consisted mostly of free whites who found that securing a job—especially a well-paying one—was more difficult than they had expected.[55] As they struggled to survive in their new surroundings,

European immigrants began to compete with slaves for some of the same jobs and occupations.[56]

The city of Baltimore similarly became an important destination for a growing population of free blacks: manumitted slaves and their descendants who turned to the city in hopes of distancing themselves further from their former owners and experiences with slavery. This migratory wave, along with the formation of a local population of manumitted slaves and their descendants, significantly changed the composition of the city's workforce. Between 1790 and 1810, free blacks in Baltimore increased in number from 323 to 5,671, surpassing in 1810 the local slave population. Moreover, experiencing an annual growth rate of 15.4 percent, nearly three times higher than that of the local white population, free blacks in Baltimore were the fastest-growing demographic in the city.[57] The free black population not only grew more numerous but also included a larger proportion of working-age adults than either the slave or the white population. Their presence thus contributed to increased competition within the city's labor market and further limited economic opportunities for Baltimore slaves.[58]

As Baltimore's workforce became more diverse and included a wider range of free labor options, the jobs and hiring positions that slave women had often held were taken up by free white and black women. Late-eighteenth-century newspapers published announcements offering slave women for hire as domestic servants adjacent to advertisements for available positions as hirelings that called for either white or black applicants. The *Federal Gazette and Baltimore Advertiser*, for instance, published in January 1796 an advertisement for "A YOUNG NEGRO WOMAN, well used to house-work, who has hitherto behaved herself soberly and honestly," "to be hired by the year or the month."[59] A few weeks later, in March, another announcement called for "A WOMAN SERVANT, white or black. Her employment will be cooking and washing." Past employers' positive testimonials of applicants' "good character" were required.[60] While slave women continued to be offered for hire by their owners, potential employers cast their offers of jobs more broadly, hoping to secure the most efficient, reliable, and cheapest worker. Seth Rockman, in his analysis of the laboring and living conditions endured by working women in early national Baltimore, shows that the rising number and different types of workers competing for the same jobs contributed to depressed salaries and poor conditions. Free white and black women, especially those who were heads of household, consequently had difficulty sustaining themselves and their families through their labor.[61] Slave women experienced greater difficulty leveraging the value or output of their labor to negotiate their freedom.

The few occupations that were available to women in Baltimore's changing urban economy further curbed slave women's ability to pursue their freedom. During the final decades of the eighteenth century and in the early nineteenth, the service sector of Baltimore's economy expanded markedly to include 47 percent of all urban households.[62] Among this group were tradesmen, professionals such as doctors and lawyers, owners of small retail businesses, and workers who hired out their labor. These occupations did not usually require an additional workforce, and, consequently, householders within this economic sector who owned slaves usually employed them in a domestic capacity. In fact, an increasing number of service-providing households employed slaves at the turn of the nineteenth century, reflecting a demand for domestic labor that became relatively widespread in Baltimore and that was met, predominantly, by slave women.[63] That women became the main providers of domestic service in the late-eighteenth and early-nineteenth centuries was a product of not only the rising demand for domestic workers but also the concomitant development of the manufacturing sector of Baltimore's economy. During that period, manufacturing businesses in Baltimore were becoming more numerous as well as more complex, creating their own demand for workers. The labor force that sustained this growth, however, was almost entirely male. Between 1790 and 1810, the population of white adult men over age sixteen was the fastest-growing segment of the Baltimore population, second only to that of free blacks.[64] The combination of an expanding labor market in manufacturing that favored male workers and a rising demand for domestic work that was met by female slaves and other working women reinforced a gendered division of labor that helped to confine women to few occupations. With few labor options available to them and facing rising competition from free women, slave women had little bargaining power when attempting to pursue the negotiation of their freedom.

During the eighteenth century, Baltimore and Sabará developed rapidly from small hamlets into important local economic centers. That transformation happened concomitantly with the expansion of their respective slave populations. Acquired to provide labor to the nascent industries that supported each town's economic growth, slaves also became relevant to the process of diversification that helped to sustain urban development in these two Atlantic localities: They contributed their labor to different economic sectors and, by supplementing household incomes, enabled their owners to pursue their own distinct specializations and investments. Women, who composed a growing segment of these slave populations, were, like their male counterparts, important actors in the process of urban development. They were employed in a variety of economic activities, contributed to the core exchanges that supported urban life, and helped to enrich their owners' households. Though many slave women found themselves providing urban residents with domestic services, the economic significance of their labor extended beyond the confines of the domestic environment in which they worked. By helping to produce goods that were commercialized by their owners, offering goods for sale in the local market, hiring out their labor, or being hired out, slave women in Baltimore and Sabará similarly contributed to the complication and expansion of these urban economic and labor practices.

The similarities that emerge from a comparison of the forms and significance of female slave labor in Baltimore and Sabará are not evident, however, when attention shifts to the implications of urban labor for bondwomen themselves. The distinctions between the two labor markets resulted in marked differences in the way slave women experienced these urban environments. In Sabará, the overwhelming presence of slaves, the gender and racial division of labor, and the informality that prevailed in certain sectors of the economy enabled slave women to have paid jobs or receive part of the income they generated for their owners. In Baltimore, a predominantly white population, incipient industrialization, and patterns of a gendered division of labor increasingly limited slave women's competitiveness in the labor market and access to the economic rewards of their labor. Consequently, whereas slave women in Sabará managed to leverage their labor when negotiating their freedom with relative frequency, in Baltimore few bondwomen had the opportunity to do the same. The comparison between the realities of urban female slave labor in Baltimore and Sabará thus supports two broad observations that seem meaningful to considerations of female urban slavery throughout the Atlantic world. First, the economic relevance of female urban labor deserves acknowledgment and inclusion in narratives of New World urban development. Second, slave women's access to the potential economic benefits of their labor varied according to the level of diversity and industrial employment that characterized a particular urban workforce. Slave women in pursuit of their manumission could thus fare better in urban environments where a racialized division of labor and preindustrial forms of production preserved demand for their work and occasionally secured for them access to the products of their labor.

NOTES

1. Barbara Bush, *Slave Women in Caribbean Society, 1650–1838* (Bloomington: Indiana University Press, 1990), 33–50; Bernard Moitt, *Women and Slavery in the French Antilles, 1635–1848* (Bloomington: Indiana University Press, 2001), 19–79; Jennifer L. Morgan, *Laboring Women: Reproduction and Gender in New World Slavery* (Philadelphia: University of Pennsylvania Press, 2004), 144–65; Gwyn Campbell, Suzanne Miers, and Joseph Miller, "Women in Western Systems of Slavery: Introduction," *Slavery and Abolition* 26 (August 2005): 161–79.

2. For a review of the scholarship on urban slavery, see Mariana Dantas, "Urban Slavery," in *Oxford Bibliography Online: Atlantic History,* ed. Trevor Burnard (New York: Oxford University Press, 2011), www.oxfordbibliographies.com/view/document/obo-9780199730414/obo-978 0199730414–0142.xml.

3. For relatively recent discussions of female urban slaves, see Cynthia M. Kennedy, *Braided Relations, Entwined Lives: The Women of Charleston's Urban Slave Society* (Bloomington: Indiana University Press, 2005), 127–56; María Elisa Velázquez, *Mujeres de Origen Africano en la Capital Novohispana, siglos XVII y XVIII* (Mexico City: Institute Nacional de Antropologia e Historia, Universidade Nacional Autónoma de México, 2006), 109–228; Richard Graham, *Feeding the City: From Street Market to Liberal Reform in Salvador, Brazil, 1780–1860* (Austin: University of Texas Press, 2010), 33–53.

4. Indeed, in my own work on urban slavery I paid greater attention to the economic significance of male slave labor than that of female slave labor. Mariana Dantas, *Black Townsmen: Urban Slavery and Freedom in the Eighteenth-Century Atlantic World* (New York: Palgrave, 2008), 47–96.

5. As Ira Berlin and Philip D. Morgan have stressed, work was a major defining element in the lives of slaves in the Americas: it shaped their activities and their routines while also being a source of affliction and privilege. See Ira Berlin and Philip D. Morgan, "The Slaves' Economy: Independent Production by Slaves in the Americas: Introduction," *Slavery and Abolition* 12 (May 1991): 1–27.

6. Important works on this topic that have framed the field are Richard S. Dunn, *Sugar and Slaves: The Rise of the Planter Class in the English West Indies, 1624–1713* (Chapel Hill: University of North Carolina Press, 1972); Stuart B. Schwartz, *Sugar Plantations in the Formation of Brazilian Society, Bahia, 1550–1835* (New York: Cambridge University Press, 1985); and Philip D. Curtin, *The Rise and Fall of the Plantation Complex: Essays in Atlantic History* (New York: Cambridge University Press, 1990). More recently, David Eltis's work portrayed plantations as the quintessential

economic environment supported by African slavery. See David Eltis, *The Rise of African Slavery in the Americas* (New York: Cambridge University Press, 2000), 193–223.

7. Gwendolyn Midlo Hall, *Africans in Colonial Louisiana: The Development of Afro-Creole Culture in the Eighteenth Century* (Baton Rouge: Louisiana State University Press, 1992), 119–55; R. Douglas Cope, *The Limits of Racial Domination: Plebeian Society in Colonial Mexico City, 1660–1720* (Madison: University of Wisconsin Press, 1994); Lyman L. Johnson, *The Development of Slave and Free Labor Regimes in Late Colonial Buenos Aires, 1770–1815* (Amherst: Latin American Studies Program, University of Massachusetts, 1997); João José Reis, *Slave Rebellion in Brazil: The Muslim Uprising of 1835 in Bahia* (Baltimore: Johns Hopkins University Press, 1993), 160–74; Robert Olwell, *Masters, Slaves, and Subjects: The Culture of Power in the South Carolina Low Country, 1740–1790* (Ithaca, NY: Cornell University Press, 1998), 141–80; Trevor Burnard and Emma Hart, "Kingston, Jamaica, and Charleston, South Carolina: A New Look at Comparative Urbanization in Plantation Colonial British America," *Journal of Urban History* 39 (March 2013): 214–34.

8. Recent literature that highlights the participation of slaves in the development and maintenance of urban life in Baltimore and Sabará includes T. Stephen Whitman, *The Price of Freedom: Slavery and Manumission in Baltimore and Early National Maryland* (Lexington: University Press of Kentucky, 1997), 33–60; Christopher Phillips, *Freedom's Port: The African American Community of Baltimore, 1790–1860* (Urbana: University of Illinois Press, 1997), 7–29; Kathleen J. Higgins, *"Licentious Liberty" in a Brazilian Gold-Mining Region: Slavery, Gender, and Social Control in Eighteenth-Century Sabará, Minas Gerais* (University Park: Pennsylvania State University Press, 1999) 43–88; Douglas Libby, "Habilidades, artífices e ofícios na sociedade escravista do Brasil colonial," in *Trabalho Livro, Trabalho Escravo: Brasil e Europa, séculos XVIII e XIX* (São Paulo: Annablume, 2006), 57–74; Dantas, *Black Townsmen,* 71–96; Seth Rockman, *Scraping By: Wage Labor, Slavery, and Survival in Early Baltimore* (Baltimore: Johns Hopkins University Press, 2009).

9. "Lista dos escravos . . . para pagarem o reaes quinto," 1720, CMS, códice 2, APM (hereinafter cited as CMS, #, APM); Waldemar de Almeida Barbosa, Dicionário Histórico-Geográfico de Minas Gerais (Belo Horizonte: Publicações do Arquivo Público Mineiro, 1971), 85; "Relação dos Habitantes da Comarca do Rio das Velhas," 1776, AHU, box (112), document 11, APM (hereinafter cited as AHU (#)#, APM).

10. List of Taxables of Deptford Hundred, 1773, BCC, Tax Lists, M 1560, MSA; Census of Deptford Hundred, Council of Safety (Census of 1776), S961-3, MSA; Assessment List of Deptford Hundred, 1783, BCC, Tax Lists, M 871, MSA; *A Century of Population Growth: From the 1st Census of the U.S. to the 12th, 1790–1900* (Washington, DC: Government Printing Office, 1909); *Population Schedules of the Second Census of the United States, 1800* (Washington, DC: National Archives and Records Service, 1960), microform.

11. At its height, the slave population in Baltimore counted 4,672 individuals and represented between 10 and 11 percent of the city's total population.

12. Dantas, *Black Townsmen,* 47–70. Richard Graham makes a similar argument about the importance of slave work to urban life in nineteenth-century Salvador. See Graham, *Feeding the City,* 19–20. For a helpful comparative discussion of slaves and other non-elites as urban economic agents in Latin America, see Mary Karasch, "Suppliers, Sellers, Servants, and Slaves,"

in *Cities and Society in Colonial Latin America,* ed. Louisa Schell Hoberman and Susan Migden Socolow (Albuquerque: University of New Mexico Press, 1986), 251–83.

13. Quantitative studies that highlight the predominance of women among urban slaves include Richard C. Wade, *Slavery in the Cities: The South 1820–1860* (New York: Oxford University Press, 1970); and Claudia D. Goldin, *Urban Slavery in the American South, 1820–1860: A Quantitative History* (Chicago: University of Chicago Press, 1976).

14. Inventários, 1750–1799, Cartório do Primeiro Ofício and Cartório do Segundo Ofício, ACBG/MOS. For this period, I consulted 350 probate records, listing a total of 5,014 slaves.

15. BCC, Register of Wills (inventories), MSA; Assessment List of 1783, BCC, Tax Lists, M 871, MSA; List of Assessed Persons, Baltimore City, 1804, BCC, Commissioners of Tax, CM 1204, MSA.

16. Wade, *Slavery in the Cities,* 23–24, 120–21; Goldin, *Urban Slavery,* 60–65; Phillips, *Freedom's Port,* 19–22; Rockman, *Scraping By,* 109–11.

17. Whitman, *Price of Freedom,* 9–13.

18. Rockman, *Scraping By,* is an exception. See 100–131, 185–91.

19. Laird W. Bergad's study of slave prices in Minas Gerais indicates that male slaves were consistently more expensive than female slaves. See Laird W. Bergad, *Slavery and the Demographic and Economic History of Minas Gerais, Brazil, 1720–1888* (Cambridge: Cambridge University Press, 1999), 173–87. In Baltimore, slave deeds of sale recorded between 1750 and 1775 indicate that adult male slaves cost an average of £48.4, while adult slave women cost, on average, £37.5. BCC, Chattel Records, MS 2865, MHS.

20. "Inventário dos Teares Existentes na Capitania de Minas Gerais, 1786," *Revista do Arquivo Público Mineiro* 40 (1995). For further discussion of the activities of these weavers and their role in the local economy, see Douglas C. Libby, "Reconsidering Textile Production in Late Colonial Brazil: New Evidence from Minas Gerais," *Latin American Research Review* 32 (Winter 1997): 88–108; and Francisco Vidal Luna and Herbert S. Klein, *Slavery and the Economy of São Paulo, 1750–1850* (Stanford, CA: Stanford University Press, 2003), 194–98.

21. André João Antonil, *Cultura e Opulência do Brasil* (Belo Horizonte: Editora Itatiaia, 1982), 169–73.

22. For a definition and discussion of *vendas* and *vendeiros(as),* see Cláudia Chaves, *Perfeitos Negociantes: Mercadores nas Minas Setecentistas* (São Paulo: Annablume, 1999), 59–61; and Júnia F. Furtado, *Homens de Negócio: A Interiorização da Metrópole e do Comércio nas Minas Setecentistas* (São Paulo: Hucitec, 1999), 230–72.

23. Slave women represented 23 percent of all women granted commercial licenses and 10 percent of all licensees found for the second half of the eighteenth century. Moreover, they constituted 80 percent of all slaves who appear in these documents. Licenses were examined for the years of 1750, 1755, 1790, 1795, and 1806. CMS, 16A, 82, 128, APM.

24. Luciano Figueiredo, in an appendix to his book on women in colonial Minas Gerais, lists several complaints, orders, and edicts issued in that region concerning the illegal activities of slave and free black women. See Luciano Figueiredo, *O Avesso da Memória: Cotidiano e trabalho da mulher em Minas Gerais no século XVIII* (Rio de Janeiro: José Olympio Editora, 1993), 205–14. Maria Odila Silva Dias found similar complaints of female vendors without licenses in

eighteenth- and nineteenth-century São Paulo. See Maria Odila Silva Dias, *Power and Everyday Life: The Lives of Working Women in Nineteenth-Century Brazil* (New Brunswick, NJ: Rutgers University Press, 1995), 35–51.

25. The relevance of slave women's labor as street and market vendors has also been noted for other Brazilian towns and cities as well as in other urban centers in the Americas. See Karasch, "Suppliers, Sellers, Servants, and Slaves," 268–72; Jane Mangan, *Trading Roles: Gender, Ethnicity, and the Urban Economy in Colonial Potosí* (Durham, NC: Duke University Press, 2005), 36–42; Graham, *Feeding the City,* 35–42; Robert Olwell, "'Loose, Idle and Disorderly': Slave Women in the Eighteenth Century Charleston Marketplace," in *More than Chattel: Black Women and Slavery in the Americas,* ed. David Barry Gaspar and Darlene Clark Hine (Bloomington: Indiana University Press, 1996), 97–110.

26. Assessment List of 1783, BCC, Tax Lists, M 871, MSA.

27. *Maryland Journal and Baltimore Advertiser,* May 20, 1783. For a description of the different tradesmen employed in shipbuilding, see R. Campbell, *The London Tradesman* (Devon, UK: Newton Abbot, David & Charles, 1969), 298–301.

28. Richard Parkinson, *A Tour in America in 1798, 1799, and 1800* (London: J. Harding and J. Murray, 1805), 175–76. Complaints to the mayor and city council of Baltimore that black women were causing disturbances in city markets suggest that slave women engaged in illegal economic exchanges in urban market spaces. "Petition by the Inhabitants near the Hanover Market House," June 17, 1805, RG 16/S.1, box 5, doc. 206A, Baltimore City Archives.

29. Between 1796 and 1810, Alexander Robinson, a doctor in Baltimore City, hired out the domestic labor of two of his slave women. Alexander Robinson Ledger, MS 699, MHS. According to a slave runaway advertisement, Frederick Delaport's slave woman, "an excellent seamstress and house wench," was used to offering herself to hire about town. See *Maryland Journal and Baltimore Advertiser,* October 5, 1784.

30. For a similar argument, see Rockman, *Scraping By,* 111–14.

31. Runaway ads, with their descriptions of the possessions—clothes in particular—that slaves took with them after fleeing their masters indicate slaves' participation, even if limited, in a local consumer market for personal goods. Dantas, *Black Townsmen,* 93–94. See also Betty Wood, *Women's Work, Men's Work: The Informal Slave Economies of Lowcountry Georgia* (Athens: University of Georgia Press, 1995), 57–61.

32. Inventário de Miguel da Silva Costa, March 12, 1761, CSO doc. (22)04, ACBG/MOS.

33. Different studies have pointed to the important participation of slave women in organizing, carrying out, and sustaining certain economic activities that contributed to the general economic well-being of urban environments. See Dias, *Power and Everyday Life,* 35–51, 96–109; Olwell, "'Loose, Idle and Disorderly,'" 97–110; Libby, "Reconsidering Textile Production"; Velázquez, *Mujeres de Origen Africano,* 161–228.

34. See, for instance, Tina Sheller, "Freemen, Servants, and Slaves: Artisans and the Evolution of Baltimore Town, 1765–1790," in *American Artisans: Crafting Social Identity, 1750–1850,* ed. Howard B. Rock, Paul A. Gilje, and Robert Asher (Baltimore: Johns Hopkins University Press, 1995), 17–32.

35. Joanne Pope Melish similarly argues that slavery was vital to the process of economic diversification in New England. See Joanne Pope Melish, *Disowning Slavery: Gradual Emanci-*

pation and "Race" in New England, 1780–1860 (Ithaca, NY: Cornell University Press, 1998), 11–21. See also Ellen Hartigan-O'Connor, "'She Said She Did Not Know Money': Urban Women and Atlantic Markets in the Revolutionary Era," *Early American Studies* 4 (October 2006): 322–52.

36. Scholars have found evidence of slaves as urban consumers in other settings as well. See Mary C. Karasch, *Slave Life in Rio de Janeiro, 1808–1850* (Princeton, NJ: Princeton University Press, 1987), 210–13; Wood, *Women's Work, Men's Work*, 128–38; Hartigan-O'Connor, "'She Said She Did Not Know Money,'" 340–42.

37. B. W. Higman, *Slave Populations of the British Caribbean, 1807–1834* (Baltimore: Johns Hopkins University Press, 1988), 379–86; David Barry Gaspar, "'To Be Free Is Very Sweet': The Manumission of Female Slaves in Antigua, 1817–26," in *Beyond Bondage: Free Women of Color in the Americas*, ed. David Barry Gaspar and Darlene Clark Hine (Urbana: University of Illinois Press, 2004), 60–81; Rosemary Brana-Shute and Randy J. Sparks, eds., *Paths to Freedom: Manumission in the Atlantic World* (Columbia: University of South Carolina Press, 2009), 161–74, 175–96.

38. Among the 513 records of manumission I consulted for Sabará, 306 (60%) referred to female slaves and 207 (40%) to male slaves. Livros de Notas L2, L56, L59, L75, L82, L89, N118, L63–67, ACBG/MOS.

39. In 1776 female slaves constituted 36 percent of the slave population of Sabará, the male-female ratio found for that population that year being 1.8. Thirty-four years later, the ratio had decreased slightly to 1.6. Mapa dos Habitantes Atuais da Capitania de Minas Gerais, 1776, AHU (110)59, APM; Recenseamento da população de alguns termos da antiga Capitania, depois Província, de Minas Gerais, 1808–1821, Arquivo da Casa dos Contos, filme 540, pl. 21115, APM.

40. Among the 305 manumission deeds I consulted for Baltimore, 134 (44%) referred to women and 171 (56%) to men. Assessment List of 1783, BCC, Tax Lists, M 871, MSA; List of Assessed Persons, Baltimore City, 1804, BCC, Commissioners of Tax, CM 1204, MSA.

41. Examining manumission deeds for Maryland, T. Stephen Whitman found that slave owners freed slave men and women in equal numbers, suggesting that manumission practices in the city of Baltimore differed from practices in other parts of the state. See Whitman, *Price of Freedom*, 95.

42. The terms under which slaves in Baltimore and Sabará obtained their freedom can be grouped into three categories: immediate, with no conditions or requirements imposed on the slave; by purchase, resulting from the slave's payment of his or her market value; and conditional, granted in exchange for a term of service. In Baltimore, 40 percent of female manumissions were immediate, 6 percent by purchase, and 54 percent conditional. In Sabará, 31 percent of female manumissions were immediate, 54 percent by purchase, and 15 percent conditional. BCC, Chattel Records, C 298, MSA; BCC, Miscellaneous Papers, MSA; BCC, Register of Wills, Certificates of Freedom, CM 820/821, MSA; BCC, Chattel Records, MS 2865, MHS; Livros de Notas L2, L56, L59, L75, L82, L89, N118, L63–67, ACBG/MOS.

43. Discussions of term slaves in Baltimore (slaves who were serving a term imposed by their manumission deeds) highlight slave owners' continued control over the conditions under which these slaves labored, as well as the frequency with which term slaves were hired out to employers in and outside of the city. Whitman, *Price of Freedom*, 110–18; Phillips, *Freedom's Port*, 42–45.

44. Colonial census records did not distinguish between slave women of African origin and those of African descent. Therefore I have used eighteenth-century probate records to deter-

mine in such detail the makeup of the slave population in Sabará. Inventários, 1750–1799, CSO, ACBG/MOS; Livros de Notas L2, L56, L59, L75, L82, L89, N118, L63–67, ACBG/MOS.

45. Similar observations were made for other parts of Minas Gerais and colonial Brazil by Stuart B. Schwartz, "The Manumission of Slaves in Colonial Brazil: Bahia, 1684–1745," *Hispanic American Historical Review* 54 (November 1974): 603–35; Karasch, *Slave Life in Rio*, 345–48; Eduardo França Paiva, *Escravidão e Universo Cultural na Colônia: Minas Gerais, 1716–1789* (Belo Horizonte, Brazil: Editora da Universidade Federal de Minas Gerais, 2006), 167–74; Douglas C. Libby and Clotilde Paiva, "Manumission Practices in a Late Eighteenth-Century Brazilian Slave Parish: São José d'El Rey in 1795," *Slavery and Abolition* 21 (April 2000): 96–127.

46. A. J. R. Russell-Wood, "Através de um prisma africano: Uma nova abordagem ao estudo da diáspora africana no Brasil Colonial," *Tempo* 12 (December 2001): 11–50; Mieko Nishida, *Slavery and Identity: Ethnicity, Gender, and Race in Salvador, Brazil* (Bloomington: Indiana University Press, 2003), 4–46; Graham, *Feeding the City*, 35.

47. For a discussion of women's work on plantations, see Morgan, *Laboring Women*, 144–65. In Sabará, slaveholdings of miners usually had a high male-female gender ratio, in some cases eight to ten slave men for every slave woman. See Dantas, *Black Townsmen*, 63.

48. For a general overview of Portuguese policies toward Brazilian manufacturing activities in the eighteenth century, see Fernando A. Novais, "A Proibição das Manufacturas no Brasil e a Política Econômica Portuguesa no Fim do Século XVIII," *Revista de História* 67 (1967): 145–66.

49. For a description of Pombal's policies and their effects on the colonial economy, see Kenneth Maxwell, *Conflicts and Conspiracies: Brazil and Portugal, 1750–1808* (Cambridge: Cambridge University Press, 1973), 33–83; Andrée Mansui-Diniz Silva, "Imperial Re-Organization, 1750–1808," in *Colonial Brazil*, ed. Leslie Bethel (Cambridge: Cambridge University Press, 1987), 261–69; Mafalda Zemella, *O Abastecimento da Capitania de Minas Gerais no Século XVIII* (São Paulo: Editora Hucitec, 1990), 226–30; Libby, "Reconsidering Textile Production," 88–108.

50. Evidence of the involvement of slave women in the local production and sales of soap and oil can be found in probate records and documents of municipal councils. Inventário de Teresa de Souza, 14 Oct. 1775, CSO (40)05, ACBG/MOS; Inventário de Antônio Duarte Couzinha, October 8, 1782, CSO (52)05, ACBG/MOS; Inventário de Inácio Pires de Miranda, May 8, 1788, CSO (63)04, ACBG/MOS; Inventário de Anselmo da Silva Diniz, November 28, 1788, CSO (62)06, ACBG/MOS; Câmara Municipal de Mariana, December 31, 1767, AHU (91)85, APM; Câmara Municipal de S. José, April 23, 1768, AHU (92)56, APM.

51. Inventário de José de Freitas Costa, June 11, 1778, CSO (46)06, ACBG/MOS.

52. As Ann Twinam has discussed for the Spanish Americas, while the notion of honor, as understood by white elites, did not apply to nonwhites, non-elites nevertheless embraced and employed those notions when negotiating a middling position in colonial society. See Ann Twinam, "The Negotiation of Honor," in *The Faces of Honor: Sex, Shame, and Violence in Colonial Latin America*, ed. Lyman L. Johnson and Sonya Lipsett-Rivera (Albuquerque: University of New Mexico Press, 1998), 68–102.

53. In general, slaves represented 40 percent of the total value of all free black estates in Sabará; real estate represented 30 percent of the total. Inventários do Cartório do Segundo Ofício, 1750–1799, ACBG/MOS. Zephyr Frank, in his study of socioeconomic mobility in nineteenth-

century Rio de Janeiro, makes a compelling case for the importance of slave ownership to free black socioeconomic status in slave societies. Zephyr L. Frank, *Dutra's World: Wealth and Family in Nineteenth-Century Rio de Janeiro* (Albuquerque: University of New Mexico Press, 2004), 96–121. See also Júnia Ferreira Furtado, *Chica da Silva: A Brazilian Slave of the Eighteenth Century* (New York: Cambridge University Press, 2009), 146–61. The importance free persons of African origin and descent placed on slave ownership has been observed in other societies in the Americas. See Edward L. Cox, *Free Coloreds in the Slave Societies of St. Kitts and Grenada, 1763–1833* (Knoxville: University of Tennessee Press, 1984), 72–75; Michael P. Johnson and James L. Roark, *Black Masters: A Free Family of Color in the Old South* (New York: Norton, 1984), 203–6; and Kimberly S. Hanger, *Bounded Lives, Bounded Places: Free Black Society in Colonial New Orleans, 1769–1803* (Durham, NC: Duke University Press, 1997), 55–87.

54. Slaves represented 9 and 10 percent of Baltimore's total population in 1790 and 1810, respectively. Free whites represented 88 and 78 percent of the city's total population in those same years. *Population Schedules of the First Census of the United States, 1790;* and *Population Schedules of the Third Census of the United States, 1810* (Washington, DC: National Archives and Record Service, 1960), microform.

55. Barbara Jeanne Fields, *Slavery and Freedom on the Middle Ground: Maryland during the Nineteenth Century* (New Haven, CT: Yale University Press, 1985), 12–14; Whitman, *Price of Freedom,* 13; Rockman, *Scraping By,* 28–33.

56. Max Grivno's examination of free and unfree labor in Maryland's northern counties reveals that the competition between different labor arrangements and its negative impact on wages was a phenomenon that, in the Upper South, extended to rural areas as well. Max Grivno, *Gleanings of Freedom: Free and Slave Labor along the Mason-Dixon Line, 1790–1860* (Urbana: University of Illinois Press), 34–60.

57. *Population Schedules of the First Census of the United States, 1790; Population Schedules of the Third Census of the United States, 1810.*

58. Dantas, *Black Townsmen,* 134–38; Jennifer Hull Dorsey, *Hirelings: African American Workers and Free Labor in Early Maryland* (Ithaca, NY: Cornell University Press, 2011), 45–60.

59. *Federal Gazette and Baltimore Daily Advertiser,* February 5, 1796.

60. Ibid., January 11, March 30, 1796.

61. Rockman, *Scraping By,* 100–131.

62. Jacob Price, in his examination of economic diversification in American urban ports, identified four main economic sectors: maritime commerce, provision of service, manufacturing businesses, and governmental jobs. I have applied his model to this discussion of Baltimore's economy. See Jacob M. Price, "Economic Function and the Growth of American Port Towns in the Eighteenth Century," *Perspectives in American History* 8 (1974): 123–86. I arrived at the percentage of service-providing households through an analysis of the Baltimore City Directory for 1800. See *The New Baltimore Directory, and Annual Register; for 1800 and 1801* (Baltimore: Warner & Hanna, 1800).

63. Charles G. Steffen, *The Mechanics of Baltimore: Workers and Politics in the Age of Revolution, 1763–1812* (Urbana: University of Illinois Press, 1984), 36–37; Phillips, *Freedom's Port,* 19–21; Dantas, *Black Townsmen,* 77–78; Rockman, *Scraping By,* 102–17.

64. *Population Schedules of the First Census of the United States, 1790; Population Schedules of the Third Census of the United States, 1810.* For a thorough analysis of the Baltimore workforce during the period of expansion of manufacturing businesses, see Steffen, *Mechanics of Baltimore,* 27–50.

"IN ALGIERS, THE CITY OF BONDAGE"

Urban Slavery in Comparative Context

CHRISTINE E. SEARS

When Ottoman Algerian corsairs seized the American ship *Dau-phin* in 1785, Richard O'Brien and his fifteen crewmen entered an urban slave system born of Old World and Greater Mediter-ranean practices. Long a "structural feature of Mediterranean society," slav-ery thrived in the many cities ringing the sea. Unlike those in the race-based Atlantic plantation complex, Mediterranean and Old World slavers bound others based on "religion and mischance" rather than "race and destiny." Thus, the enslavable Other claimed both a different religion and a different polity. Unfortunately for O'Brien and his crew, the Ottoman Algerian government declared war against the United States as they set sail, and O'Brien and his men were at least nominally Christian. This system of slave-taking—enslaving prisoners of war—existed alongside other slave-making practices in the Otto-man and Greater Mediterranean worlds, yielding the ethnically diverse slave population that O'Brien and his crew found in Algiers. The *Dauphin* sailors joined six previously captured American men and about three thousand Eu-ropean men in what was, from an Algerian point of view, a highly successful, long-practiced form of urban slavery.[1]

Since Richard Wade's 1964 landmark work *Slavery in the Cities,* many scholars have described cities as hostile, even anathema, to slavery and posited that slavery there met its demise owing to urban conditions. In cities, they have argued, slaves moved, congregated, and organized more easily than in rural settings. City slaves developed a taste for freedom as they hired them-selves out, interacted with free people, and directly experienced "cash power."

Inevitably, these scholars assert, slaves' relative liberty and masters' decreased control over them brought about the demise of urban slavery.[2]

In the work of Wade and other scholars, greater freedom of movement, less control, and access to markets made up the "urban nature" of slavery. But these characteristics were not confined to urban settings. Historians have exposed how rural slaves, like urban bondmen, interacted with free people, frequently bought and sold goods, and were often hired out. Like their urban counterparts, country owners struggled with divided mastery and the ever-present problems of slave discipline and control. In fact, recent scholarship highlights how "rural slavery" covered widely divergent experiences. Country slaves labored on large holdings and small, toiled over radically different tasks and crops, experienced varying degrees of autonomy and mobility, and were located in different states, countries, and continents. Increasingly, historians agree that no single "rural slavery" existed. Indeed, understanding any particular slavery requires investigating the specific time, place, labor, related populations, and other aspects of the society in which slavery was practiced.[3]

Like rural bondage, urban slavery has commanded increased attention during the past thirty years. Scholars have examined urban slavery in New York, Richmond, Baltimore, Cape Town, Havana, Bursa, and many other locations. Studies of single locations point to urban slavery's diversity and indicate how closely each slave system was woven into the society, economy, and culture of each city. Wade and other scholars separated "urban society" from the slave system embedded in it. But these studies demonstrate, as one historian put it, that "slavery was, in fact, part of the 'nature' of many urban societies." Slavery in its various forms was frequently utilized by city dwellers, but one cannot "abstract a city from its context."[4]

Richard Wade noted slavery's long urban history, while Claudia Goldin argued that city slavery illustrated the "capacity of slavery to adapt to a wide variety of special conditions." Perhaps Goldin had it backward: Plantation slavery showcased slavery's ability to adapt from its pervasive urban forms. Slavery and cities coexisted from humanity's earliest history, a fact obscured by the frequent focus on antebellum U.S. plantation slavery. When examined in a world-historical context, plantation slaveries in the American South and across the New World plantation complex emerge as outliers rather than "typical" forms of enslavement. Reexamining urban slavery requires dislodging antebellum southern slavery from its pedestal as the quintessential slavery. In fact, this line of inquiry—urban slavery's eventual demise—arises from U.S.-focused slave studies.[5]

Recent slave studies provide reasons to reexamine any pat divisions between city and country slavery. Using what Peter Kolchin termed a "soft approach" of comparison, I examine the late-eighteenth- and early-nineteenth-century Ottoman Algerian enslavement of Christians—Americans and Europeans—to illuminate the specific conditions of slavery in that urban system. This "soft approach" applies a broadly comparative lens that highlights how slave systems depended on temporal and regional conditions rather than merely a city or country address. The comparative method employed here indicates that slavery and cities were not incompatible as a matter of course; slavery was far too flexible an institution. Rather, slave systems' longevity, whether urban or rural, depended upon historically contingent variables.[6]

I find that Ottoman Algerian Christian slavery was well suited to its urban setting. In fact, the very qualities that contributed to slavery's denouement in other cities—the ability to receive and spend money or the relative day-to-day autonomy paired with the chance to earn privileged positions and preferred treatment—nurtured the Ottoman Algerian slave system. Ottoman Algerian enslavement of Christians did not die out because of "urban conditions"; instead, those conditions maintained and supported the Ottoman Algerian form of bondage.

O'Brien and his largely American crew would have quickly seen how their Algerian enslavement differed from slavery's other variants in the New World. Most Ottoman Algerian slaves were state-owned, and the few privately owned bondpeople were treated like the state-owned. Most worked, but not all. Several served as administrators and a small number were released from labor altogether. As in Mediterranean and Ottoman forms of slavery, Ottoman Algerian Christian slavery tended to be temporary rather than lifelong and hereditary. Christian slaves received and sent mail, were encouraged to get and spend money, and congregated easily with fellow slaves. Moreover, O'Brien and his men swiftly perceived the futility of escape attempts. They could not elude notice by blending in with freedmen, since almost none populated the city. Nor did either the Algerian countryside or the greater Mediterranean world offer freedom. In short, redemption by the U.S. government—or death—was their surest way out of Algiers.[7]

Like most eighteenth-century Christian slaves, O'Brien and his men were claimed by the Algerian Regency and the Dey (the council and the king, respectively). In Ottoman Algiers, government-owned slaves resided with and worked alongside a few privately held bondmen and thus experienced a similar slavery. Though not unheard of, public or state ownership of slaves was by no means the norm for urban slavery. Private ownership of bondmen predominated in most U.S. locales, notably Baltimore, New York, Philadelphia, and Richmond.[8]

In urban areas where individual masters claimed slaves, bondmen were distributed throughout the city, held in small groups, and toiled at a wide variety of work in diverse settings. In post-Revolutionary Baltimore, for example, artisans and manufacturers made up 20 to 30 percent of slaveholders and collectively possessed one-third of the city's slaves. By 1800, close to 30 percent of Baltimore households listed one or more enslaved individuals. Most held few slaves, so bondpeople lived in small groups with their owner or hirer. Enslaved people labored in shipyards, in artisans' workshops, in merchant establishments, and in homes as domestic workers. In cities such as Baltimore, where small holdings predominated, slave labor involved "greater individualized work" than in those urban areas where individual owners held larger numbers of enslaved people.[9]

In Ottoman Algiers and other urban locales, states or companies often owned a majority of the enslaved. Those bondmen worked, recreated, and slept together. In sixteenth-century Havana, the Crown claimed most of the city's slaves, while in eighteenth-century Cape Town, the Dutch East India Company (in Dutch, the Vereenigde Oostindische Compagnie, or VOC) held a majority of the city's enslaved persons. Where states or companies owned slaves, bondmen were often housed together and toiled alongside one another. Government-owned slaves in Havana resided in separate quarters, away from privately held bondmen, but with convicts and other condemned persons joining them at their daily tasks. VOC-owned slaves were locked nightly in the Slave Lodge and completed largely manual labor in gangs. State slaves in Rio de Janeiro were similarly sheltered in barracks and reported to quarries and public works in gangs.[10]

Ten of O'Brien's fifteen-member crew were assigned to a *bagnio*, one of the prisons where three-fourths of the Christian slaves were housed. In 1785 four Algerian *bagnios* accommodated between 1,000 and 1,800 slaves apiece. Most of the captives were Spanish, though their number included some French,

Portuguese, Genoan, Sardinian, Neapolitan, and a few American prisoners as well. Like government-owned slaves in colonial Havana, *bagnio* slaves were locked in barracks overnight and called out each morning to work in gangs, in Algiers under the supervision of Turkish soldiers.[11]

In single-owner slave systems such as those in Havana and Algiers, bondmen shared a generally common enslavement that might have provided a base for communal action. After all, *bagnio* slaves spent most of their time together, much of it free from supervision. Every night, they were confined with hundreds of their fellow slaves and were monitored only by a handful of Algerian-appointed Christian slaves. They might have planned insurrections or made nocturnal arrangements to resist their masters in other ways, but such plans rarely materialized, a testament to the Ottoman Algerian Christian slave system's organization. Although most slaves belonged to a single owner and were housed in *bagnios,* the Ottoman Algerian government nevertheless drew some distinctions among its captives. Government officials carefully noted their Christian slaves' rank and nationality and then divided slaves into three categories—*papalunas,* elite slaves, and *bagnio* slaves—based on rank and access to funds.

From the start, then, Christian slaves were identified as "those who worked"—*bagnio* and elite slaves—or as "those who waited," the *papalunas.* Former officers were designated *papalunas;* a monthly fee kept them from working and from *bagnio* residency. Elite slaves worked within the Ottoman Algerian system as administrators and officials, while *bagnio* slaves inhabited the barracks after their assigned labors. In single-owner urban environments, slaves' lives and labor often converged more than they diverged. Ottoman Algerians' cultivation of different Christian-slave "tracks" hindered slaves from making common cause, despite their considerable autonomy.[12]

If, as Ira Berlin noted, "labor defined slaves' existence," then describing urban slaves' work can illuminate a particular slave system. Of course, the "when, where, and especially how" slaves worked depended on many factors that go beyond a country or city setting. In Ottoman Algiers, *papalunas* did little work, while elite slaves performed specialized tasks. *Bagnio* slaves usually worked at physically demanding, daylong tasks. In some cities, slaves were jacks of all trades; in others, they filled manufacturing or artisanal positions. In late-eighteenth-century Baltimore, 35 percent of slave owners were artisans and manufacturers who, together, held about one-third of Baltimore's bondmen. One scholar found that between 1718 and 1834, 58 percent of Bridgetown, Barbados, slaves were employed as skilled laborers. In Richmond, Virginia, slaves were so often hired out and used in so many different capacities that Midori Takagi argued that Richmond did not possess a uniform slave system at all.[13]

In other urban systems, slaves were assigned unskilled tasks. Slaveholders in the medieval city of Ragusa (modern Dubrovnik in Croatia) desired unskilled domestic laborers, a need they filled by capturing and enslaving rural young women. Female slaves performed household work individually in private homes. The most tractable were rewarded with "prerogatives and rewards" that seldom resulted in freedom or permission to live in the city. Similarly, late-eighteenth-century royal slaves in Havana built and maintained fortifications, resided in barracks, and could not be hired out.[14]

As in Richmond, Virginia, slaves in Ottoman Algiers worked and served in widely different capacities. Despite these great differences, *papalunas*, elite slaves, and *bagnio* slaves were integral parts of the same slave system. Most toiled daily on public works, but some (officers) worked seldom or not at all. Still others did lighter tasks for which they earned remuneration. That is, Ottoman Algerians removed officers from living and laboring with seamen but provided opportunities to those few seamen inclined to complete administrative tasks rather than manual labor.

Like domestic slaves in Ragusa, Christian *bagnio* slaves in Ottoman Algiers functioned as an "alternative for the organization of unskilled labor." Most Christian slaves toiled in gangs from sunup to sundown at the "Sisyphaean labour" required to repair or extend the *mole*, the man-made barrier protecting the Algerian harbor. Gangs of Christian slaves quarried rock, carried stones, and built and rebuilt the *mole* under the supervision of Turkish overseers. They unloaded and outfitted corsair ships, carted dung, and performed other manual tasks, often in gangs. In essence, *bagnio* slaves labored on the "urban plantation" of Algiers, a pattern repeated in other systems in which bondmen were principally state-owned, community housed, and tasked with unskilled gang labor. Three-fourths of Algerian Christian slaves worked at unskilled, manual labor in groups, just as three-fourths of antebellum U.S. slaves toiled together in the fields. That is, despite their urban location, most Christian slaves in Algiers did not do specialized jobs that offered valuable knowledge or the ability to purchase their own freedom. Instead, they slogged daily at manual, tedious, unskilled tasks more akin to what historians have described in rural areas than that in cities.[15]

A few *bagnio* bondmen filled specialized niches, though they reported nightly to a *bagnio*. Some worked in the Ottoman Algerian Marine as coopers, carpenters, turners, sailmakers, and blacksmiths. Six to twelve Christian slaves served in the slave hospital, where they cared for fellow slaves under the direction of Spanish monks. Less than one hundred were assigned to the palace, where some maintained the Dey's gardens, cleaned livestock stalls, and manned the kitchens. American seaman James Cathcart initially served in the Dey's garden, but he and other palace workers bedded each evening with fellow *bagnio* slaves. Only kitchen drudges escaped *bagnio* residency; they were "closely but comfortably lodged" in small rooms near the kitchen.[16]

In Ottoman and other Middle Eastern slave systems, a handful of elite bondmen escaped unskilled, manual work and instead filled administrative or palace posts. Elite slaves chose to work within the Ottoman Algerian system and earned particular perks for doing so. For example, two *cofeegi* made and served coffee to the Dey and his guests. Generously tipped by the Dey and his coffee-drinking guests when their services were required, they accrued significant amounts of money. Like other elite slaves, *cofeegi* ate in the palace, but they bunked in the *bagnios*. Elite slaves shared *bagnio* accommodations with their fellow bondmen unless they were assigned to the palace kitchen or were one of two *captains a proa*, who roomed in the cooks' gallery.[17]

Some elite bondmen administered the Christian slave system. A Christian clerk—always a slave—was assigned to each *bagnio*. The clerk mustered slaves morning and night, reported those sick, dead, or missing, and ordered rations distributed. The secretary of the Marine commanded six to eight bondmen who cared for his goods, waited upon his guests, and served bread and oil to other slaves. One Christian secretary to the Dey acted as head of the slave department. Among other duties, he made a daily report to the Dey that accounted for the Christian slaves and their activities.[18]

Willing slaves competed for these elite and administrative positions; more to the point, they competed for the perks attendant to these positions. Slaves willing to work for the Regency were freed from manual labor, got better housing, had less supervision, enjoyed considerable autonomy, and were tipped in cash. Like the *cofeegi*, these elite slaves might live "better than in their own country." If assigned to the secretary of the Marine, a slave ate well, received some "emolument," had Fridays off, and answered only to the secretary. The *Bagnio Gallera's* clerk was permitted to own a *bagnio* tavern but only required to pay one-half the regular duty on it. The Christian secretary to the Dey, the top administrative slave position, collected exceptional bonuses. This secretary operated a tavern free of duty charges and paid no fee for his *bagnio* suite, which included two rooms with a kitchen, four large windows for ventilation, and a private terrace.[19]

Any slave, regardless of his previous rank, might gain elite slave status, but only officers were accorded *papaluna* status in Ottoman Algiers. *Papalunas* paid a monthly fee to the Algerian Regency. In return, they rarely worked and arranged living quarters outside of the crowded *bagnios*. Though they swore not to escape, the Algerian Regency required a European guarantor who would reimburse the state if a *papaluna* absconded. Only officers were permitted this status in the late eighteenth century. From an Ottoman Algerian point of view, a slave merited this status only if he could command funds enough to pay for it, which officers could do more readily than most seamen. In addition to a monthly fee, *papalunas* footed costs for their room, board, and clothing. Officers, especially captains, might have accumulated the wealth or cultivated the social networks that would aid them in paying the monthly fee. In addition, the U.S. and European governments offered more support for officers than they did for seamen.[20]

As was typical with officers, Captain O'Brien and his passenger Captain Coffin experienced preferential treatment in Algiers. Initially, English Consul Charles Logie rented them from the Regency. They lived in the consular house and did minimal work. Not long after their 1785 capture, however, the Spanish consul Miguel D'Expilly vouched for the two men, provided them with funds, and helped them rent an Algerian house for American officers. As *papalunas*, the officers, funded through D'Expilly, paid a monthly fee to the Regency and fed, housed, and clothed themselves.

European consuls and merchants frequently supported captured captains and officers, perhaps as a courtesy extended to men of rank. Consuls acted with the understanding that the officer's government would reimburse them, an expectation that was not always met. Consuls most readily covered costs for their own countrymen, both because their own governments charged them to provide such care and because they would be compensated for it. The United States lacked a diplomatic presence in Algiers, leaving the Americans at a disadvantage. Expecting that the United States would reimburse him, D'Expilly extended an allowance to the enslaved Americans. When, after several years, the government hinted that it would not, the American slaves reverted to their former protector, English consul Charles Logie.[21]

By 1793, corsairs claimed 130 crewmen from thirteen American ships. Of those 130, roughly 40, all of whom were officers, were classified as *papalunas* at some point. That is, about 31 percent of enslaved Americans were captains or mates, and about the same percentage were afforded *papaluna* status. Officers' protected position meant that they were free to "walk about the streets," patronize Algerian markets, and consult with European merchants and consuls, as could any elite American slaves freed from their administrative labors during the day.[22]

In the late eighteenth century, recurring plague and redemptions shrank the Christian slave population, and Ottoman Algerian leaders reassessed their labor needs. In 1787 Christian slaves numbered about 3,000, but by 1790, only 780 remained. *Papalunas* were henceforth required to serve in the sail loft, but they did not report to the quarries or *mole*. The single-owner system— the Ottoman Algerian government owned most and oversaw all Christian slaves—meant that slaves' work and status could be easily reallocated. If more slaves were needed to outfit a ship, the Regency diverted slaves to the Marine. When more laborers were required, *papalunas* were put to work. Should slaves be too numerous, more could be authorized for *papaluna* standing. Even when working in the sail loft, however, *papalunas* exercised far greater autonomy than did their *bagnio*-assigned crewmen. Furthermore, they were spared the cramped conditions that facilitated the plague's spread among slaves housed in *bagnios*.[23]

Dividing Christian slaves into the categories of *bagnio, papaluna,* and elite slaves prevented bondmen from discerning a shared slavery. Tracking slaves in this way, along with the possibility of redemption, may have quelled slaves' perceptions of a similar slave experience and thus muted the desire to act communally. To be sure, other slave owners used similar strategies to divide slaves. In Cape Town, for instance, some company-owned slaves were awarded privileges and administrative positions. Ottoman Algerians separated slaves based in part on prior status and rank, an effective strategy given that the slaves themselves willingly enforced these hierarchies. In the many late-eighteenth- and early-nineteenth-century wars, American officers balked when housed with seamen as prisoners of war. Algerians freed captains and mates from working and living with sailors, thus maintaining their separate statuses. As *papalunas,* officers achieved great self-determination and autonomy. This, when paired with their likely redemption, at least partially explains why few officers during this period fomented revolt or mounted escape attempts. Algerians held forth incentives for seamen as well: Those who wished might achieve success as elite slaves, gaining privileged living conditions and freedoms that differentiated their experience of slavery from that of others.[24]

Regardless of their status, all Christian slaves could communicate with family, friends, government officials, or others, without Ottoman Algerian interference or oversight. Algiers attracted European merchants who delivered funds, news, and correspondence regularly. Bondmen received letters, newspapers, and even money from outside the city. They dispatched correspondence to family members, government officials, and business connections. For example, seaman John Foss and Captain O'Brien penned letters to their mothers; the *Maria's* first mate, Andrew Forsythe, obtained letters from an aunt and an uncle. Enslaved Americans also directed missives to the president, Congress, consuls, and other officials. In their correspondence, they requested financial assistance and pushed for redemption arrangements on their behalf. Ottoman Algerians facilitated their Christian bondmen's requests for money to spend in Algiers as well as their pleas for redemption. Because slaves anticipated their probable redemption and created and maintained ties with those outside of Algiers, they perhaps relied less on fellow bondmen than they would have otherwise.[25]

In addition to letters and newspapers, all Christian slaves could receive and spend cash. Bondpeople in many times and places procured and spent funds or bartered goods. Slaves in and outside of Havana participated in markets and a "monetary economy" as other slaves did in both rural and urban areas. In most locations and times, slaves earned money when they were hired out or when they sold livestock they raised, produce they grew, or crafts they made. Theft marked another important source of funds.[26]

By the late eighteenth century, enslaved whites in Ottoman Algeria could not sell items they manufactured, and they could not raise livestock or vegetables in the *bagnios.* Administrative or elite Christian slaves in Algiers received money through their work, however. Former seaman Cathcart, for example, earned cash in elite positions such as *cofeegi* or from the *bagnio* taverns that he owned. Some enslaved Christians accepted funds from business connections, family, and charitable groups. Still others borrowed or stole from their fellow slaves and workplaces.[27]

Christian slaves in Algiers could procure funds from outside the city. This feature of Ottoman Algerian bondage was not found in the New World but was sometimes employed in older, Mediterranean slave systems. The Ottoman Algerian Regency allowed, even encouraged, slaves' governments, families, and charities to send them money. The American government, following existing European protocol, provided enslaved Americans with a stipend between 1785 and 1789 and again from 1793 to 1796. In 1794 the Swedish consul meted out stipends of $8 per month for American masters, $6 for mates, and $3 for seamen. According to one American diplomat, enslaved Americans were paid the same amount Spain allowed its men. On the other hand, a French Trinitarian pointed to the Americans' "liberal allowance" when compared to what the French supplied their enslaved countrymen.[28]

The Ottoman Algerian slave system promoted slaves' use of money to buy provisions and granted privileges such as *papaluna* status and private rooms. Ottoman Algiers boasted many markets that Christian slaves visited habitually. *Papalunas* and elite slaves patronized these markets during the day, but even *bagnio* slaves had free time to roam through marketplaces. Once released from daily labor, *bagnio* slaves were free until final roll was called in their assigned *bagnio*. During that time, slaves might patronize a market and buy food. Or they might frequent one of the many *bagnio* taverns run by privileged slaves and visited by Christian slaves and others in Algiers. Though alcohol and no doubt sexual services were available, enslaved Americans mentioned spending their funds on food rather than alcohol, sex, or luxury items. Ottoman Algerians were not threatened by slaves' use of cash and "cash power"; on the contrary, slaves' buying and selling played a crucial role in the functioning of the slave system.[29]

When captured in 1785, O'Brien and his crew were aware that redemption might free them from their Algerian enslavement. They spent more than a decade in Algiers, however, and during that time met Christian slaves who spent their lifetimes enslaved in the city. Surely they entertained fantasies of escape, but few Christian slaves attempted absconding in reality. Several characteristics made escape difficult and inhibited all but those who despaired of ransom from trying.

The absence of freedmen in Algiers was significant. According to some scholars, American cities encouraged slavery's demise because slaves could blend into urban life with relative ease. Throughout the Caribbean, the "free colored population was largely urban-based," so escaped slaves, in merging with free peoples, might convincingly pass as free. Historians have charted the rising free black and enslaved populations of late-eighteenth-century U.S. cities as threats to a clear two-race system. After the Revolutionary War, for example, African Americans made up the fastest-growing segment of Baltimore's population. In cities like Baltimore, with a concentration of freedmen, escaped slaves found jobs to support themselves, especially if they possessed a skill or specialized training. Most free Barbadian blacks lived in Bridgetown, where free and escaped Africans mingled in maritime trades or in the hawking of goods.[30]

In Ottoman Algiers, a runaway Christian slave could not blend into the city's populace. Few free Europeans, and no free Americans, lived in Algiers. Europeans in Algiers occupied high-profile trading or consular posts or were well-known renegades. Renegades were Christians who "turned Turk," or converted to Islam, settled in the city, and often worked for the Regency. The Dey's two chamberlains were renegades. O'Brien mentioned two slaves, neither American, who, in 1790, also turned Turk. But by the late eighteenth century, very few Christian slaves chose this path. Those who did were well known in Algiers and, as new converts, strived to prove their loyalty to Islam and to Ottoman Algiers. Any would-be escaped slaves were unlikely to find protection or aid from the one or two renegades living in the city.[31]

Christian slaves could neither blend into the city's populace nor expect assistance from a sympathetic free population of Europeans or Americans. Nor could slaves find freedom outside Algiers. Walls surrounded the famously well-guarded city. Christian slaves were driven in and out of Algiers through a small number of gates and were supervised by Turkish overseers while working. The heavily fortified port fended off attack and prevented slaves from reaching European ships. Should a slave reach a ship, he would likely be returned, since the Regency negotiated treaties with trading partners, requiring them to return fugitive slave property. In the unlikely event that a slave escaped into the Algerian interior, he was usually reenslaved and resold either in Algiers or farther into the African interior. O'Brien and his crew would leave the city only by death or redemption.[32]

Fortunately for them, most late-eighteenth-century Christian slaves were ransomed and returned to their homes. As in other slave systems, redemption functioned as a management technique by holding out the promise that bondage would be temporary. In Algiers, Christian slaves were redeemed via a treaty in which their countries of origin arranged ransom payment. Surviving enslaved Americans were ransomed in a 1796 U.S.-Algerian treaty. According to the treaty, the United States paid 4,000 sequins (roughly $7,200) per captain and 1,500 to 2,000 sequins ($2,700 to $3,600) to free each mariner. Overall, 76 percent of captured Americans were redeemed; the rest died in Algiers. O'Brien's crew had unusually good luck and bad: Five were redeemed early by friends, but eight died, leaving only two for redemption in 1796.[33]

Algerian urban slavery flourished in the late eighteenth and early nineteenth centuries owing to many factors, all of which show how well this slave system was honed to fit its urban location. As Pedro Welch noted, "the urban environment represents a theater in which specific challenges/adjustments to the authority structure . . . may be viewed." Using Christian slaves, Algerians solved their need for unskilled laborers and administrators for their slave system. They also brought in income through monthly *papaluna* fees, private room rentals, ransom funds, and other fees.[34]

The Ottoman Algerian system of enslaved Christians was in some ways a high-risk project. Slaves lived together, most worked in gangs, and they might have made common cause in their considerable unobserved free time. Bondmen were, however, divided by nationality, work assignments, rank, status, and access to money. Easing the severity of their bondage, they maintained connections to and communication with distant countrymen and kinsmen and received news and funds from outside Algiers. The absence of a freed slave or European population and the presence of impediments to escape or maroonage also contributed to the system's success. Most importantly, Christian slaves counted on redemption. As redemption held forth the promise of eventual liberation, *papaluna* and elite slave status offered some bondmen a comparatively palatable period of enslavement. Thus, the urban conditions in Algiers were entirely compatible with this system of slavery; rather than causing its demise, they sustained it into the nineteenth century.

NOTES

I am deeply grateful to Jeff Forret, John Davies, Katie Turner, Alan Meyer, Tina Manko, and the University of Alabama, Huntsville, writing group for their insights, feedback, and support.

1. Richard O'Brien et al. to Congress, December 20, 1788, Miscellaneous Papers, 1770–1789, Papers of the Continental Congress, 1774–1789, NARA, Washington, DC, 3:181, http://gwpapers .virginia.edu/documents/pirate/documents/irwin_enc.html; Jeffrey Flynn-Paul, "Empire, Monotheism, and Slavery in the Greater Mediterranean Region from Antiquity to the Early Modern Era," *Past and Present* 205 (December 2009): 4; Gillian Weiss, *Captives and Corsairs: France and Slavery in the Early Modern Mediterranean* (Stanford. CA: Stanford University Press, 2011), 3 (quotations); Halil Sahillioğu, "Slaves in the Social and Economic Life of Bursa in the Late 15th and Early 16th Centuries," *Turcica* 17 (1985): 47, 63.

2. Richard Wade, *Slavery in the Cities: The South, 1820–1860* (New York: Oxford University Press, 1964); Douglas R. Egerton, "Slaves to the Marketplace: Economic Liberty and Black Rebelliousness in the Atlantic World," *Journal of the Early Republic* 26 (Winter 2006): 618 (quotation); Barbara Jeanne Fields, *Slavery and Freedom on the Middle Ground: Maryland during the Nineteenth Century* (New Haven, CT: Yale University Press, 1985), 48–51. See also Jonathan D. Martin, *Divided Mastery: Slave Hiring in the American South* (Cambridge, MA: Harvard University Press, 2004).

3. Mariana L. R. Dantas, *Black Townsmen: Urban Slavery and Freedom in the Eighteenth-Century Americas* (New York: Palgrave Macmillan, 2008), 3. Wade addressed only antebellum southern cities in his argument, though other scholars have extended his thesis considerably. See also Donnie D. Bellamy, "Macon, Georgia, 1823–1860: A Study in Urban Slavery," *Phylon* 45 (4th Quarter 1984): 298–302; Martin, *Divided Mastery;* Keith C. Barton, "'Good Cooks and Washers': Slave Hiring, Domestic Labor, and the Market in Bourbon County, Kentucky," *Journal of American History* 84 (September 1997): 436–60; Michael V. Kennedy, "The Hidden Economy of Slavery: Commercial and Industrial Hiring in Pennsylvania, New Jersey, and Delaware, 1728–1800," *Essays in Economic and Business History* 21 (2003): 115–25; Loren Schweninger, "The Underside of Slavery: The Internal Economy, Self-Hire, and Quasi-Freedom in Virginia, 1780–1865," *Slavery and Abolition* 12 (September 1991): 1–22; J. Elliott Russo, "'Fifty-Four Days Work of Two Negroes': Enslaved Labor in Colonial Somerset County, Maryland," *Agricultural History* 78 (Autumn 2004): 466–92; Ira Berlin, *Many Thousands Gone* (Cambridge, MA: Harvard University Press, 1998); Philip D. Morgan, *Slave Counterpoint* (Chapel Hill: University of North Carolina Press, 1998).

4. Dantas, *Black Townsmen,* 96 (first quotation); Fields, *Slavery and Freedom,* 51 (second quotation). See also Ehud R. Toledano, "The Concept of Slavery in Ottoman and Other Muslim Societies: Dichotomy or Continuum," in *Slave Elites in the Middle East and Africa: A Comparative Study,* ed. Miura Toru and John Edward Philips (New York: Kegan Paul International, 2000), 159–75; Linda Colley, *Captives* (New York: Random House, 2004), 58–60; Seth Rockman, "Work in the Cities of Colonial British North America," *Journal of Urban History* 33 (September 2007): 1021–32; Leslie M. Harris, *In the Shadow of Slavery* (Chicago: University of Chicago Press, 2003); Shane White, "Slavery in New York State in the Early Republic," *Australasian Journal of American Studies* 14 (December 1995): 1–29; Robert S. Shelton, "Slavery in a Texas Seaport: The Peculiar Institution in Galveston," *Slavery and Abolition* 28 (August 2007): 155–68; Mary C. Karasch, *Slave Life in Rio de Janeiro, 1808–1850* (Princeton, NJ: Princeton University Press, 1987); Yvonne Sent, "Fugitives and Factotums: Slaves in Early Sixteenth-Century Istanbul," *Journal of the Economic*

and *Social History of the Orient* 39 (May 1996): 136–69; Kristin Mann, *Slavery and the Birth of an African City: Lagos, 1760–1900* (Bloomington: Indiana University Press, 2007).

5. Wade, *Slavery in the Cities,* vii; Claudia Dale Goldin, *Urban Slavery in the American South, 1820–1860: A Quantitative History* (Chicago: University of Chicago Press, 1976), 124 (quotation). As Ronald L. Lewis explained, "too often historians write about 'slavery,' when they really mean the slavery they mean." Lewis, "Industrial Slavery in the African American Urban Experience," in *The African American Urban Experience: Perspectives from the Colonial Period to the Present,* ed. Joe Trotter (New York: Palgrave Macmillan, 2004), 39. See also Ehud Toledano, *Slavery and Abolition in the Ottoman Middle East* (Seattle: University of Washington Press, 1998), 158–61; Christine E. Sears, *American Slaves and African Masters* (New York: Palgrave Macmillan, 2012), 16–23; Weiss, *Captives and Corsairs,* 3–5, 20–22; Peter Kolchin, "The Big Picture: A Comment on David Brion Davis's 'Looking at Slavery from Broader Perspectives,'" *American Historical Review* 105 (April 2000): 467–71; Pierre Dochis, *Medieval Slavery and Liberation,* trans. Arthur Goldhammer (Chicago: University of Chicago Press, 1979), 4–5; Gwyn Campbell and Edward A. Alpers, "Introduction: Slavery, Forced Labour and Resistance in Indian Ocean Africa and Asia," *Slavery and Abolition* 25 (August 2004): ix–x; Alessandro Stanziani and Gwyn Campbell, eds., *Debt Slavery in the Mediterranean and the Atlantic Worlds* (London: Pickering and Chatto, 2013), 1.

6. Peter Kolchin, *A Sphinx on the American Land: The Nineteenth-Century South in Comparative Perspective* (Baton Rouge: Louisiana State University Press, 2003), 3–4; Kolchin, "Comparing American History," *Reviews in American History* 10 (August 1982): 64–65; White, "Slavery in New York State," 10.

7. Weiss, *Captives and Corsairs,* 20–21; Sahillioğu, "Slaves in the Social and Economic Life of Bursa," 63–67; Robin Blackburn, "The Old World Background to European Colonial Slavery," *William and Mary Quarterly,* 3rd ser., 54 (January 1997): 66–67; Tal Shuval, "Poor Quarter/Rich Quarter: Distribution of Wealth in the Arab Cities of the Ottoman Empire, the Case of Eighteenth Century Algiers," *Turcica* 32 (2000): 178–82, 189; William Spencer, *Algiers in the Age of the Corsairs* (Norman: University of Oklahoma Press, 1976), 27–29.

8. Thomas Jefferson, "Memoranda concerning Algiers, [ca. January 1788]," in *The Papers of Thomas Jefferson,* ed. Julian P. Boyd (Princeton, NJ: Princeton University Press, 1955), 12:549–51.

9. Pedro L. V. Welch, "The Urban Context of the Life of the Enslaved: Views from Bridgetown, Barbados, in the Eighteenth and Nineteenth Centuries," in *Slavery without Sugar: Diversity in Caribbean Economy and Society since the 17th Century,* ed. Verene A. Shepherd (Gainesville: University Press of Florida, 2002), 194 (quotation); Midori Takagi, *Rearing Wolves to Our Own Destruction: Slavery in Richmond, Virginia, 1782–1865* (Charlottesville: University Press of Virginia, 2002), 1; Dantas, *Black Townsmen,* 58; T. Stephen Whitman, *The Price of Freedom: Slavery and Manumission in Baltimore and Early National Maryland* (Lexington: University Press of Kentucky, 1997), 16–23.

10. State-owned and individually owned slaves existed side-by-side in most of these locations, including Ottoman Algiers. Elizabeth Grzymala Jordan, "'Unrelenting Toil': Expanding Archaeological Interpretations of the Female Slave Experience," *Slavery and Abolition* 26 (August 2005): 218–19; Alejandro de la Fuente, *Havana and the Atlantic in the Sixteenth Century* (Chapel Hill: University of North Carolina Press, 2008), 152–53; Gerald Groenewald, "Slaves and Free Blacks

in VOC Cape Town, 1652–1795," *History Compass* 8 (September 2010): 964, 967–68; Robert C. Davis, *Christian Slaves, Muslim Masters* (New York: Palgrave Macmillan, 2003), 12; Ellen G. Friedman, "Christian Captives at 'Hard Labor' in Algiers, 16th-19th Centuries," *International Journal of African Historical Studies* 13, no. 4 (1980): 618; Karasch, *Slave Life in Rio de Janeiro,* 56, 113, 118.

11. Sears, *American Slaves and African Masters,* 48–49; Richard B. Parker, *Uncle Sam in Barbary: A Diplomatic History* (Gainesville: University Press of Florida, 2004), 11; Daniel Panzac, *Barbary Corsairs: The End of a Legend, 1800–1820* (Boston: Brill, 2005), 108–10; Robert C. Davis, "Counting European Slaves on the Barbary Coast," *Past and Present* 172 (August 2000): 99.

12. Weiss, *Captives and Corsairs,* 20 (quotations); de la Fuente, *Havana,* 152, 159; Groenewald, "Slaves and Free Blacks," 967–68.

13. Berlin, *Many Thousands Gone,* 179–80, 5 (quotation); Christopher Phillips, *Freedom's Port: The African-American Community of Baltimore, 1790–1860* (Urbana: University of Illinois Press, 1997), 16, 23; Whitman, *Price of Freedom,* 19; Welch, "Urban Context," 185, 192, 194; Takagi, *Rearing Wolves,* 45, 23.

14. Susan Mosher Stuard, "To Town to Serve: Urban Domestic Slavery in Medieval Ragusa," in *Women and Work in Preindustrial Europe,* ed. Barbara A. Hanawalt (Bloomington: Indiana University Press, 1986), 39, 44 (quotation); de la Fuente, *Havana,* 153.

15. Stuard, "To Town to Serve," 39 (first quotation); John Foss, *A Journal of the Captivity and Sufferings of John Foss,* 2nd ed. (Newburyport, MA: Angier March, 1798), 12, 21–25; James Wilson Stevens, *An Historical and Geographical Account of Algiers* (Philadelphia: Hogan and M'Elroy, 1797), 77 (second quotation); Parker, *Uncle Sam in Barbary,* 10; Groenewald, "Slaves and Free Blacks," 967 (third quotation); Evelyn Powell Jennings, "War as the 'Forcing House of Change': State Slavery in Late Eighteenth-Century Cuba," *William and Mary Quarterly,* 3rd ser., 62 (July 2005): 414; Evelyn Powell Jennings, "State Enslavement in Colonial Havana, 1763–1790," in Shepherd, *Slavery without Sugar,* 153, 156–59.

16. James Cathcart, Papers of James L. Cathcart, 1785–1817, Library of Congress, Manuscript Reading Room, Washington, DC, 86, 114 (quotation), 123–24; Foss, *Journal of the Captivity,* 22–23, 28; Ellen G. Friedman, *Spanish Captives in North Africa in the Early Modern Age* (Madison: University of Wisconsin Press, 1983), 91–98.

17. Cathcart, Papers, 120, 155, 19–20; Filippo Pananti, *Narrative of a Residence in Algiers* (London: Henry Colburn and Richard Bentley, 1830), 85; Richard O'Bryen to William Carmichael, June 24, 1790, Thomas Jefferson Papers, ser. 1, General Correspondence, 1651–1827, http://memory.loc.gov/ammem/collections/jefferson_papers/index.html, image 581; Parker, *Uncle Sam in Barbary,* 90.

18. Cathcart, Papers, 134; Foss, *Journal of the Captivity,* 73; Parker, *Uncle Sam in Barbary,* 90–91; Davies, *Christian Slaves, Muslim Masters,* 118.

19. Cathcart, Papers, 19, 136 (quotations); James Leander Cathcart, *The Captives* (La Porte, IN: J. B. Newkirk, 1899), 117–18, 157; Davis, *Christian Slaves, Muslim Masters,* 98–99; Sears, *American Slaves and African Masters,* 82–83.

20. Dr. Warner from Algiers, January 1788, The Thomas Jefferson Papers, ser. 1, General Correspondence, 1651–1827, http://memory.loc.gov/cgi-bin/ampage?collId=mtj1&fileName=mtj1p

age006.db&recNum=965; William Carmichael to Thomas Jefferson, August 13, 1789, with Accounts and Sums Advanced by D'Expilly for the Americans Held in Algiers, *Papers of Thomas Jefferson,* ed. Julian P. Boyd (Princeton, NJ: Princeton University Press, 1958), 15:340–41; Parker, *Uncle Sam in Barbary,* 10; Davis, *Christian Slaves, Muslim Masters,* 106; Sears, *American Slaves and African Masters,* 67.

21. Sears, *American Slaves and African Masters,* 94; Thomas Jefferson to David Humphreys, July 13, 1791, "Message from the President of the United States to Congress, Relative to Morocco and Algiers, 16 December 1793, Report from Secretary of State Jefferson," in *State Papers and Publick Documents of the United States from the Accession of George Washington* (Boston: Thomas B. Wait, 1819), 259–60; "Instructions to Robert Montgomery from David Humphreys," in *American State Papers: Foreign Relations, Documents Legislative and Executive of the Congress of the United States,* ed. Walter Lowrie and Matthew St. Clair (Washington, DC: Gales and Seaton, 1833), 1:419; "Extract of a Letter from William Penrose," *Philadelphia Independent Gazette,* March 21, 1794, 3.

22. P. R. Randall to his Father, enclosure, April 2, 1786, in *Papers of Thomas Jefferson,* vol. 9, *September 1785–June 1786,* ed. Julian P. Boyd (Princeton, NJ: Princeton University Press, 1954), 526–36; Richard O'Bryen et al., August 28, 1785, Petitions Address to Congress, 1775–1789, Papers of the Continental Congress, NARA, 6:118, www.fold3.com/image/438526/.

23. Sears, *American Slaves and African Masters,* 66–69. In 1787, three thousand Christian slaves populated Algiers. By 1790, hundreds had died of the plague, and the Neapolitan, Spanish, and other governments had ransomed their men, leaving only 780 Christian slaves. Richard O'Bryen to Thomas Jefferson, July 12, 1790, in *Papers of Thomas Jefferson,* ed. Julian P. Boyd (Princeton, NJ: Princeton University Press, 1965), 17:29–34. The Christian slave population dipped to 700 in 1791 but rose to 1,342 in 1799. Parker, *Uncle Sam in Barbary,* 9.

24. Sears, *American Slaves and African Masters,* 43–64; Groenewald, "Slaves and Free Blacks," 968; Karasch, *Slave Life in Rio de Janeiro,* 325; Peter Kolchin, *American Slavery,* 2nd ed. (New York: Hill and Wang, 2003), 149.

25. Sears, *American Slaves and African Masters,* 33; Lawrence A. Peskin, *Captives and Countrymen: Barbary Slaves and the American Public, 1785–1816* (Baltimore: Johns Hopkins University Press, 2009), 27.

26. De la Fuente, *Havana,* 157–160 (quotation 160); Dantas, *Black Townsmen,* 92–94. See also Lawrence T. McDonnell, "Money Knows No Master: Market Relations and the American Slave Community," in *Developing Dixie: Modernization in a Traditional Society,* ed. Winfred B. Moore Jr., Joseph F. Tripp, and Lyon G. Tyler Jr. (Westport, CT: Greenwood Press, 1988), 31–44.

27. Sears, *American Slaves and African Masters,* 96; Foss, *Journal of the Captivity,* 122; Pananti, *Narrative,* 350; Richard O'Bryen, *Charleston Evening Gazette,* February 17, 1786, 2; Richard O'Bryen to George Washington, November 5, 1793, Founders Online, National Archives, http://founders.archives.gov/documents/Washington/05-14-02-0227, from David R. Hoth, ed., *The Papers of George Washington,* Presidential Series, vol. 14, *1 September–31 December 1793* (Charlottesville: University of Virginia Press, 2008), 338–40.

28. Sears, *American Slaves and African Masters,* 94; Parker, *Uncle Sam in Barbary,* 67; Paul R. Randall to his Father, Extracted and Annotated by William Short, April 2, 1786, Letters Received

by Thomas Jefferson, 1785–1789, Papers of the Continental Congress, 1774–1789, 1:404, www.fold
3com/image/257743; United States Congress, Instructions to Robert Montgomery, Consul of
the United States of America at Alicant, n.d., in Walter Lowrie and Matthew St. Clair Clarke,
eds., *American State Papers, Foreign Relations,* Class I (Washington, DC: Gales and Seaton, 1832),
11:419; Thomas Jefferson to George Washington, December 28, 1790, Founders Online (quotation), http://founders.archives.gov/?q=to%20george%20washington%20from%20thomas%20
jefferson%20Author%3A%22Jefferson%2C%20Thomas%22&s=1111311111&sa=&r=216&sr=; John
Jay to George Washington, November 16, 1789, The Papers of John Jay, Columbia University Libraries, Jay Papers ID 2389, wwwapp.cc.columbia.edu/ldpd/jay/item?mode=item&key=columbia.
jay.02390; "Boston, January 2, Extract of Letter from Captain Isaac Stephens," *Newport (RI)
Mercury,* January 9, 1786, 3.

    29. Foss, *Journal of the Captivity,* 24, 70; John Burnham, "The Curse of Slavery," *Rural Maga-
zine or Vermont Repository* (March 1795): 120; Sears, *American Slaves and African Masters,* 87,
105–6; Shuval, "Poor Quarter/Rich Quarter," 178–89; Egerton, "Slaves to the Marketplace," 618
(quotation).

    30. Welch, "Urban Context," 185 (quotation), 184–88, 190–92; Dantas, *Black Townsmen,* 97,
128; Phillips, *Freedom's Port,* 16; Seth Rockman, *Scraping By: Wage Labor, Slavery, and Survival in
Early Baltimore* (Baltimore: Johns Hopkins University Press, 2009), 34.

    31. Cathcart, Papers, 33; Richard O'Bryen, *Remarks and Observations in Algiers, 1789–1791*
(Philadelphia: Historical Society of Pennsylvania, 1989), entries for February 24, 28, March 1, 1791;
James L. Cathcart, Undated on Irish Renegade Carr, Cathcart Papers, box 1, Folder Correspon-
dence 1785–1794, New York Public Library. See also Weiss, *Captives and Corsairs,* 23–25; Linda
Colley, "Going Native, Telling Tales: Captivity, Collaborations, and Empire," *Past and Present* 168
(August 2000): 170–93.

    32. Pananti, *Narrative,* 356–57; O'Bryen, *Remarks,* January 10, 23, 1791; September 5, 1790;
Cathcart, Papers, 91; Sears, *American Slaves and African Masters,* 49; Friedman, *Spanish Captives,*
65–66; Weiss, *Captives and Corsairs,* 39–40.

    33. Sears, *American Slaves and African Masters,* 66, 20–21; Parker, *Uncle Sam in Barbary,* 199;
Phillips, *Freedom's Port,* 43–45; Martin, *Divided Mastery,* 66; Stephen Whitman, "Diverse Good
Causes: Manumission and the Transformation of Urban Slavery," *Social Science History* 19 (Fall
1995): 333–334; Bernard Moitt, "Freedom from Bondage at a Price: Women and Redemption from
Slavery in the French Caribbean in the Nineteenth Century," *Slavery and Abolition* 26 (August
2005): 247–56; Stanley Engerman, "Pricing Freedom," in *Working Slavery, Pricing Freedom: Per-
spectives from the Caribbean, Africa, and the African Diaspora,* ed. Verene A. Shepherd (New York:
Palgrave, 2002), 273–89; Pál Fodor, "Piracy, Ransom Slavery, and Trade," *Turcica* 33 (2001): 119–34.

    34. Welch, "Urban Context," 185.

THE NINETEENTH-CENTURY "OTHER SOUTHS," MODERNIZATION, AND NATION-BUILDING

Expanding the Comparative Perspective

ENRICO DAL LAGO

I n his seminal work *A Sphinx on the American Land* (2003), Peter Kolchin termed "other souths" the regions of the world that shared broadly similar historical, economic, and/or sociopolitical features with the U.S. South.[1] Comparative historical studies focusing on the U.S. South and those regions have a great deal to offer in terms of improving our understanding of the relationship between nineteenth-century American slavery and modernity, an issue currently at the heart of debates among scholars of slave societies and slave systems.[2] Significant new scholarship on the "second slavery" has broken new ground by identifying the specific modern features of nineteenth-century New World slave societies within the context of world economic transformations. In particular, Dale Tomich and Michael Zeuske have pointed out how modern "world historical processes . . . transformed the Atlantic World between the 1780s and 1888" and created "highly productive new zones of slave commodity production," specifically in the U.S. South, with commodities such as cotton and sugar; Cuba, with sugar; and southern Brazil, with coffee.[3] In these three regions of the New World, the nineteenth century witnessed the rise of highly centralized and organized forms of slave management that shared common features with modern industrial capitalist practices. In each case, the primary objective was to produce valuable staple crops for sale on the world market.[4]

In the nineteenth-century U.S. South, Cuba, and Brazil, this process, together with the consequent pervasiveness of slavery in the economy and society, led to the formation of new and increasingly larger, more powerful, and more aggressive slaveholding elites whose class interests wholly identified with a flourishing slave system.[5] In all three regions, slaveholders held a high degree of political power, which they wielded to produce central governments that defended their interests. As a result, in the United States, Cuba, and Brazil, attempts to move toward a nationalization of slavery—that is, toward the creation of a national polity wholly and permanently committed to slavery—characterized nineteenth-century national political life in general and the national politics of the slaveholding elites in particular.[6]

Since the appearance of the groundbreaking studies by Benedict Anderson, Eric Hobsbawn, and Ernest Gellner from the 1980s onward, scholarship on nationalism has succeeded in demonstrating the fundamentally modern features of the nineteenth- and twentieth-century phenomena of nation-building.[7] Slaveholding elites' attempts at nationalizing slavery were modern "inventions of traditions" that were eventually defeated as opposition movements labored to nationalize freedom rather than slavery, culminating in slave emancipation in the United States (1863–65), Cuba (1886), and Brazil (1888). Though ultimately defeated, those attempts to nationalize slavery are worth investigating as possible alternative paths to modern nation-building in the three countries where the "second slavery" thrived until its final abolition.[8]

When considering the tortured relationship between slavery and U.S. southern nation-building, Peter Kolchin has stated that "in comparative context, the 'creation of Confederate nationalism' appears a more problematic venture than many scholars have recognized."[9] Studies on U.S. southern nationalism, secession, and the Confederate experience—notably by Drew Faust and, more recently, by Don Doyle, Stephanie McCurry, Paul Quigley, and André Fleche—have extended the comparative focus to Europe, looking at these phenomena in a much wider context. In doing this, these scholars have confirmed Kolchin's intuition that, even though southerners saw the creation of the Confederate nation as part of a common age of nation-building on both sides of the modern Atlantic, slavery distinguished and rendered problematic their particular brand of southern nationalism, in comparison with both previous and contemporary ideas and efforts at achieving national self-determination by other people, particularly in Europe.[10]

Yet, if this is true in regard to the comparative perspective with Europe, the case is hardly the same when we look in comparative perspective at other areas of the American hemisphere. In those areas, as in the United States, slaveholding was mostly seen as one of several forms of property not necessarily incompatible with ideas and practices of national self-determination, some of which might even advocate nation-building through secession as a blatant means to defend the right to property. To date, there are no comparative studies that have placed secession and Confederate nationalism within the context of other separatist movements in the nineteenth-century Americas. And yet, the story of a "legitimate" centralizing government, such as the Union, defeating a centrifugal separatist movement by a "rebel" region or nation-state, such as the Confederacy, was not peculiar to the United States; rather, it was an integral part of modern nation-building in the New World in the middle decades of the nineteenth century. From this perspective, building on the important intuitions by scholars of the "second slavery" on the shared modern features between the U.S. southern, Cuban, and Brazilian slave systems, it is worthwhile to compare the process of creation of the Confederate nation, with its defense of slavery and its alternative version of modernization and nation-building, with other separatist movements led by powerful peripheral elites. It was not only in the South but in other parts of the nineteenth-century Americas as well that elites sought national independence from centralizing governments as a means to defend property rights.[11]

This chapter will focus specifically on two instances of comparative nation-building in historical perspective. The first comparison is between the long-term process of regional secession in South Carolina (1832–60), in itself the indispensable prequel for the creation of the Confederate nation, and the long-term causes of the temporary regional secession of the Rio Grande do Sul province from the Brazilian Empire occasioned by the *Farroupilha* Revolt (1835–45). This first comparison focuses on the attempts by two regional slaveholding elites—South Carolina slaveholders and *riograndense* property owners—to protect their economic interests through nation-building. The outcomes were ultimately similar, the consequence of comparable defeats, in both cases, of regional movements for secession or separation from their respective central governments. The second comparison traces the rise and fall of the Confederacy in the U.S. Civil War era (1861–65) and eastern Cuba's attempted separation from the Spanish Empire during the Ten Years' War (1868–78). Here, the focus turns specifically on the opposite attitudes of the Confederate and Cuban slaveholding elites toward slavery and the relation between the large-scale civil wars that they triggered and the unintended consequences that the two events had on the future of slavery. In fact, in both the Confederate and the Cuban cases, the wars inflicted a fatal blow on slavery and ultimately led to its unexpected and relatively sudden demise, despite different timings and characteristics.

A study comparing the causes of secession in the Confederate South with those of other separatist movements within the three regions of the Americas encompassed by the "second slavery"—the United States, Cuba, and Brazil—bears particular significance if it focuses specifically on the regional features of South Carolina and Rio Grande do Sul. In the first half of the nineteenth century, both South Carolina and Rio Grande do Sul were smaller regions within larger polities. Yet, unlike South Carolina, which was a state within the federal system of the early American republic, Rio Grande do Sul was a province within the Brazilian imperial system and had been governed by a constitutional monarchy since 1824. In both cases, specific social and economic features combined to provide the property-owning elite with a peculiar identity in political terms and lent impetus to a very distinctive type of regionalism. Specific regional features and identities were, effectively, the prime causes behind South Carolina's 1860–65 movement for secession from the United States and Rio Grande do Sul's 1835–45 *Farroupilha* Revolt aimed at separation from the Brazilian Empire. At the heart of the regional identities of both South Carolina and Rio Grande do Sul at the time of their separatist revolts were the characteristics of their "slave societies"—that is, societies in which slavery was pervasive, slaves were a large part of the population, and slaveholders were the elite in charge of politics and society—even though in very different ways.[12]

The elites of South Carolina and Rio Grande do Sul had a different relationship with two of the three economic heartlands of the "second slavery" in the U.S. South and Brazil. South Carolina's slaveholders formed a composite elite of rice and cotton planters whose wealth and power derived from the state's position between the old rice-plantation area of the Atlantic seaboard and the main expanding area of cotton production and large plantations run with slave labor in the U.S. South. In contrast, Rio Grande do Sul's elite, even though equally composite, was made up mostly of large-scale and powerful landed proprietors and owners of cattle and of establishments for the production of dried beef. Although factory owners exploited substantial numbers of bondpeople to process foodstuffs, they remained at the margins of the main area of exploitation of slave labor: the coffee plantations of the São Paulo and Rio de Janeiro provinces. In similar fashion, however, at different points in the nineteenth century, both South Carolina's slaveholders and Rio Grande do Sul's property owners faced the challenge of centralizing initiatives by their respective national governments—the American republic and the Brazilian Empire—in the form of legislative measures that threatened their economic and social power and privileges. In response, both elites promoted nation-building through regional independence as the most effective means to defend those privileges.

The slaveholding elite of South Carolina had initially built its strong regional identity in relation to the production of rice in large plantations worked by slaves and located on the Atlantic coast around Charleston. As a result of the profitability of low-country rice on the world market, by the early eighteenth century a wealthy planter class dominated the colony of South Carolina, which was not only a "slave society" but also had a majority black population.[13] After American independence and the temporary setback that resulted from the devastations wrought by the Revolution and from widespread antislavery feelings, slavery in South Carolina rebounded with the invention of the cotton gin in 1793 and the consequent colonization of the up country by both small farmers and large planters seeking land for growing short-staple cotton. By the early nineteenth century, up-country South Carolina—ideally situated within one of the three regions in the Americas encompassed by the phenomenon of the "second slavery"—was an integral part of a rapidly expanding plantation area that supplied British and northern U.S. textile mills with cotton.[14] As these crucial economic changes unfolded, the slaveholding elite of South Carolina strengthened its regional identity through the creation of a political system that allowed the old aristocracy of low-country rice planters and the new gentry of up-country cotton slaveholders to share political representation in the state's Senate and House of Representatives and the effective control of membership in the legislature. The result was a peculiarly aristocratic system of government. Through this system and through frequent intermarriages between low-country and up-country families, South Carolina's slaveholding elite solidified unparalleled control over local politics and formed the basis for the state's uniquely regional elitist culture—a phenomenon known as "the problem of South Carolina," studied by a number of scholars.[15]

More than other slaveholding elites in the U.S. South, the slaveholding elite of South Carolina gave birth to some of the most ardent and articulate spokesmen for the proslavery argument, such as James Henry Hammond. In fact, South Carolina's defenders of slavery came closer than most proslavery ideologues to providing an alternative idea of modernization for the U.S. South that was based on the need to keep or even expand the South's paternalistic slave system, an indispensable part of the "modern" phenomenon of the market revolution and of the "second slavery."[16] Yet, theirs was an idea of modernization that was strictly regional. Therefore, it was bound to clash with an opposite view of modernization that saw the process of constructing a strong American republic as achieving national cohesion through administrative centralization and other measures that inevitably harmed the interests of the elites of peripheral regions. Confrontation between the extreme regionalism of the slaveholding elite of South Carolina and American national policies began with the nullification crisis (1828–33) when, supported by the state-focused political theory of John C. Calhoun, South Carolina's slaveholders led the movement to veto "the federal government's protective tariff policies, which discriminated against agricultural, staple-exporting southern states in favor of northern manufacturing industries."[17] The crisis pitted two opposite ideas of modernization—regional agrarianism and national centralization—against each other for the first time. It reached its apex in 1832 when the South Carolina state convention threatened to nullify the 1828 federal tariff law at the heart of the controversy and, if necessary, secede from the United States. Yet, in March 1833, as President Andrew Jackson stood ready to intervene militarily, Congress passed a compromise tariff that satisfied the nullifiers, thus averting a possible civil war.[18]

After the U.S. conquest of the western territories in the Mexican War (1846–48) and the growth of political antislavery in the North, the issue of modernization through governmental centralization versus modernization through the respect of regional interests became entirely focused on the controversy over the expansion of slavery and was instrumental as an agent of cohesion around a southern nationalism based on the defense of the slave system. Once again, South Carolina's slaveholding elite was at the vanguard of a movement of regional opposition to U.S. federal provisions, and in 1850 it promoted a concrete move toward the unity of a southern nation based on Calhoun's ideas. The resulting pair of southern conventions held at Nashville,

Tennessee, rejected the federal government's interference with southern plans to expand slavery in the West and advocated secession.[19] Despite the failure of both conventions to create a unitary secession movement in the South, in May 1851 South Carolina's planters and politicians stood ready to secede, confirming the state's reputation for extreme regionalist and separatist politics. South Carolina's eventual secession on December 20, 1860, therefore marked the final act in a long confrontation with the U.S. federal government that had progressively radicalized the regional separatist tendencies of the state's slaveholding elite.[20]

Even though the election of Republican and antislavery president Abraham Lincoln precipitated South Carolina's extreme act, the "Declaration of the Immediate Causes of Secession" explained that the reason for it was that the nonslaveholding states had "assumed the right of deciding upon the propriety of our domestic institutions": slavery.[21] Thus, in 1860, South Carolina's slaveholding elite perceived and rejected through secession Lincoln's Republican program of declared opposition to slavery's expansion. Although the Republican platform did not call for abolition, regional elites nevertheless perceived a dangerous attempt at enforcing modernization through governmental centralization antithetical to their interests, specifically their right to hold property in slaves. Ultimately, South Carolina's extreme regionalism could and did find its fulfillment only as part of the broader movement for the independence of a slaveholding southern nation. On February 4, 1861, the states that had joined South Carolina in secession united to create the Confederate States of America.[22] It is certainly true, as William Barney has remarked, that during the secession crisis, "South Carolina created the model of [regional] popular mobilization followed by other states in the Lower South."[23] The American Civil War, as the final struggle between the two opposite ideas of modernization, witnessed the final defeat in 1865 not only of South Carolina's regionalism but also of the southern slaveholding elites' alternative view of an American republic as a modern nation based on slavery, and specifically on the distinctive capitalist and profit-seeking type of economic enterprise that characterized the "second slavery."

Similar to the slaveholding elite of South Carolina, the cattle-owning elite of Rio Grande do Sul began its ascent to power during the colonial period. It was tightly related to the discovery of gold in the province of Minas Gerais and the consequent economic boom of the eighteenth-century Brazilian min-

ing industry. As Herbert S. Klein and Ben Vinson have noted, "the gold mining boom of Minas Gerais powerfully shifted the center of gravity of Brazilian
economy and population from the north to the center and south," where the
province of Rio Grande do Sul was located.[24] Not only did the mines demand
a constant supply of workers, leading to an increase of imports of African
slaves into southern Brazil, but also they equally required a constant supply
of cattle and mules for food and transportation. The resulting rise of a flourishing grazing industry in the southern Brazilian frontier led to the region's
rapid colonization by enterprising farmers and property owners. Thus, in a
few decades, slavery reached Rio Grande do Sul, where slaves rapidly became
the staple labor force employed on both farms and cattle-raising enterprises.
Ranches dominated a landscape characterized by enormous expanses of open
land, the majority of it owned by a few very wealthy families. Already by the
end of the eighteenth century, Rio Grande do Sul had 21,000 slaves out of a
population of 71,000 (almost 30%).[25] The work of the slaves was strictly related
to the export economy, since they were employed by the thousands in large
factories, called *charqueadas,* that produced the popular dried beef (*charque*)
for an external market reaching as far as the Caribbean. As a result, explained
Gabriel Aladrén, "between the last decade of the eighteenth century and the
Independence [of Brazil, in 1822], the province of Rio Grande do Sul ceased
to be a 'society with slaves' and"—more than a century after South Carolina—
"turned into a 'slave society.'"[26]

As these momentous changes took place, the propertied elite of Rio
Grande do Sul acquired progressively the control of the economy, the society,
and the politics of the region and fashioned a distinctive regional identity. Unlike the slaveholding elites in other regions of Brazil, the elite of Rio Grande
do Sul consisted of large-scale land and cattle owners (*estancieiros*) and owners
of dried-beef factories (*charqueadores*), all of whom were slaveholders. Moreover, the *estancieiros* and *charqueadores* all lived in a frontier zone—similar, to
a certain extent, to the cotton frontier of the U.S. South—where war with
neighboring countries for the same resources was a very likely prospect. Yet,
despite Rio Grande do Sul's characteristics as a "slave society"—which, in areas
such as Piratiní, even had a black majority, as did South Carolina—the region's
property owners had a more indirect relationship than South Carolina's slaveholders with the nearest core region of the "second slavery." In the Brazilian
case, the core was the coffee-producing region centered around Rio de Janeiro

and São Paulo. Still, in comparable ways, the broad world economic changes that led to the rise of the cotton production associated with the "second slavery" in the U.S. South and with the rise of coffee production in southern Brazil also had a major impact on the rise to power of the Rio Grande do Sul's property owners.[27]

In fact, it was the flourishing, profitable "second slavery" in nineteenth-century Brazil that guaranteed that first the Portuguese government (1808–22) and then the Brazilian Empire (from 1822 onward) protected the slave system as an essential part of the national economy, much to the advantage of the slaveholding elites of Rio Grande do Sul and other regions of Brazil.[28] Even though they did not articulate a "proslavery argument" as the slaveholding elite did in South Carolina, implicitly the Rio Grande do Sul property owners also advanced their claim to modernization based on specific features of their regional identity. In fact, their idea of slavery, and the master-slave relationship in particular, had some features in common with the regional paternalistic ideology of U.S. planters.[29] At the same time, the Rio Grande do Sul property owners' employment of slave labor was linked to the process of modernization of their region, in that it was both tied to the highly profitable cattle trade and related to the factory production of dried beef in the large establishments that provided a form of early industrialization in Rio Grande do Sul.[30] Yet, similarly to the regional project of modernization of South Carolina's slaveholders, the regional project of modernization undertaken by Rio Grande do Sul's property owners required a central government that would not enforce the cohesiveness of the nation through administrative centralization at the expense of the interests of the regional elites.[31]

To be sure, the constant state of war at the southern frontier of the Brazilian Empire allowed Rio Grande do Sul's property owners the possibility of expanding the control of land and of the cattle business, reinforcing their power and their regional identity as a slaveholding class and also tying together military status and landownership. Simultaneously, however, it had disastrous consequences, especially when trade was disrupted during the Cisplatine War (1825–28) with the United Provinces of Rio de la Plata. The war eventually led to the independence of Uruguay and the loss of Brazilian control over the vast territory of the *Banda Oriental* region, formerly owned by Rio Grande do Sul.[32]

A further blow came to Rio Grande do Sul's elite with the 1831 law on the abolition of the slave trade, even though it had little practical effect after the first few years. A subsequent legislative enactment, however, was ultimately devastating. As Spencer Leitman explained, Brazil's central government, based in Rio de Janeiro, "taxed cattle coming from neighboring states, reducing the cattle flow, thus retarding the expansion of the *riograndense* cattle industry, and continued with a tariff system which discriminated against Rio Grande do Sul's products on the national market."[33] The pattern of confrontation between center and periphery resembled the nullification crisis in South Carolina.[34]

Eventually—unlike South Carolina's nullifiers, but similar to South Carolina's 1860 secessionists—Rio Grande do Sul's property owners decided to respond to the centralizing measures enacted by Brazil's imperial government. In 1835 they seceded and created a new nation, the autonomous Republic of Rio Grande do Sul. This major act of revolt led to a long separatist war with the Brazilian Empire called *Farroupilha,* from the derogatory term that described the rebels as *farrapos,* or "ragamuffins."[35] Legendary *riograndense* president and large-scale cattle-owner Bento Gonçalves led the revolt. The war lasted ten years, until 1845, partly as a result of Brazil's institutional crisis during the period of the Regency (1831–40), in which Emperor Dom Pedro II, a minor, held the throne. In addition, a series of major revolts exploded in different regions of Brazil, such as Parà, Maranhão, and Bahia, during the 1830s and early 1840s. But by the mid-1840s, Brazil's imperial government had succeeded in reining in the centrifugal revolts, and by 1845 even Rio Grande do Sul's property owners, tired after ten years of war, renounced all pretensions of national independence and allowed their regional identity to be part of a centralized project of Brazilian modernization and nation-building.[36]

Thus, over the course of the nineteenth century, both the U.S. federal government and the Brazilian imperial government implemented policies of modernization through the enforcement of centralization. These policies increased the pressure on regional ruling classes and provoked changes in the distribution of power between centers and peripheries. Governmental measures harmed the economic interests of South Carolina's planters and Rio Grande do Sul's property owners, two equally powerful slaveholding elites, primarily through taxation and, in the United States in 1860, political opposition to slavery. Such developments ultimately provoked an acceleration in the two elites' moves toward regional secessionist and separatist politics as protective measures against either perceived or real governmental interferences in local affairs. The ultimate outcome of this process, though with important differences, was both similar and comparable in the two cases. South Carolina's regional secession from 1860 to 1865, spearheaded by the state's planters (as in the previous attempts of 1832 and 1850), and Rio Grande do Sul's separatist attempt with the 1835–45 *Farroupilha* were both temporarily successful. Whereas South Carolina slaveholders achieved success through fusion with the U.S. South's Confederate cause, the elite of Rio Grande do Sul did not blend with a larger separatist movement. They nonetheless achieved temporary success as a result of both the relative weakness of the Brazilian government at the time of the Regency and the effect of other revolts taking place in other provinces of the Brazilian Empire. Yet, in both South Carolina and Rio Grande do Sul, secession was ultimately defeated at the end of a long war.

If we widen the scope of the comparative study of Confederate secession with other separatist movements from the regional to the national, but still within the boundaries of the three great regions encompassed by the "second slavery," we can fruitfully compare the U.S. Civil War (1861–65) with Cuba's Ten Years' War (1868–78). This is a particularly enlightening case study for several reasons. At a general level, an important difference is in the fact that, from the Union government's point of view, the U.S. Civil War was an internal affair within an American republic that had been independent from the British Empire for almost a hundred years. In contrast, Cuba's Ten Years' War was, first and foremost, a rebellion of Spain's most profitable Latin American colony for independence from the Spanish Empire. Yet in both cases, the actual events and the courses they took, despite significant differences, bear important similarities. Particularly striking is the fact that, in both cases, the slaveholding elites who controlled half of the country—the Confederate South and the eastern portion of Cuba—rose in secessionist and separatist rebellion, creating a new republican nation against the legitimate national government that controlled the other half. In so doing, both Confederate and eastern Cuban slaveholders ignited civil wars that lasted for several years and that ultimately ended not only with the defeat of the rebellious sides and their separatist projects of nation-building by the legitimate national governments, but also with the collapse of the slave system altogether.

In the United States, the birth of the Confederate States of America on February 4, 1861, from the seven southern states that had initially seceded from the Union (soon to be joined by four more states after the April 14 fall of Fort Sumter) divided the American republic in half, igniting the American Civil War through the creation of a new republican nation wholly committed to the defense and preservation of slavery.[37] In the famous words of Confederate Vice President Alexander Stephens, slavery was the "cornerstone" of the Confederacy, and the justification of the nation's existence depended upon the perpetuation of the slave system in the South, which was officially protected in the Confederate Constitution.[38] Yet, during its brief existence, the Confederate government, under increasing pressure from the Union, was forced to adopt harsher and more drastic centralizing policies aimed at making the best use of the limited resources available to fight a modern type of war in which technology and manpower, both insufficient in the Confederacy, were key components for victory. In fact, according to Emory Thomas, the consequences of Confederate President Jefferson Davis's adoption of centralized nationalism in an attempt to cope with the Union's more powerful war machinery were nothing short of revolutionary. They prompted sudden and profound changes in both southern economy and southern society, privileging manufacturing and urbanization over plantation agriculture and ultimately creating large pockets of resentment among southern slaveholders, many of whom increasingly saw their Confederate government as delegitimated by these policies.[39]

As war progressed and the carnage continued, the Confederate government could not prevent the departure for the front of an increasing number of slaveholders and their sons, leaving numerous slaveholding women with the difficult task of running plantations and farms.[40] At the same time, the continuous flow of tens of thousands of runaway slaves to the Union lines brought enormous disruption to the plantation economy and increased the pressure on the heavily agricultural, minimally industrialized southern states. Thus, by the time President Abraham Lincoln signed the Emancipation Proclamation, which nominally freed slaves on January 1, 1863, in Confederate territories actively in rebellion, the Confederacy's agricultural economy was already under enormous pressure. Most of its resources had been diverted to support the Confederate Army, with disastrous consequences for cities such as Richmond, where food riots broke out the same year. By the time Union general William Tecumseh Sherman embarked upon his famous "March to the Sea" in 1864, destroying the rich agricultural countryside of Georgia before moving northward into South Carolina, the southern slave system was in ruins. The slaveholding elite had lost its grip on most Confederate territory.[41]

As early as the end of 1863, in response to the Union's creation of black regimental units and, above all, in response to the Confederacy's worrying lack of necessary manpower, some commissioned Confederate officers envisioned the recruitment of black Confederate troops among southern slaves. In particular, General Patrick Cleburne of the Army of Tennessee had written a memorandum in which he recommended that the Confederacy "immediately commence training a large reserve of the most courageous of our slaves," whose loyalty to the Confederate cause would earn them freedom as their reward.[42] Continuous resistance from the majority of the planters in the Confederacy, however, delayed a serious discussion of Cleburne's proposal for a crucial year and a half, during which time the prospect of a Confederate victory in the Civil War became less and less likely. By the time the Confederate Congress passed the law that allowed the Confederate Army to recruit black volunteers in infantry units, on March 13, 1865, it was too late for it to be enacted, since by then the Confederacy had effectively lost the war. Moreover, Cleburne's original plan had been changed a great deal by the time the 1865 law was drafted. As Bruce Levine has remarked, in practice, "by refusing to guarantee the freedom of black volunteers—much less of their family members, and much less of the slave population in general—the Confederate government demonstrated that it could not, even at the brink of defeat and destruction, bring itself to initiate an effective revolution from above."[43] Nevertheless, there is no doubt that, even if only discussed at this late hour and implemented too late to be of any use, the 1865 law deriving from the Confederate Congress's decision to arm the slaves ultimately signaled the complete failure by the Confederate government to protect the very basis of power of the slaveholding elite that formed the economic and social backbone of the Confederate nation.

Comparable to the birth of the Confederate nation and the consequent Civil War that divided the United States in two for four years, the first major movement for Cuban independence from the Spanish Empire began with the separation of the eastern part of Cuba and led to the Ten Years' War, a civil war that divided the island in half for the duration of the conflict. At the time of the war, Cuba was the largest slave society in the Caribbean, and the profit-seeking, capitalist-oriented "second slavery" thrived on it, thanks to an ever-increasing number of sugar mills and sugar plantations geared to production for the world market.[44] Still, the days of Cuban slavery were numbered, as first the rise of the first Spanish abolitionist society in 1864 and then the Spanish government's abolition of the Atlantic slave trade in 1867 clearly showed. It was, however, the creation of the first Spanish republic in 1868 that precipitated slavery's fate on Cuba.[45] That same year, a Creole planter named Carlos Manuel de Cespedes launched the movement for Cuban independence. On October 10, 1868, as he prepared to fight against the Spanish Empire, Cespedes gathered slaves on his sugar plantation in the eastern part of the island. "Addressing them as 'citizens,'" explain Matt Childs and Manuel Barcia, "he told them they were now 'free' to join the fight to 'conquer liberty and independence' for Cuba."[46]

The Ten Years' War thus began between the eastern part of Cuba, which proclaimed itself an independent republic, and the Spanish Empire, which continued to control the western part of the island, still loyal to Spain. Cespedes's decision to free his slaves in the early part of the Ten Years' War would seem a significant difference from the Confederacy's late decision to emancipate its slaves only at the end of the U.S. Civil War. Yet there are several factors to consider in order to understand better the context and motivations of Cespedes's action. First of all, Cespedes and the planters who joined him in the rebellion were all prominent members of the slaveholding elite of the eastern part of Cuba, where slaves were only 10 percent of the population. The eastern Cuban elite was resentful of the much richer slaveholders of the western half of the island, where the center of sugar production, the largest sugar plantations, and the largest number of slaves were located. The rebels' objective was, first and foremost, to build a new Cuban nation that evened out the differences between eastern and western Cuba by severing the connections with the Spanish Empire while maintaining the fundamental social structure based on the respect of private property. This is evident in the actual plans that Cespedes had for the concrete steps toward the abolition of slavery.[47]

In fact, although he freed his slaves and asked them to join the cause of Cuban independence, Cespedes was hardly an abolitionist, defined as an advocate of the immediate emancipation of slaves. Instead, to achieve the goal of independence, he and the planters of the eastern part of the island were prepared to promise reforms leading to the abolition of slavery, provided that masters were given compensation in some form. According to Ada Ferrer, "abolition . . . would be gradual; it would indemnify owners; and it would occur only after the successful conclusion of the war."[48] Moreover, similar to the Confederacy in the late stages of the U.S. Civil War, independent Cuba desperately needed soldiers and was thus forced to recruit them among the slaves by promising them liberation as a reward in exchange for their services in the cause of Cuban freedom. Cuban slaves, however, gave their own radical interpretation to the mild provisions of the independent Cuban government, and by fleeing the plantations and joining the rebel army, they effectively "helped transform a separatist struggle led by white slaveholding elites in eastern Cuba into a war for personal liberation."[49] Finally, in 1870, to curb Cuba's separatist effort, the Spanish government issued the Moret Law, which unilaterally declared that the children born of slave mothers since September 1868 and slaves aged sixty or older were free. The conclusion of the ten-year Cuban civil war in 1878 witnessed not only the Spanish Empire's defeat of the eastern Cuban planters' separatist efforts and attempts at nation-building but also, through the Moret Law, the defeat of their attempt to postpone the enactment of only a mild form of abolition designed to preserve the social and economic status quo.[50]

In retrospect, it appears that the different relationships that the elites of the Confederate South and of Cuba's eastern half had with their respective heartlands of the "second slavery" is of paramount importance in explaining their different handling of the issue of slavery. In fact, with the secession of the South from the United States and the creation of the Confederacy, southern planters temporarily succeeded in fashioning a slaveholding nation out of the largest cotton-producing area in the world and out of one of the three main regions of the Americas encompassed by the "second slavery." Conversely, with their separation from Cuba's western half, eastern Cuban planters severed their ties with the heart of the largest area of slave-based sugar production, with the most modernized plantation economy of the Caribbean, and with one of the three main regions of the Americas encompassed by the "second slavery." This fundamental difference explains why slave emancipation was never an option for Confederate southerners until the very end of the U.S. Civil War, whereas in the independent eastern half of Cuba, plans for at least a mild form of abolition figured prominently soon after the start of the Ten Years' War.

I n both of the comparisons outlined above, powerful peripheral elites, mostly made up of large-scale slaveholders, instigated a form of secession or separation as an extreme attempt to defend their socioeconomic interests against perceived hostile policies of a centralizing government. In each instance, elites struggled to create their own version of a modern nation, which, significantly, entailed the creation of new republican institutions that prioritized the utmost respect for private property in all its forms. In the first comparison, in both South Carolina and Rio Grande do Sul, the existence of strong regional features that characterized the elite in power and the "slave society" over which it ruled (even though in different ways and with a different relationship with the phenomenon of the "second slavery") provided the basis for political separatism in reaction to efforts by a relatively weak national government to centralize the administration and control the development of specific peripheral issues. In the second comparison, the different relationships of the Confederate and eastern Cuban secessionist elites with the nearest heartlands of the "second slavery" was the determining factor in their divergent attitudes toward abolition. In fact, Confederate planters, in command of the largest area of cotton production in the world, were reluctant even to propose some form of emancipation for their indispensable enslaved workforce until the end of the U.S. Civil War. Conversely, eastern Cuban planters, living in the less prosperous part of the sugar-producing island, considered from the start of the Ten Years' War the possibility of a mild form of emancipation for what was only a minority of enslaved workers.

Ultimately, these two comparative examples show that the case of Confederate secession and the U.S. Civil War was hardly an isolated incident of separatist politics leading to a military conflict between center and periphery, or between two different visions of modern nation-building in New World "slave societies," especially in the three areas where the "second slavery" thrived. At the same time, though, both of these comparisons show that, in the context of the nineteenth-century Americas, all the regionalist/nationalist movements of secession/separation that the slaveholding elites triggered as a means to defend their own interests ultimately ended in failure, failure with profound long-term consequences. In fact, not only were these movements all defeated by the legitimate national/central governments, but also they all witnessed, in different ways and degrees, either the demise or the beginning of the end of the slave systems over which the slaveholding elites ruled, whether in the U.S. South, Cuba, or Brazil. The complete emancipation of the enslaved workforce was the eventual consequence in all three regions.

NOTES

1. Peter Kolchin, *A Sphinx on the American Land: The Nineteenth-Century South in Comparative Perspective* (Baton Rouge: Louisiana State University Press, 2003), 74.

2. See especially the essays in *The Old South's Modern Worlds: Slavery, Region, and Nation in the Age of Progress,* ed. L. Diane Barnes, Brian Schoen, and Frank Towers (New York: Oxford University Press, 2011).

3. Dale Tomich and Michael Zeuske, "Introduction, the Second Slavery: Mass Slavery, World Economy, and Comparative Microhistories," *Review, a Journal of the Fernand Braudel Center* 31, no. 2 (2008): 91.

4. Dale W. Tomich, *Through the Prism of Slavery: Labor, Capital, and World Economy* (Lanham, MD: Rowman & Littlefield, 2004), 56–71; Anthony E. Kaye, "The Second Slavery: Modernity in the Nineteenth-Century South and the Atlantic World," *Journal of Southern History* 75 (August 2009): 627–50.

5. Enrico Dal Lago, *American Slavery, Atlantic Slavery, and Beyond: The U.S. "Peculiar Institution" in International Perspective* (Boulder, CO: Paradigm, 2012), 63–91.

6. Edward B. Rugemer, "Why Civil War? The Politics of Slavery in Comparative Perspective: The United States, Cuba, and Brazil," in *The Civil War as Global Conflict: Transnational Meanings of the American Civil War,* ed. David T. Gleeson and Simon Lewis (Columbia: University of South Carolina Press, 2014), 14–35; Don E. Fehrenbacher, *The Slaveholding Republic: An Account of the United States Government's Relation to Slavery* (New York: Oxford University Press, 2001), esp. 49–89; Márcia Berbel, Rafael de Bivar Marquese, and Tâmis Parron, *Escravidão e política. Brasil e Cuba, 1790–1850* (São Paulo: Editora Hucitec, 2010).

7. Benedict Anderson, *Imagined Communities* (London: Verso, 1983); E. J. Hobsbawm, *Nations and Nationalism since 1780: Programme, Myth, Reality* (Cambridge: Cambridge University Press, 1990); and Ernest Gellner, *Nations and Nationalism* (Oxford: Blackwell, 1983).

8. Eric Hobsbawm, "Introduction: Inventing Traditions," in *The Invention of Traditions,* ed. Eric Hobsbawm and Terence Ranger (Cambridge: Cambridge University Press, 1983), 1–14.

9. Kolchin, *Sphinx on the American Land,* 93.

10. Drew Gilpin Faust, *The Creation of Confederate Nationalism: Ideology and Identity in the Civil War South* (Baton Rouge: Louisiana State University Press, 1988); Don H. Doyle, *Nations Divided: America, Italy, and the Southern Question* (Athens: University of Georgia Press, 2003); Stephanie McCurry, *Confederate Reckoning: Power and Politics in the Civil War South* (Cambridge, MA: Harvard University Press, 2010); Paul Quigley, *Shifting Grounds: Nationalism and the American South, 1848–1865* (New York: Oxford University Press, 2011); André M. Fleche, *The Revolution of 1861: The American Civil War in the Age of Nationalist Conflict* (Chapel Hill: University of North Carolina Press, 2012).

11. See the essays in *The Second Slavery: Mass Slaveries and Modernity in the Americas and in the Atlantic Basin,* ed. Javier Laviña and Michael Zeuske (Berlin: LIT, 2013).

12. For the definition of "slave societies," see especially Ira Berlin, *Many Thousands Gone: The First Two Centuries of Slavery in North America* (Cambridge, MA: Harvard University Press, 1998), 10–11.

13. S. Max Edelson, *Plantation Enterprise in Colonial South Carolina* (Cambridge, MA: Harvard University Press, 2006), 1–12.

14. On the expansion of the cotton South, see especially Adam Rothman, *Slave Country: American Expansion and the Origins of the Deep South* (Cambridge, MA: Harvard University Press, 2007), 37–73.

15. James M. Banner, "The Problem of South Carolina," in *The Hofstadter Aegis: A Memorial*, ed. Stanley Elkins and Eric McKitrick (New York: Knopf, 1974), 60–93; David Moltke-Hansen, "Protecting Interests, Maintaining Rights, Emulating Ancestors: U.S. Constitution Bicentennial Reflections on 'the Problem of South Carolina,' 1787–1860," *South Carolina Historical Magazine* 89 (July 1988): 160–82.

16. Lacy K. Ford, *Deliver Us from Evil: The Slavery Question in the Old South* (New York: Oxford University Press, 2009), 449–535.

17. Quigley, *Shifting Grounds*, 45.

18. On the nullification crisis, see especially William W. Freehling, *The Road to Disunion*, vol. 1, *Secessionists at Bay, 1776–1854* (New York: Oxford University Press, 1990), 253–86.

19. On the southern conventions and southern nationalism in the 1850s, see especially John McCardell, *The Idea of a Southern Nation: Southern Nationalists and Southern Nationalism, 1830–1860* (New York: Norton, 1979), 308–19. See also Robert E. Bonner, *Mastering America: Southern Slaveholders and the Crisis of American Nationhood* (New York: Cambridge University Press, 2009).

20. On this process, see especially Manisha Sinha, *The Counterrevolution of Slavery: Politics and Ideology in Antebellum South Carolina* (Chapel Hill: University of North Carolina Press, 2000), 95–255.

21. "South Carolina's Declaration of the Immediate Causes of Secession (1860)," in *Slavery and Emancipation*, ed. Rick Halpern and Enrico Dal Lago (Oxford: Blackwell, 2002), 348.

22. See especially William W. Freehling, *The Road to Disunion*, vol. 2, *Secessionists Triumphant, 1854–1861* (New York: Oxford University Press, 2007), 343–442.

23. William L. Barney, "Rush to Disaster: Secession and the Slaves' Revenge," in *Secession Winter: When the Union Fell Apart*, ed. Robert J. Cook, William L. Barney, and Elizabeth R. Varon (Baltimore: Johns Hopkins University Press, 2013), 29.

24. Herbert S. Klein and Ben Vinson III, *African Slavery in Latin America and the Caribbean* (New York: Oxford University Press, 2007), 68.

25. Herbert S. Klein and Francisco Vidal Luna, *Slavery in Brazil* (New York: Cambridge University Press, 2010), 62–63.

26. Gabriel Aladrén, "*Sem Respeitar fé nem tratados:* Escravidão e guerra na formação histórica da fronteira sul do Brasil (Rio Grande de São Pedro, c. 1777–1835)" (PhD diss., Universidade Federal Fluminense, 2012), 254.

27. Ibid., 338–43; Fernando Henrique Cardoso, *Capitalismo e escravidão no Brasil meridional: O negro na sociedade escravocrata do Rio Grande do Sul* (1962; Rio de Janeiro: Civilização Brasileira, 2003).

28. Berbel, Marquese, and Parron, *Escravidão e política*, 95–257.

29. Luís Augusto Ebling Farinatti, "Os compadres de Estêvão e Benedita: Hierarquia social, compadrio e escravidão na fronteira meridional do Brasil (1821–1845)," *Anais do XXI Simposio Nacional de Historia—ANPUH* (July 2011): 1–3, 14–15.

30. Stephen Bell, "Early Industrialization in the South Atlantic: Political Influences on the *charqueadas* of Rio Grande do Sul before 1860," *Journal of Historical Geography* 19 (October 1993): 399–411.

31. Luciano Campelo Bornholdt, "What Is a *Gaúcho*? Intersections between State, Identities, and Domination in Southern Brazil," *(Con)textos. Revista d'antropologia i investigacão social* 4 (May 2010): 23–41.

32. On some of these issues, see Leslie Bethell and José Murilo de Carvalho, "1822–1850," in *Brazil: Empire and Republic, 1822–1930,* ed. Leslie Bethell (New York: Cambridge University Press, 1989), 71–72.

33. Spencer L. Leitman, "Cattle and *Caudillos* in Brazil's Southern Borderland, 1828–1850," *Ethnohistory* 20 (Spring 1973): 192.

34. I wish to thank Rafael de Bivar Marquese for his suggestion to compare Rio Grande do Sul's *Farroupilha* with South Carolina's nullification crisis.

35. On the *Farroupilha,* see especially Moacyr Flores, *A Revolução Farroupilha* (Porto Alegre: UFRGS Editora, 1990); and Sandra Jatahy Pesavento, *Historia do Rio Grande do Sul* (Porto Alegre: Mercado Aberto, 2002).

36. See especially Roderick J. Barman, *Brazil: The Forging of a Nation, 1798–1852* (Stanford, CA: Stanford University Press, 1988), 189–245.

37. William W. Freehling, *The South vs. the South: How Anti-Confederate Southerners Shaped the Civil War* (New York: Oxford University Press, 2001), 33–44.

38. Faust, *Creation of Confederate Nationalism,* 22–40; Anne Sarah Rubin, *A Shattered Nation: The Rise and Fall of the Confederacy, 1861–1868* (Chapel Hill: University of North Carolina Press, 2007), 11–49.

39. Emory M. Thomas, *The Confederacy as a Revolutionary Experience* (Columbia: University of South Carolina Press, 1991), 134–35. See also Paul D. Escott, *The Confederacy: The Slaveholders' Failed Venture* (Santa Barbara, CA: ABC-CLIO, 2010), 21–64.

40. Drew Gilpin Faust, *Mothers of Invention: Women of the Slaveholding South in the American Civil War* (Chapel Hill: University of North Carolina Press, 1996), 9–20.

41. McCurry, *Confederate Reckoning,* 310–58. On the destruction of slavery in the South, see Ira Berlin, Barbara J. Fields, Steven F. Miller, Joseph P. Reidy, and Leslie S. Rowland, *Slaves No More: Three Essays in Emancipation and the Civil War* (New York: Cambridge University Press, 1992), 1–76; and James Oakes, *Freedom National: The Destruction of Slavery in the United States, 1861–1865* (New York: Norton, 2013), 340–488.

42. Quoted in Bruce Levine, *The Fall of the House of Dixie: The Civil War and the Social Revolution That Transformed the South* (New York: Random House, 2013), 167.

43. Bruce Levine, *Confederate Emancipation: Southern Plans to Free and Arm Slaves during the Civil War* (New York: Oxford University Press, 2006), 147.

44. On Cuban slavery in the nineteenth century and the "second slavery," see Michael Zeuske, "Comparing or Interlinking? Economic Comparisons of Early Nineteenth-Century Slave Systems in the Americas in Historical Perspective," in *Slave Systems: Ancient and Modern,* ed. Enrico Dal Lago and Constantina Katsari (New York: Cambridge University Press, 2008), 148–83.

45. Christopher Schmidt-Nowara, "Empires against Emancipation: Spain, Brazil, and the Abolition of Slavery," *Review, a Journal of the Fernand Braudel Center* 31, no. 2 (2008): 101–20.

46. Matt D. Childs and Manuel Barcia, "Cuba," in *The Oxford Handbook of Slavery in the Americas*, ed. Mark M. Smith and Robert L. Paquette (New York: Oxford University Press, 2010), 104.

47. Ada Ferrer, *Insurgent Cuba: Race, Nation, and Revolution, 1868–1898* (Chapel Hill: University of North Carolina Press, 1999), 22–31; Ada Ferrer, "Cuban Slavery and Atlantic Antislavery," *Review, a Journal of the Fernand Braudel Center* 31, no. 3 (2008): 267–96.

48. Ferrer, *Insurgent Cuba*, 22.

49. Childs and Barcia, "Cuba," 103. See also Ada Ferrer, "Armed Slaves and Anticolonial Insurgency in Late Nineteenth-Century Cuba," in *Arming Slaves: From Classical Times to the Modern Age*, ed. Christopher Leslie Brown and Philip D. Morgan (New Haven, CT: Yale University Press, 2006), 304–29.

50. Rebecca J. Scott, *Slave Emancipation in Cuba: The Transition to Free Labor, 1860–1899* (Princeton, NJ: Princeton University Press, 1985), 45–62.

"WHEN I THINK HOW OUR FAMILY IS SCATTERED"

Comparing Forced Separation among Antebellum Slave Families

DAMIAN ALAN PARGAS

One day near the end of March 1846, Juliet Grimshaw, a young slave woman from Virginia, sat down and pondered the separation of her entire family. Originally slaves of Mount Airy Plantation, the Grimshaws had all been removed by 1845 save the family matriarch, Esther, and her youngest son Henry, who was only eight years old. Juliet herself had been sold locally to one Mrs. Tyler. Her sister Winny and brother James had been sent to Alabama, her sister Lizza had been sent to Washington, D.C., and her father had absconded and was presumed to have made it to a free state. In a dictated letter to Lizza, Juliet lamented: "Dear Sister you can not imagine how lonely I feel sometimes when I think how our family is scattered, my father I know not where nor how he is whether dead or alive, one sister in Alabama[,] mother at home alone with out any of her children with her [except for Henry], and we never hear from you. This is enough to make me low spirited is it not?"[1]

Like all families of all times and places, slave families in the American South were not static social units but rather evolved and devolved over time, constantly changing as unions were established and then broken, as members were added and then lost. Unlike most families, however, the dismemberment of slave families was often the result of forcible and arbitrary separation by their owners, a frequent source of anxiety and personal tragedy in slave quarters from Maryland to Texas. From 1800 to 1860, an era that witnessed not only the spectacular expansion of human bondage in the southern states but also the rise of an active and lucrative domestic slave trade, virtually no slave family was completely safeguarded from the prospect of being "torn asunder."

The extent of forced breakups of slave families throughout the antebellum South is still far from clear. Much of the scholarly debate has centered on the issue of long-distance sale, which in the nineteenth century was certainly the most widely discussed method of forced separation and far and away the most feared by slaves. Cliometric historians Robert Fogel and Stanley Engerman argued in *Time on the Cross* (1974) that in the antebellum period long-distance sales as a whole accounted for a mere 2 percent of dissolved marriages among slaves, suggesting that forced separation was far from a legitimate threat for most bondpeople. Their methodology and results were widely criticized as a drastic underestimate, most aptly by Michael Tadman, who estimated in *Speculators and Slaves* (1989) that long-distance sales probably destroyed about one in three first marriages among slaves in the Upper South, and that they may have separated as many as one in five slave children from both parents. The domestic slave trade was not the only threat to family stability; estate divisions and local sales also disrupted domestic arrangements and the nature of family contact throughout the South. These factors are given due consideration in recent localized studies by historians such as Emily West and Wilma Dunaway, but as yet few if any historians have approached the issue of permanent forced separation from an intraregional comparative perspective.[2]

A closer inspection of various southern communities reveals that families in certain agricultural regions were more at risk than others. Time and place mattered; the specific labor demands and nature of slaveholding in specific localities could make forced separation a vague yet real possibility or a constantly recurring nightmare. In an attempt to shed light upon the regional variations in the long-term stability of slave families throughout the antebellum South, as well as to illuminate the importance of economic developments in causing such variations, this study will examine the extent to which family bonds were forcibly and permanently ruptured by estate divisions and sale (both local and long-distance) in two distinct agricultural regions: northern Virginia's Fairfax County and Georgetown District in the South Carolina low country. Attention will also be paid to the ways in which enslaved people in these localities reacted to forced separation or the prospect thereof. Dissolution surely haunted slave families everywhere, but this chapter makes clear that the threat of forced separation differed across time and space according to the nature of slave-based economies.

* * *

A thriving and healthy agricultural sector was most conducive to long-term stability among slave families throughout the South, because economic success favored the expansion of slaveholdings rather than their dissolution through sale or estate divisions. Enslaved people in antebellum northern Virginia, however, found themselves living in a region struggling to maintain its slave economy. Typical of the statewide trend yet atypical for the South as a whole, Fairfax County moved in the direction of a society with slaves during the nineteenth century, despite having once been a thriving slave society. Tobacco culture had brought wealth and prosperity to the county's original settlers, but as a result of declining productivity triggered by tobacco's severe exhaustion of the soil and the disastrous effects of the Revolutionary War on the Chesapeake's tobacco economy, tobacco was already in marked decline by the second half of the eighteenth century. By the dawn of the nineteenth century, most planters had abandoned their traditional staple crop and had desperately begun to intensify their truck farming and commercial cultivation of mixed grains: wheat, corn, rye, and oats. "The staple commodity or most general crop is wheat and corn," observed one visitor in a letter home to his family in Vermont in 1810. "They have abandoned the cultivation of Tobacco in a great degree, it requiring a very rich soil and much attention, they do not find it profitable." The new cash crops did not make many planters rich, and with time it became increasingly difficult for slaveholders to keep their account books in the black. Continued low crop yields, soil depletion, and the failure to employ progressive fertilizing techniques until the 1840s and 1850s exacerbated their economic woes. Moreover, the new crops were not traditional plantation crops and did not necessarily demand much slave labor. Planters in the region therefore found themselves burdened with surplus slaves on failing estates. Many abandoned the region altogether and moved west.[3]

The retrogression that characterized slave-based agriculture was visible in the diminishing sizes of slaveholdings during the antebellum period. Tobacco did not necessarily require economies of scale, and most slaveholdings in Fairfax had never really been very large to begin with, though there were a few notable exceptions such as George Washington's Mount Vernon and William Fitzhugh's Ravensworth, each of which counted well over one hundred slaves at its peak. By the eve of the Civil War, slaveholdings had shrunk dramatically. Between 1810 and 1860 the percentage of slaves living on plantations, defined as holdings containing more than twenty slaves, dropped from 42 percent to only

16 percent, while the percentage of slaves living on farms containing twenty or fewer slaves increased from 58 percent in 1810 to 84 percent in 1860. Indeed, by the outbreak of the Civil War, a majority of slaves (58%) lived on tiny holdings of fewer than ten slaves. Slaveholdings that recalled the wealth of the tobacco era had by that time vanished from the Fairfax County landscape. In 1810 the largest slaveholding was Ravensworth, boasting some 235 bondpeople. Fifty years later, in contrast, the largest plantation was Bush Hill, owned by Virginia Gunnell Scott and containing only 43 slaves, most of whom she annually hired out because she could find no use for them at home. Such developments had important consequences for enslaved people's social landscapes and family structures. The dwindling size of local slaveholdings created a social landscape in which cross-plantation marriages among slaves were especially prevalent. Enslaved men frequently lived on separate holdings from their wives and children. Families were thus often forcibly separated from the outset.[4]

The nature and development of regional agriculture in Georgetown District in the South Carolina low country created a world that bore a marked contrast to Fairfax County. Whereas nineteenth-century Fairfax County transitioned from a slave society into a society with slaves, Georgetown District, long one of the wealthiest and most firmly rooted slave societies of the South, showed no signs of decline in the antebellum period. The rice-producing low country remained one of the most successful agricultural regions in the slave South.

By 1800, while planters in northern Virginia were desperately abandoning tobacco and turning their resources to mixed farming, rice planters in Georgetown District were in the process of significantly expanding and consolidating their operations, as the geographic center of the rice industry shifted from the inland swamps to the more efficient river plantations near the coast. The result of this shift was a dramatic growth in plantation and slaveholding size and the virtual elimination of inland competition as smaller-scale planters sold out to the larger-scale planters along the rivers and emigrated. As the rice industry became consolidated in their hands, planters in Georgetown grew unimaginably wealthy, a fact reflected in their vast slaveholdings. As early as 1810, a majority of enslaved people in the district lived on plantations containing more than one hundred slaves, and 30 percent lived on holdings with more than two hundred slaves. The size of local slaveholdings grew consistently over time. At their peak of wealth and power in 1850, the rice masters held 74 percent of the local slave population on holdings with more than one hundred slaves and

46 percent on holdings of more than two hundred. Some estates controlled several hundreds of slaves; one counted more than one thousand. Indeed, the expansion of operations became a near obsession among local planters. One nineteenth-century resident claimed that her neighbors were interested only in "mak[ing] Rice to buy Negroes and Buy[ing] Negroes to make Rice."[5]

The vast size of slaveholdings in Georgetown District had important consequences for slave family structure. Whereas in Fairfax County most slave families were divided from the outset, as slaves from small farms were forced to marry across plantation lines, in Georgetown District bondpeople had more opportunities to form coresident families and two-parent households. Ample slave inventories and plantation records confirm that most slaves in the district lived in coresidential nuclear families. The 1819 inventory of slaves belonging to the estate of Benjamin Allston Jr., for example, indicates a prevalence of coresidential couples and two-parent households. Of the 132 slaves listed in Allston's inventory, 113 were grouped into one of seventeen family units, each with a collective value. Fourteen of these families—containing an aggregate 108 slaves, or 82 percent of the total—were headed by coresidential couples. On Weehaw plantation, which contained 265 slaves in 1855, both parents were present in 67 of the 69 households (97%). At White House plantation, owned by Julius Izard Pringle and containing 110 slaves in May 1858, coresidential couples headed 15 of 17 households (88%). So it was throughout the district.[6]

E state divisions in particular confronted local enslaved people with formidable obstacles to maintaining stable domestic arrangements and social relationships, and predictably the death of a slaveholder usually wrought havoc in the slave quarters. Primogeniture law was no longer practiced in the nineteenth century; the property of the deceased, including slaves, was therefore divided more or less equally among several heirs. This was true throughout the South, but because of the unusually small number of slaves living on most holdings in northern Virginia, severing at least some family ties during estate divisions was practically unavoidable in antebellum Fairfax County. There the forced separation of family members during estate divisions was the rule, not the exception, and it only worsened over time.[7]

Joshua Buckley owned only eight slaves upon his death in 1821: three men, a woman named Fann, and her four children. With exactly eight heirs, Buckley's

slaves were all separated from each other, including Fann's four small children from their mother. In 1825 James Turley also bequeathed his seven slaves,
consisting of a complete coresidential family, to his seven children, separating
them all from each other. The three female-headed families owned by Peter
Coulter likewise failed to escape forced separation. In his last will and testament, Coulter specified that his daughter Margaret receive "a negro woman
call'd Mary & all her increase except a negro boy called William." His daughter Cordelia was to receive "one negro woman call'd Rachael & all her increase
except Eliza, Winny & Joseph." And John Coulter, the only male heir, was to
inherit "old Jinny, her son James, little Mary, Hannah & all her increase, also a
negro boy called Joe." Joe was presumably Joseph, the above-mentioned son of
Rachael. Finally, Coulter specified his wish that the remaining slaves—Mary's
son William, Rachael's daughters Eliza and Winny, and a fourth bondperson
named Henry—be sold in order to pay off his outstanding debts. Such cases
appear in the will books with staggering frequency and appear even more
frequently in the late antebellum period, when most slaveholdings had shrunk
to miniscule proportions. In estate inventories slaves were almost always listed
and appraised individually, indicating they were to be bequeathed as such.[8]

Slave families were not passive when faced with the prospect of forced
separation through an estate division. Threatened with the erection of physical boundaries between themselves and their family members, they often attempted to negotiate with the heirs of their masters to be bequeathed together, or at least with their youngest children. Yet their negotiating power
was circumscribed by the size of slaveholdings and the number of heirs. The
scattering of families locally, as often happened upon estate divisions, softened
the blow of separation by permitting contact across property lines, such as
weekend visits. Some risked truancy to spend additional time with their families. Harriet Williams, who absconded in 1855, was suspected of hiding out in
Washington, where "she has relations." An advertisement for a runaway named
Daniel Solomon hinted that he had extensive "relations in Fairfax County and
the District." Nelly Williams was suspected of having run to any one of her
"relatives and acquaintances in Washington, Georgetown, Baltimore, Dum-
fries and Stafford court house Va." Baltimore and Stafford were certainly not
close. Family members who were removed beyond a radius of ten to fifteen
miles could not be visited with regularity, but even then some slaves struck
deals with their masters to traverse great distances to see them. Nelly Shanks,

an elderly slave at Bush Hill, was separated from her daughter Clarissa and her grandchildren in an estate division, the latter being sent to Farmington, some one hundred miles distant. In October 1827, Clarissa obtained special permission from her master to travel all the way to Fairfax County with her husband and three youngest children in order to see her mother. Such cases demonstrate that whenever possible slaves attempted to make the best of a bad situation by seizing opportunities to maintain family contact.[9]

Slave families in Georgetown District were less often disrupted or forcibly divided during estate divisions than their Fairfax County counterparts; in many cases they did not even change residence. Large slaveholdings and the profitability of economies of scale in rice cultivation largely safeguarded slave families in the low country from forced ruptures. The case of Henry Augustus Middleton is illustrative. Seeking a pardon after the Civil War, Middleton pleaded that while he had owned more than three hundred slaves in 1861, all of his slaves and their ancestors had been owned by the family since 1735. He had personally never bought or sold anybody, but rather had inherited them all with the plantation. This was not particularly unusual for Georgetown District. Indeed, local slaveholdings were remarkably stable from generation to generation, and visitors and residents alike frequently commented on the continuity of slave ownership within certain families. One former resident recalled long after the Civil War that most of the plantations in his neighborhood "had been in the possession of the same family for several generations, and the negroes had been born and bred upon them." J. Motte Alston claimed, "Most of [my grandfather's] large number of negroes lived and died in the same family." Laurence Oliphant, who visited Georgetown District just before emancipation, noted that the slaves on one plantation "recall reminiscences of three or four generations back of the family to which they have belonged for nearly a century."[10]

Multiple-plantation ownership among many local rice planters often made it possible to bequeath entire plantations with their slave populations largely intact to their heirs, or at least greatly reduce the breakup of slave populations during estate settlements. For example, rice planter Plowden Weston, upon his death in 1827, bequeathed a plantation and more than 250 slaves *each* to each of his two sons. William Alston in 1838 bequeathed to each of his three sons a complete plantation, and one of his sons even received two plantations. In 1853 Joshua John Ward likewise left his six plantations and more than a thousand slaves to be divided equally among his three sons, with each son receiving two plantations. And Robert F. W. Allston willed to each of his five children a plantation and approximately one hundred slaves.[11]

Slaveholdings were, moreover, large enough that it was possible in most cases to keep families intact even when they did have to change residence. It is significant to note that in the inventories of Georgetown's grandees, slaves are frequently listed and appraised in simple family groups, whereas in northern Virginia they were usually listed singly, and family ties were rarely mentioned. This suggests that slaveholders in Georgetown District in fact intended to keep families together during estate divisions, as it facilitated the equal division of such large groups of bondpeople. Benjamin Alston Jr., for example, who owned 144 slaves when he died, only specified his wishes concerning eighteen domestic slaves in his will; the rest, numbering 126, were to be divided equally among his seven heirs, "share and share alike." In a subsequent inventory made in 1819, all but nineteen slaves were listed and appraised in collective family groups. In the slave inventories accompanying the will of Frances Withers, the owner of both Friendfield and Northampton estates, which together contained some 468 bondpeople in 1841, the slaves were also appraised collectively in family units. The 185 slaves living on Hagley plantation and owned by Plowden C. J. Weston during the Civil War were listed in family groups and collectively appraised at $370,000 for the lot. Evidence from throughout the antebellum period suggests that this was the rule rather than the exception. When enslaved people in Georgetown District were transferred from one holding to another during estate divisions, it did not often result in the destruction of simple family ties or marital arrangements.[12]

With slave-based agriculture in decline and the number of slaves that could efficiently be employed in mixed farming limited, it is unsurprising that the heirs of Fairfax County slaveholders did not always wish to hold on to their inherited bondpeople. After estate divisions, slave sales were the order of the day, as local residents quickly converted their inheritance into cash. This enabled them to pay off debts and spared them the financial burdens of having to maintain surplus slaves. In the process, they ruptured countless slaves' family ties.

Many transactions were local affairs, with slaves being sold at auction locally, to new masters in northern Virginia or Washington, D.C. Sometimes slave women were sold along with their infants, but only rarely were they sold with older children. The eight slaves owned by Edward Blackburn were sold by his heirs to four different local buyers. Two mothers were purchased with only one infant each. Similarly, eight of the eleven slaves attached to the estate of John Summers were sold to six different local buyers. Again, two mothers were each sold together with only their youngest child. Children past infancy were usually sold apart from their parents. Members of a slave family owned by the heirs of Wormley Carter—a man and his wife, their two young children, and an elderly woman—were sold to three different local buyers. The man and his wife were sold to one William Weir, their two children to Catherine Lane, and the elderly woman to Robert Robinson. Such cases appear with frequency in the estate accounts of Fairfax County slaveholders.[13]

Fairfax County slaves had methods of keeping contact with family members who had been sold locally. On the weekends they requested and received passes to visit those who had been removed to other holdings. Therefore, the result of local sales, as with local estate divisions, was often not the destruction of slaves' family ties, but rather the destruction of their domestic arrangements. Coresidential families were turned into cross-plantation families, and cross-plantation families became even more scattered across the landscape. But the real danger in local slaveholders' eagerness to rid themselves of surplus slaves lay in the prospect of being sold to interstate traders and sent to the Deep South, where able-bodied slaves, commanding higher prices, never saw their family members again.

Indeed, the rise of cotton presented the most significant threat to slave-family stability in the Upper South. The insatiable demand for labor in the southern interior, combined with the abolition of the Atlantic slave trade in 1808, neatly dovetailed with the interests of slaveholders in struggling and overstocked regions where the demand for slave labor was diminishing. The most recent estimates by Steven Deyle suggest that between 1820 and 1860 some 875,000 slaves were forcibly removed from the Upper South. Between 60 and 70 percent of those were transported via the domestic slave trade. Along with this massive forced migration came the unspeakable devastation for slave families in the exporting states. Michael Tadman has estimated that the domestic slave trade probably destroyed one in three first slave marriages in the Upper South. The proportion of children separated from at least one parent may also have been as high as one in three, and that of children separated from both parents one in five.[14]

Population data indicates that large numbers of slaves were forcibly removed from Fairfax County during the antebellum period. Census returns show that the local slave population was reduced by no less than 47 percent between 1810 and 1860—not in relative numbers, but in absolute numbers. If projected population growth is taken into account, the decline was in fact much greater. In the decade preceding the Civil War, for example, the slave population declined by only 2 percent, but considering local mortality rates and birthrates during the 1850s, the real decline was probably more like 16 percent.[15]

Not all of these slaves were sold. A few were emancipated, and many others, especially in the early decades of the nineteenth century, were forced to migrate west with their masters. There can be no doubt, however, that the vast majority of slaves who left the county during the antebellum period did so in chains, sold to the burgeoning plantations of Georgia, Alabama, Mississippi, Louisiana, and Arkansas. Local traders and southern planters alike ran countless advertisements in the *Alexandria Gazette* promising distressed slaveholders cash for likely young hands under the age of thirty. Franklin & Armfield offered sellers in 1828 "Cash for one hundred likely YOUNG NEGROES of both sexes, between the ages of 8 and 25," adding that since the "negroes are wanted immediately," they would "give more than any other purchasers that are in the market or may hereafter come into the market." Price, Birch & Co. wished "to purchase any number of NEGROES, of both sexes, for cash." And Joseph Bruin offered to "pay liberal prices" for "any number of NEGROES," not specifying age or sex.[16]

Such ads had the desired effect on the local slaveholding population. During estate divisions, many heirs of unwanted bondpeople immediately delivered them to interstate traders or sold them at auction to agents of southern planters. The five slaves owned by the estate of William Lane in 1829 were sold to slave trader Alexander Grigsby for a total of $1,287. In 1835 the five heirs of Francis Lightfoot Lee of Sully plantation instructed an agent to "see if it will be possible to get any or all of those negroes off. The sooner the arrangements are made, the better." And the heirs of several local slaveholders sold their inherited chattel to local trader Joseph Bruin in the 1850s, as estate records testify.[17]

Many slaveholders did not wait for their heirs to dispose of their surplus bondpeople. There is ample evidence that farmers and planters culled their labor forces in times of economic difficulty. One resident of Alexandria told

British visitor E. S. Abdy in the 1830s that "if it were not for this detestable traffic, those who have a large number of slaves upon poor land (such is most of the soil near Washington), would not long be enabled to hold them; as it generally takes the whole produce of their labor to clothe and support them." Bushrod Washington, president of the American Colonization Society, an organization dedicated to repatriating free blacks to Africa, sold fifty-five of his slaves to a Louisiana planter in 1821 for the sum of ten thousand dollars. As justification he claimed that he had struggled for twenty years to turn a profit from the "products of their own labor," but with slaves who were "worse than useless," and a plantation losing between five hundred and one thousand dollars per year, he felt he had no choice. This act broke up several families. The slaves who remained told Abdy "that the husbands had been torn from their wives and children; and that many relations were left behind." Washington's neighbor Lawrence Lewis, master of Woodlawn, was compelled to do the same. In 1837, a year marked by the onset of a nationwide panic, Lewis wrote to an agent in Louisiana about the "prospect . . . of either selling [the slaves] or hireing them out; the loss I have met with will make me prefer the former rather than the latter." "Indeed," he continued, "my income is nothing. . . . Woodlawn is worse than nothing, . . . It is best to sell the negroes as early as possible."[18]

Enslaved people confronted with the reality of long-distance sale encountered few opportunities to prevent it, but many nevertheless risked desperate attempts to escape their lot, attempting to negotiate local sales or flee the grasp of their captors. A few even maimed their valuable bodies or chose suicide, literally destroying their salability in southern markets. When slaveholder Elizabeth Tyler died, for example, one of her slaves named Henry fled immediately in order to escape sale to the Deep South. He was caught in Baltimore and sent back to Fairfax County, upon which he chopped off his own hand, apparently to render himself worthless for sale. Even this did not save Henry. He was sold anyway, presumably at a greatly reduced price. One slave woman named Anna, having been separated from her husband and sold to traders in Washington, jumped out of an upper window of the jail where she was being held, in an attempt to kill herself. She survived but broke her limbs "in a shocking manner," leaving her a "helpless cripple." Attempts to prevent deportation were the exception rather than the rule, however, and were usually unsuccessful. Most slaves sold south had little choice but to accept their fate.[19]

Although many low-country rice planters were wealthy beyond the wild-est dreams of most American slaveholders, and certainly those in northern Virginia, slave sales were not uncommon in Georgetown District. Auctions were held with some regularity, especially to settle estates or to fund the retire-ment of some planters. Many such auctions consisted of small groups of slaves whose sale was intended to round out partitions or pay off outstanding debts. The Georgetown *Winyah Intelligencer* ran numerous advertisements for local estate auctions. In one, "8 prime and very valuable NEGROES, the property of the Estate of the late Francis Brudot," were offered for sale. "FOUR NEGROES, belonging to the Estate of O. Potter, deceased," were advertised prior to their sale in January 1829. Other sales were much larger. The heirs of planter Thomas F. Goddard offered for sale "from FIFTY to SIXTY PRIME NEGROES" in 1832.[20]

Labor demands within Georgetown District were such that relatively few slaves were sold away from their homes, and local planters, constantly watch-ful for bargains, eagerly snatched up a majority of those who were. Indeed, continuous purchasing by the most successful planters resulted in significant consolidation and growth of local slaveholdings during the antebellum period. The account books belonging to planter Stephen D. Doar, for example, in-dicate that he was a regular frequenter of his neighbors' estate sales. In 1855 he spent $1,963 on a group of slaves sold by the estate of L. D. Desaussure. That same year he bought 4 more from the heirs of J. Gourdin and another 17 at James Jinkler's estate sale. Before the year was out, he had acquired an additional 25 slaves from the Skinning estate. Many of the most prominent planters in the district also acquired slaves at local auctions, some of them in relatively large groups. Robert Allston, for one, continuously expanded his la-bor force through local purchases during his long career. In 1828, he bought 32 slaves from the estate of William and Sarah Allen. In the 1850s he purchased 42 bondmen from Thomas Pinckney Alston, whose sons did not want to take over the family business when he retired, inducing him to sell 177 of his slaves. In 1857 Allston bought another group of 53 Waccamaw slaves. Two years later, he purchased Pipe Down plantation in its entirety, complete with 109 slaves, from the widow Mary Ann Petigru, who wished to cash in on her estate when her husband died. Thirty-six of these slaves were transferred to Guendalos, the plantation Allston was setting up for his son Benjamin. Finally, at the auction of one Mrs. Withers in 1859, Allston bought an additional 41 bondpeople for his son Benjamin.[21]

As was the case in northern Virginia, slaves who were sold locally at‐
tempted to maintain family contacts by requesting passes for weekend visiting.
But a handful of runaway slave advertisements illustrate that bondpeople who
had been removed beyond a reasonable distance sometimes risked truancy to
visit with family and friends left behind, not unlike their counterparts in Fair‐
fax. Paddy was owned by a Black River planter but suspected of lurking about
the Pee Dee River plantation of John D. Witherspoon, "who I understand
owns two of his brothers." One missing man named Adam had been "bought
in 1811, of the Estate of John Bowman, of South Santee, by the late major
Joseph Allston," from whom the subscriber had subsequently acquired him.
Adam had presumably returned to the Santee area to visit family and friends.
Another missing slave who absconded with his wife and four children was
suspected of being harbored by extended family or friends near "the plantation
of Thomas W. Price Esq, at the sale of whose negroes he was purchased about
two years ago." Sammy, who was owned by a planter on the Sampit River, had
"a mother at Rose Hill (Waccamaw) where the subscriber understands he is."[22]

If incidents of truancy to see friends and family appear to have occurred
with less frequency in Georgetown District than they did in northern Virginia,
however, perhaps this was because it was less necessary. As was the case during
estate divisions, slave families in the low country were usually sold in family
groups, a rare phenomenon that has caught the attention of other historians.
Larry Hudson, for one, found that "as the antebellum period wore on, it was
clear that slave masters in South Carolina were making efforts to keep slave
families together." This is evident in Georgetown District from a wide variety
of sources. In the records of Paul D. Weston, for example, an inventory of 145
slaves to be sold listed and appraised them all as families. Likewise, the slaves
belonging to the estate of E. J. Heriot were all sold in family groups. Sale ad‐
vertisements often announced slaves in family units. The auction house of John
Shackleford & Son in Georgetown advertised in 1819 the sale of "Nine valu‐
able Negroes," adding that "these negroes being one family, cannot be sepa‐
rated." William Belluney offered for sale "a family of eight Negroes." Richfield
plantation was advertised for sale along with "a gang of about 111 Negroes . . .
to be sold in Families." Purchasers advertised to buy slaves in family groups as
well. One planter wanted "a family of 6 or 8 Negroes." Another promised "cash
. . . for a family of 8 to 10 healthy negroes."[23]

Far from passive victims in the buying, selling, and trading of human property, enslaved people throughout the low country created opportunities to keep simple families intact by making it unattractive to acquire them otherwise. Bondpeople in Georgetown District protested the separation of family members during sales and estate divisions. Historian Leslie Schwalm found that in the low country "the pending sale and separation of members of a slave community created a 'general gloom' that settled on the plantation slaves 'at the idea of parting with each other.'" Their reaction had a negative effect on plantation labor, and indeed "so disrupted the peace and efficiency of the slave workforce that it became common wisdom among nineteenth-century rice planters that slaves should be purchased and sold in intact family groups." Doing otherwise could have disastrous consequences for the slave owner. According to one planter, if slaves were bought individually and thrown "all together among strangers, they don't assimilate, & they ponder over former ties, of family, &c., & all goes wrong with them." Adjusting to the demands of the market, auctioneers and sellers of slaves offered them in family groups. On rare occasions low-country bondpeople even succeeded in keeping entire plantation communities intact.[24]

The threat of long-distance sale did not loom over slave families in Georgetown District to the extent that it did in northern Virginia. In such a wealthy district as Georgetown, planters were not hard-pressed to rid themselves of their bondpeople. Indeed, most constantly sought to expand their slaveholdings. Population data indicates that few slaves were sold outside of the district during the antebellum period. Unlike the Fairfax County slave population, which plummeted by 47 percent between 1810 and 1860, the Georgetown slave population increased by 53 percent during the antebellum period, despite far higher mortality rates and lower birth rates.[25]

Yet certainly not all local slaves were spared deportation during the antebellum period, even in Georgetown District. It is important not to exaggerate their protection from the interstate trade. Local planters could always sell to interstate traders based in Charleston or elsewhere, and many did so with few qualms about forever separating their bondpeople from family and friends. In 1855 one trader operating out of Sumterville made a special detour to Georgetown District when he heard of a promising "Sale of negros" that was to take place there. When Thomas Pinckney Alston retired to Georgia in 1859, he decided to sell 177 of his slaves and pocket the proceeds. Forty-two were bought by Robert Allston, but the rest were scattered across the state. Robert Allston himself was forced to sell 59 slaves when he inherited his brother's Waverly plantation in 1834, which was encumbered with a heavy debt of more than fifty thousand dollars. Plowden Weston sold in excess of 100 of his slaves from his plantation Laurel Hill, which he decided to get rid of in 1856 in order to concentrate his holdings around Hagley, his resident plantation. The purchaser of the plantation, Daniel Jordan, offered to buy the slaves as well, but Weston decided instead to sell most of them to the Deep South where they could command a higher price. Their departure by riverboat was recorded by Weston's wife Emily: "The vessel steamed along for a little while very slowly. Tears filled my eyes as I *looked* and *listened* to the wail from those on shore echoed by those on board." Her husband was less perturbed. And although these slaves were sold to traders in family groups, there was no guarantee that families would be kept intact at auctions in the Deep South. Most slaves were spared such a horrible fate in antebellum Georgetown District, however.[26]

The stability of enslaved people's family structures and domestic arrangements over time differed across space and depended heavily on both the nature of slaveholding and the labor markets of different slave societies. In Fairfax County, small slaveholdings and the decline in regional agriculture proved disastrous for slave families as estate divisions and local sales severed domestic arrangements and the domestic slave trade ruptured many families permanently. The nature of forced separation in Georgetown District was fundamentally different. Multiple-plantation ownership and large slaveholding size cushioned the effects of estate divisions, and the profitability of rice cultivation safeguarded many families from sale.

In neither of these regions were slaves passive when confronted with the threat of forced separation, even if they were not always successful in avoiding it. They negotiated to be sold together, ran away, and in Georgetown District even collectively protested to an extent that made it unattractive for slaveholders to separate families. Inevitably, however, enslaved families' boundaries and opportunities to avoid separation and maintain a degree of stability varied from region to region according to the nature of regional agriculture.

* * *

NOTES

1. Juliet Grimshaw to Lizza Grimshaw, March 27, 1846, in Richard S. Dunn, "Winney Grimshaw, a Virginia Slave, and Her Family," *Early American Studies* 9 (Fall 2011): 507–8.

2. Robert William Fogel and Stanley L. Engerman, *Time on the Cross: The Economics of American Negro Slavery* (Boston: Little, Brown, 1974), 49; Michael Tadman, *Speculators and Slaves: Masters, Traders, and Slaves in the Old South* (Madison: University of Wisconsin Press, 1989), 134, 170–71, 178; Emily West, *Chains of Love: Slave Couples in Antebellum South Carolina* (Urbana: University of Illinois Press, 2004), 141–56; and Wilma Dunaway, *The African-American Family in Slavery and Emancipation* (New York: Cambridge University Press, 2003), 53–62.

3. Nan Netherton, Donald Sweig, Janice Artemel, Patricia Hickim, and Patrick Reed, *Fairfax County, Virginia: A History* (Fairfax, VA: Fairfax County Board of Supervisors, 1978), 152–70; Avery Odelle Craven, *Soil Exhaustion as a Factor in the Agricultural History of Virginia and Maryland, 1606–1860* (Urbana: University of Illinois Press, 1926), 72–121; Lewis Cecil Gray, *History of Agriculture in the Southern United States to 1860* (Washington, DC: Carnegie Institution of Washington, 1933), 2:589–92, 811–20; Allan Kulikoff, *Tobacco and Slaves: The Development of Southern Cultures in the Chesapeake, 1680–1800* (Chapel Hill: University of North Carolina Press, 1986), 157–58; Elijah Fletcher to Jesse Fletcher Sr., August 4, 1810, in *The Letters of Elijah Fletcher*, ed. Martha von Briesen (Charlottesville: University Press of Virginia, 1965), 8 (quotations); Arthur G. Peterson, "The Alexandria Market Prior to the Civil War," *William and Mary Quarterly* 12 (April 1932): 104–14; Lorena S. Walsh, "Plantation Management in the Chesapeake, 1620–1820," *Journal of Economic History* 49 (June 1989): 404.

4. U.S. Bureau of the Census, Population Census, 1810–1860 (microfilm), NARA, Washington, DC; Richard Marshall Scott Jr., Diary, January 1, 1859 (typescript), FCRL; Brenda E. Stevenson, *Life in Black and White: Family and Community in the Slave South* (New York: Oxford University Press, 1996), 206–25.

5. Gray, *History of Agriculture*, 2:721–22; Joyce E. Chaplin, "Tidal Rice Cultivation and the Problem of Slavery in South Carolina and Georgia, 1760–1815," *William and Mary Quarterly* 49 (January 1992): 31–34, 39; U.S. Census, 1800–1860 (microfilm), NARA; Dale E. Swan, "The Structure and Profitability of the Antebellum Rice Industry: 1859," *Journal of Economic History* 31 (March 1973): 322; Charlotte Petigru Allston cited in Leslie A. Schwalm, *A Hard Fight for We: Women's Transition from Slavery to Freedom in South Carolina* (Urbana: University of Illinois Press, 1997), 8 (quotation).

6. "Appraisement of Slaves Belonging to the Estate of Benjamin Allston, Jr., 1819," in *The South Carolina Rice Plantation as Revealed in the Papers of Robert F. W. Allston*, ed. J. H. Easterby (Chicago: University of Chicago Press, 1945), 331–32; List of Weehaw People, December 31, 1855, Henry A. Middleton Jr., Weehaw Plantation Journal, 1855–1861, Cheves-Middleton Papers, SCHS; List of Negroes at the White House, May 1858, Julius Izard Pringle, White House Plantation Book, 1857, Pringle Family Papers, SCHS; Larry E. Hudson Jr., *To Have and to Hold: Slave Work and Family Life in Antebellum South Carolina* (Athens: University of Georgia Press, 1997), 149. On White House plantation, three young, single mothers were listed under their coresidential parents' names.

7. Netherton, *Fairfax County*, 161; Joan E. Cashin, "Landscape and Memory in Antebellum Virginia," *Virginia Magazine of History and Biography* 102 (October 1994): 431; Donald M. Sweig, "Northern Virginia Slavery: A Statistical and Demographic Investigation" (PhD diss., College of William and Mary, 1982), 158.

8. The cited examples are from the 1820s, but similar examples can be found throughout the antebellum period. Testament of Joshua Buckley, Fairfax County Will Book (hereinafter Will Book) M-1, 249–50 (microfilm), FCRL; Testament of James Turley, Will Book O-1, 71 (microfilm), FCRL; Testament of Peter Coulter, Will Book P-1, 242–43 (microfilm), FCRL.

9. *Alexandria Gazette and Virginia Advertiser,* August 24, 1855 (first quotation), May 9, 1822 (second quotation), September 14, 1824 (third quotation); Richard Marshall Scott Sr., Diary, October 27, 1827 (typescript), FCRL.

10. George C. Rogers Jr., *The History of Georgetown County, South Carolina* (1970; reprint, Spartanburg, SC: Reprint, 1990), 426; Sherman L. Richards and George M. Blackburn, "A Demographic History of Slavery: Georgetown County, South Carolina, 1850," *South Carolina Historical Magazine* 76 (October 1975): 215; H. Hasell Wilson, in Elizabeth Deas Allston, *The Allstons and Alstons of Waccamaw* (Charleston, SC: Walker, Evans & Cogswell, 1936), 88 (first quotation); J. Motte Alston, *Rice Planter and Sportsman: The Recollections of J. Motte Alston, 1821–1909,* ed. Arney R. Childs (1953; reprint, Columbia: University of South Carolina Press, 1999), 56 (second quotation); Laurence Oliphant, *Patriots and Filibusters; or, Incidents of Political and Exploratory Travel* (London: Blackwood, 1860), 140 (third quotation).

11. Rogers, *History of Georgetown County,* 258, 259–61; Will of William Alston, 1838, Charleston County Will Book 41, 939, Charleston County Court House, Charleston, SC; Rogers, *History of Georgetown County,* 267–68; Alberta Morel Lachicotte, *Georgetown Rice Plantations* (Georgetown, SC: Georgetown County Historical Society, 1993), 122; Michael Trinkley, ed., *An Archaeological Study of Willbrook, Oatland, and Turkey Hill Plantations, Waccamaw Neck, Georgetown County, South Carolina* (Columbia, SC: Chicora Foundation, 1987), 52. For a genealogical overview of estate acquisition and subsequent division in antebellum Georgetown District, see Rogers, *History of Georgetown County,* ch. 13.

12. "Appraisement of the Slaves Belonging to the Estate of Benjamin Alston, Jr., 1819," in Easterby, *South Carolina Rice Plantation,* 331–32 (quotation); "List of Negroes belonging to my [Francis Withers's] Friendfield Estate, including Mount Pleasant, Midway and Canaan Plantations, July 1841," James Ritchie Sparkman Papers, in *Records of Ante-Bellum Southern Plantations from the Revolution through the Civil War,* ed. Kenneth M. Stampp, series A, part 2 (microfilm), LSU; "List of Negroes for Northampton Estate, Including Westfield and Bonny Neck, July 1841," James Ritchie Sparkman Papers; "Negroes Belonging to Hagley Plantation, 1864," Estate of Plowden C. J. Weston (microfilm), Georgetown County Courthouse, Georgetown, SC.

13. Estate Account of Edward Blackburn, Will Book P-1, 286 (microfilm), FCRL; Estate Account of John Summers, Will Book O-1, 12, 28 (microfilm), FCRL; Estate Account of Wormley Carter, Will Book N-1, 261 (microfilm), FCRL.

14. Steven Deyle, *Carry Me Back: The Domestic Slave Trade in American Life* (New York: Oxford University Press, 2005), 41–46, 283–89; Gray, *History of Agriculture,* 2:650; Tadman, *Speculators and Slaves,* 170–72.

15. Vital statistics for census years 1850 and 1860 indicate that many slaves were sold or left the state during that decade. In 1850, when the slave population was at 3,178, there were 74 births and 29 deaths. If 1850 was a typical year, the slave population should have grown to 3,628 by 1860. Instead it declined absolutely by 2 percent, from 3,178 to 3,116. Considering projected population growth, however, this amounted to a decline of 16 percent. Calculations based on data from the Historical Census Browser, University of Virginia, Geospatial and Statistical Data Center (2004), http://fisher.lib.virginia.edu/collections/stats/histcensus/index.html.

16. Netherton, *Fairfax County,* 156, 263; *Alexandria (VA) Phenix Gazette,* December 25, 1828 (first quotation); *Alexandria Gazette and Daily Advertiser,* November 24, 1859 (second and third quotations).

17. Estate Account of William Lane Sr., Will Book P-1, 247 (microfilm), FCRL; Robert S. Gamble, *Sully: The Biography of a House* (Chantilly, VA: Sully Foundation, 1973), 65 (quotation); Estate Account of Ann Mason, Will Book Z-1, 153 (microfilm), FCRL; Estate Account of John Huntington, Will Book W-1, 145 (microfilm), FCRL; Estate Account of James Potter, Will Book X-1, 423 (microfilm), FCRL; Estate Account of Sarah McInteer, Will Book X-1, 120 (microfilm), FCRL.

18. E. S. Abdy, *Journal of a Residence and Tour in the United States of North America, from April 1833 to October 1834* (1835; reprint, New York: Negro Universities Press, 1969), 2:98–99 (first quotation), 177–78 (fourth quotation); Bushrod Washington cited in Frederic Bancroft, *Slave-Trading in the Old South* (1931; Columbia: University of South Carolina Press, 1996), 15 (second and third quotations); Lawrence Lewis to Major Edward G. W. Butler, January 18, 1837, Custis-Lee Family Papers, LC (fifth and sixth quotations). See also letter of November 2, 1836.

19. Estate Account of Elizabeth Tyler, Will Book O-1, 424 (microfilm), FCRL; *Alexandria (VA) Phenix Gazette,* January 31, 1826; Ethan Allen Andrews, *Slavery and the Domestic Slave Trade in the United States, in a Series of Letters Addressed to the Executive Committee of the American Union for the Relief and Improvement of the Colored Race* (1836; Freeport, NY: Books for Libraries Press, 1971), 112–13 (quotations). For examples of slave responses to potential forced separation, see John W. Blassingame, ed., *Slave Testimony: Two Centuries of Letters, Speeches, Interviews, and Autobiographies* (Baton Rouge: Louisiana State University Press, 1977), 87; John Hope Franklin and Loren Schweninger, *Runaway Slaves: Rebels on the Plantation* (Oxford: Oxford University Press, 1999), 53; William Still, *The Underground Railroad: A Record of Facts, Authentic Letters, Etc.* (1872; New York: Arno Press, 1968), 391. Historian Steven Deyle found that slaves sometimes used physical violence to resist sale. See Deyle, *Carry Me Back,* 245–75.

20. *Georgetown (SC) Winyah Intelligencer,* February 20, 1830 (first quotation); January 3, 1829 (second quotation); October 6, 1832 (third quotation).

21. Stephen D. Doar, Account Book 1, Papers of Stephen D. Doar, Manuscript Collection, LC. For the slave purchases of Robert F. W. Allston, see William Dusinberre, *Them Dark Days: Slavery in the American Rice Swamps* (New York: Oxford University Press, 1996), 402–3, 524; "Slave Bill of Sale, 1828," in Easterby, *South Carolina Rice Plantation,* 337; Slave Sale Broadside, January 27, 1857, Cleland Kinloch Huger Papers, SCL; "Slave Bill of Sale, 1 February 1859," in Easterby, *South Carolina Rice Plantation,* 353–54; "Agreement to Purchase Slaves, January 25, 1859," in Easterby, *South Carolina Rice Plantation,* 351–52.

22. *Georgetown (SC) Winyah Intelligencer,* February 13, 1819 (first quotation); January 7, 1829 (second quotation); February 6, 1830 (third quotation); September 29, 1830 (fourth quotation).

23. Hudson, *To Have and to Hold,* 175 (first quotation); Slave Inventory of the Paul D. Weston Estate, Paul D. Weston Papers, in Stampp, *Records of Ante-Bellum Southern Plantations,* series B (microfilm), LSU; "Sales of Negroes of the Estate of E. J. Heriot," October 4, 1859, James Ritchie Sparkman Papers; *Georgetown (SC) Winyah Intelligencer,* March 31, 1819 (second and third quotations), January 12, 1819 (fourth quotation); Slave Sale Broadside, January 27, 1857, and Slave Sale Broadside, March 1, 1854, James Ritchie Sparkman Papers (fifth quotation); *Georgetown (SC) Winyah Intelligencer,* November 10, 1819 (sixth quotation), November 24, 1819 (seventh quotation).

24. Schwalm, *Hard Fight for We,* 56 (all quotations); Elizabeth W. Allston Pringle, *Chronicles of Chicora Wood* (1922; reprint, Atlanta: Cherokee, 1976), 10–11.

25. Hudson, *To Have and to Hold,* 175; Rogers, *History of Georgetown County,* 343. The George-town slave population increased by 6,218 between 1800 and 1860, from 11,816 to 18,034. U.S. Census Schedules, 1800–1860, NARA. According to vital statistics, the Georgetown slave population counted 318 births and 288 deaths in 1850, a difference of only 30. If 1850 was a normal year, the slave population should have grown by 300 by 1860; instead it grew by only 140 (from 17,894 in 1850 to 18,034 in 1860), with approximately 160 slaves unaccounted for. This could be explained by exceptionally high mortality rates during the 1850s or by long-distance sales. Even in the case of the latter, however, these statistics still suggest that only a tiny fraction of the total slave population was sold away during the last decade of the antebellum period. For vital statistics in 1850, see the Historical Census Browser, University of Virginia, Geospatial and Statistical Data Center (2004): http://fisher.lib.virginia.edu/collections/stats/histcensus/index.html.

26. A. J. McElveen to Z. B. Oakes, February 6, 1855, in *Broke by the War: Letters of a Slave Trader,* ed. Edmund L. Drago (Columbia: University of South Carolina Press, 1991), 116 (first quotation); Easterby, *South Carolina Rice Plantation,* 29–48; Dusinberre, *Them Dark Days,* 298–99, 305, 402–3; Emily Weston cited in Dusinberre, *Them Dark Days,* 402.

CONTRIBUTORS

ENRICO DAL LAGO is lecturer in American history at the National University of Ireland, Galway. He is the author of *Agrarian Elites: American Slaveholders and Southern Italian Landowners, 1815–1861* (2005); *American Slavery, Atlantic Slavery, and Beyond: The U.S. "Peculiar Institution" in International Perspective* (2012); and *William Lloyd Garrison and Giuseppe Mazzini: Abolition, Democracy, and Radical Reform* (2013).

MARIANA DANTAS is associate professor of history at Ohio University. Her first book was *Black Townsmen: Urban Slavery and Freedom in the Eighteenth-Century Americas* (2008). She is presently researching a book on multiple generations of mixed-race families in a colonial Brazilian mining town to investigate the social meanings of racial categories.

JOHN DAVIES is adjunct instructor in the history department at the University of Delaware. He is currently revising for publication his doctoral dissertation, "Class, Culture, and Color: Black Saint-Dominguan Refugees and African-American Communities in the Early Republic."

JEFF FORRET is professor of history at Lamar University. His publications include *Race Relations at the Margins: Slaves and Poor Whites in the Antebellum Southern Countryside* (2006), the textbook *Slavery in the United States* (2012), and *Slave against Slave: Plantation Violence in the Old South* (2015).

KENNETH S. GREENBERG is distinguished professor of history and dean of the College of Arts and Sciences at Suffolk University. He is the author of

Masters and Statesmen: The Political Culture of American Slavery (1985) and *Honor and Slavery: Lies, Duels, Noses, Masks, Dressing as a Woman, Gifts, Strangers, Humanitarianism, Death, Slave Rebellions, the Proslavery Argument, Baseball, Hunting and Gambling in the Old South* (1996). He is also the editor of *The Confessions of Nat Turner and Related Documents* (1996) and *Nat Turner: A Slave Rebellion in History and Memory* (2003).

KATHLEEN M. HILLIARD is associate professor of history at Iowa State University. She is the author of *Masters, Slaves, and Exchange: Power's Purchase in the Old South* (2014). Her next book, *Bonds Burst Asunder: The Transformation of Southern Exchange in War and Freedom*, examines the effects of the Civil War and emancipation upon the exchange relations cultivated during slavery.

ANTHONY E. KAYE is associate professor of history at Pennsylvania State University, University Park. He is the author of *Joining Places: Slave Neighborhoods in the Old South* (2009) and a coeditor of *Land and Labor, 1866–1867* (2013), a volume in the series Freedom: A Documentary History of Emancipation, 1861–1867. He is presently at work on a book about the Nat Turner revolt.

BONNIE MARTIN was Cassius Marcellus Clay Fellow at the Gilder Lehrman Center for the Study of Slavery, Resistance, and Abolition and the Department of History at Yale University. Currently an independent scholar, she is coediting a collection of essays on slavery in North America from prehistoric time to the present and writing a manuscript on the capital raised by mortgaging slaves in colonial and antebellum America.

DAMIAN ALAN PARGAS is associate professor of history at Leiden University in the Netherlands. Author of *The Quarters and the Fields: Slave Families in the Non-Cotton South* (2010), he has also published *Slavery and Forced Migration in the Antebellum South* (2015).

KAREN RYDER is adjunct instructor of history at Central Connecticut State University. Her dissertation is titled "'Permanent Property': Slave Life Insurance in the Antebellum Southern United States, 1820–1866."

CALVIN SCHERMERHORN is associate professor of history at Arizona State University. He is the author of *Money over Mastery, Family over Freedom: Slavery in the Antebellum Upper South* (2011) and *The Business of Slavery and the Rise of American Capitalism, 1815–1860* (2015). He is also coeditor of *Rambles of a Runaway from Southern Slavery,* by Henry Goings.

CHRISTINE E. SEARS is associate professor of history at the University of Alabama, Huntsville. She has published *American Slaves and African Masters: Algiers and the Western Sahara, 1776–1820* (2012) and is currently examining sailors and their definitions of citizenship during the late-eighteenth and early-nineteenth centuries.

WITHDRAWN